Andreas Röthig

Microeconomic Risk Management and Macroeconomic Stability

Springer

Dr. Andreas Röthig
Darmstadt University of Technology
Residenzschloß
64283 Darmstadt
Germany
roethig@vwl.tu-darmstadt.de

ISSN 0075-8442
ISBN 978-3-642-01564-9 e-ISBN 978-3-642-01565-6
DOI 10.1007/978-3-642-01565-6
Springer Dordrecht Heidelberg London New York

zgl.Dissertation, Darmstadt University of Technology, 2009, D17

Library of Congress Control Number: 2009926242

Cover design: SPi Publishing Services

Printed on acid-free paper

Springer is part of Springer Science+Business Media (www.springer.com)

To my parents, Christa and Wolfgang Röthig

Acknowledgements

This dissertation was written while I was a research and teaching assistant at Darmstadt University of Technology. I thank the people who have contributed to the development of this thesis.

First and foremost, I thank my principal advisor Professor Ingo Barens for his permanent support and encouragement. His open-mindedness and the willingness to share his great ideas, enthusiasm and broad knowledge of micro- and macroeconomics created a friendly and productive working atmosphere.

I am deeply grateful to my second advisor Professor Willi Semmler for his always prompt and excellent advise. He led me into the field of macro-finance when I was studying economics at Bielefeld University, and always reminded me of the importance of both theoretical and empirical economic research.

I have also benefited from insightful discussions with Professors Volker Caspari, Carl Chiarella, Peter Flaschel and Günther Rehme. I am particularly grateful to Carl Chiarella and Harald Uhlig for the invitations to the University of Technology, Sydney, and to the Humboldt University, Berlin.

Special thanks are to my friends and colleagues at Darmstadt University of Technology and Bielefeld University, especially Olaf Münster, Christian Proaño and Jens Rubart for the many stimulating and encouraging discussions.

Darmstadt, February 2009

Andreas Röthig

Contents

Part I Preliminary Explorations

1 Introduction 3
1.1 Literature Review and Motivation 3
1.1.1 Why Should Firms Hedge? 4
1.1.2 How Much Do Firms Hedge? 7
1.2 Outline 9

Part II A Micro View: Optimal Risk Management

2 Backwardation and Optimal Hedging Demand in an Expected Utility Hedging Model 15
2.1 Introduction 15
2.2 The Expected Utility Hedging Model 17
2.2.1 Optimal Long Hedging 17
2.2.2 Hedging Costs and Optimal Hedging 20
2.3 Empirical Investigation 21
2.3.1 Data and Summary Statistics 21
2.3.2 Vector Autoregression and Vector Error Correction Analysis 24
2.4 Discussion 30

3 Mean-Variance Versus Minimum-Variance Hedging 31
3.1 Introduction 31
3.2 The Mean-Variance Approach to Hedging 32
3.2.1 The Model 32
3.2.2 Optimal Hedging 33
3.2.3 Pure Hedging and Speculative Demand 38
3.2.4 The Value of the Futures Market 41

3.3 Minimum-Variance Hedging and Hedging Effectiveness 42
3.3.1 Deriving the Pure Hedge 42
3.3.2 Hedging Effectiveness and Correlation 44
3.3.3 Optimal Hedge Ratios by Linear Regression 45
3.4 Discussion 47

Part III A Macro View: Economic Stability

4 Corporate Risk Management in Balance-Sheet Triggered Currency Crises 51
4.1 Introduction 51
4.2 The Basic Mundell–Fleming–Tobin Model 53
4.2.1 The Goods Market 53
4.2.2 The Financial Markets 56
4.2.3 The Multiple Equilibria MFT Model 57
4.3 Linear Hedging and Speculation in the MFT Model 58
4.3.1 The Hedging Methodology and the Investment Function 58
4.3.2 Speculation and the Investment Function 62
4.3.3 Simulation of the Basic Model 63
4.3.4 Simulation of Hedging Activity 64
4.3.5 Simulation of Speculation 65
4.3.6 The Role of Trading Costs: Forwards Versus Futures 66
4.4 A Nonlinear Hedging Strategy Using Options 73
4.4.1 Options Hedging and Investment 73
4.4.2 Simulation of Options Hedging 76
4.4.3 Linear Versus Nonlinear Hedging Strategies 78
4.5 Economic Implications 81
4.5.1 Corporate Hedging and Economic Stability 81
4.5.2 Capital Flight and Private Asset Allocation 83
4.6 Discussion 86

5 Arbitrage Pressure, Positive Feedback Speculation, Selective Hedging, and Economic Stability: An Empirical Analysis and Catastrophe Modelling 87
5.1 Introduction 87
5.2 Arbitrage Pressure and Noise Trading 89
5.2.1 Arbitrage with Transaction Costs 89
5.2.2 Arbitrage with Holding Costs 91
5.2.3 Noise, Positive Feedback Trading, and Herding 92
5.3 Vector Autoregression Analysis of Futures Trading Activity 94
5.3.1 Data 94
5.3.2 Speculation Versus Hedging 95
5.3.3 Long Versus Short Speculation 97
5.4 Logistic Smooth Transition Regression Analysis of Long Speculation 98
5.4.1 The LSTR Model 102
5.4.2 Testing Linearity Against LSTR 102

5.4.3 Estimation Results ... 103
5.4.4 Misspecification Tests ... 112
5.5 A Catastrophe Theory Approach ... 113
5.5.1 The Cusp Catastrophe Model and Underlying Hypotheses ... 115
5.5.2 The Chain of Events ... 116
5.6 Discussion ... 118

6 Conclusions ... 121

A A Geometric Approach to the Hedgers' Surplus ... 125

B Stability Analysis ... 127

C The Computation of the Catastrophe Surface ... 131

Bibliography ... 133

List of Figures

1.1 Value of the firm and risk 5
1.2 Positions of hedgers (*light grey*) and speculators (*dark grey*) in currency futures markets as reported by the COT report 8

2.1 Impulse response functions: Effects of weak (*BW*) and strong (*BS*) backwardation on short (*Short*) and long (*Long*) hedging activity. *Asterisks* *, **, and *** indicate that the null hypothesis of no Granger causality can be rejected on the 10%, 5%, and 1% levels, respectively 27
2.2 Impulse response functions (continued): Effects of weak (*BW*) and strong (*BS*) backwardation on short (*Short*) and long (*Long*) hedging activity. *Asterisks* *, **, and *** indicate that the null hypothesis of no Granger causality can be rejected on the 10%, 5%, and 1% levels, respectively 28

3.1 Hedging costs and the optimal hedge ratio 35
3.2 Risk aversion and the optimal hedge ratio 36
3.3 Backwardation and the optimal hedge ratio 37
3.4 Speculative and pure hedging demand. The optimal hedge ratio h/x is the *straight black line*. Return is defined as $\tilde{f}_1 - f_0 - c$. The speculative demand is the *dashed line* and the pure hedging demand is the *straight gray line* 39
3.5 The hedgers' surplus 40
3.6 The hedgers' surplus as a function of risk aversion and hedging costs 43
3.7 Estimated hedging regression lines and data 46

4.1 The Krugman type investment function 55
4.2 The IS-AA model 57
4.3 Firm's payoff depending on e 59
4.4 Firm's perfectly hedged payoff 61
4.5 Firm's payoff plus speculation 62
4.6 ArcTan investment function and IS curve 63

4.7 Investment function and IS curve with linear hedging, $h_{fut} = 0$ (*black line*), $h_{fut} = 0.5$ (*dashed line*), and $h_{fut} = 1$ (*gray line*) 64
4.8 IS-AA model with linear hedging, $h_{fut} = 0$ (*black line*), $h_{fut} = 0.5$ (*dashed line*), and $h_{fut} = 1$ (*gray line*) 65
4.9 IS-AA model with h_{fut} ranging from 0 to 1 65
4.10 IS-AA model with speculation, $h_{fut} = 0$ (*black line*), $h_{fut} = -0.5$ (*dashed line*), and $h_{fut} = -1$ (*gray line*) 66
4.11 IS-AA model with h_{fut} ranging from -1 to 0 67
4.12 Investment functions with linear hedging 71
4.13 Perfectly hedged economy with hedging costs $c_{fut} = 0$ (*black line*), $c_{fut} = 50$ (*dashed line*), and $c_{fut} = 100$ (*gray line*) 72
4.14 Perfect hedge ($h_{fut} = 1$; *gray line*) with $c_{fut} = 200$ and "no hedge" ($h_{fut} = 0$; *black line*) 72
4.15 Nonlinear hedging strategy with strike price = e_0 73
4.16 Investment function and IS-AA model with option hedging: $h_{opt} = 0$ (*black line*), $h_{opt} = 0.5$ (*dashed line*), $h_{opt} = 1$ (*gray line*) 76
4.17 IS curve with option hedging and h_{opt} ranging from 0 to 1 77
4.18 IS curves with futures, forwards, and options hedging strategies 79
4.19 Futures versus options hedging strategies from different viewpoints 80
4.20 Forwards versus options hedging strategies from different viewpoints. (Options trading costs: $c = 50$) 81
4.21 Investment and IS-AA dynamics without hedging, with linear hedging, and with nonlinear hedging 82
4.22 Capital flight in the IS-AA diagram 84
4.23 Capital flight in the IS-AA diagram with linear hedging 85
4.24 Capital flight in the IS-AA diagram with nonlinear hedging 85

5.1 Price path with and without arbitrage 90
5.2 Arbitrage with transaction costs 90
5.3 Arbitrage with transaction and holding costs 92
5.4 Impulse responses: Effect of price shocks on the "speculation-hedging-ratio" 97
5.5 Impulse responses: Effect of price shocks on the "long-short-speculation-ratio" 100
5.6 AUD transition function plotted against transition variable Δp_t 105
5.7 CHF transition function plotted against transition variable Δp_t 107
5.8 EUR transition function plotted against transition variable Δp_{t-9} 108
5.9 JPY transition function plotted against transition variable Δp_t 110
5.10 MXP transition function plotted against transition variable Δp_{t-1} 112
5.11 The catastrophe model, bifurcation, and divergence 115
5.12 The chain of events in the cusp catastrophe model 117

B.1 The trace-determinant plane 128
B.2 The "neighborhood" of E_2 130

List of Tables

2.1 Summary statistics for backwardation and hedging activity 22
2.2 Unit root tests 24
2.3 Tests for cointegrating rank 25
2.4 Lags and Granger causality test 26
2.5 Diagnostic tests 29

3.1 Variances and covariances 35
3.2 Full, over-, and underhedging 40
3.3 Correlation and pure hedge ratios 47

4.1 Competitiveness vs. balance sheet effects and output 58
4.2 Linear hedging and the investment function 61
4.3 Relative OTC to CME FX futures contract size (08/04/2005) 67
4.4 CME currency futures: Performance bond requirements (07/26/2005) ... 69
4.5 Premiums of PHLX foreign currency call options 78
4.6 Payoffs of different hedging strategies 79

5.1 Summary statistics, ARCH-LM, and unit root tests for the VAR analysis of speculation versus hedging 96
5.2 Granger causality test for the "speculation-hedging-ratio" 97
5.3 Summary statistics, ARCH-LM, and unit root tests for the VAR analysis of long versus short speculation 99
5.4 Granger causality test for the "long-short-speculation-ratio" 100
5.5 Summary statistics, ARCH-LM, and unit root tests for the LSTR analysis 101
5.6 Testing linearity against LSTR 103
5.7 Test for no remaining nonlinearity and parameter constancy 113

Part I
Preliminary Explorations

Chapter 1
Introduction

> *"The essence of a hedging contract is a coincident purchase and sale in two markets which are expected to behave in such a way that any loss realized in one will be offset by an equivalent gain in the other. If such behavior follows a perfect hedge has been effected."*
>
> Hardy and Lyon (1923, p. 276).

1.1 Literature Review and Motivation

In the traditional hedging literature, the two markets in which hedgers trade are spot and futures markets. The trader's position in the spot market is generally considered as given. According to Johnson (1960), hedging can be meaningfully defined only if the spot market is regarded as the trader's primary market. The futures market is used solely to counterbalance an existing position in the spot market. Speculators, in contrast, do not have a commitment in the spot market. They take on risk in futures markets in order to profit from expected price changes. The hedger synchronizes his trading activities in spot and futures markets in order to reduce spot risk. In the literature this approach to hedging is labeled risk reduction concept. Risk reduction will be achieved if spot and futures prices move more or less in parallel. If prices are perfectly correlated, risk is abolished, since losses in one market are perfectly offset by profits in the other market. However, as Hardy and Lyon (1923) point out, any divergence from perfect correlation results in an imperfect hedge. The less futures and spot prices move in parallel, the more imperfect the protection offered by hedging is. According to Kobold (1986), spot and futures prices generally do not move exactly in parallel. In fact, futures and spot markets are separate markets. Even speaking of a single spot market may be misleading, since, in general, most commodities are traded in many different places. The futures market, on the contrary, is generally highly centralized. Telser (1986) points out that each futures contract is a perfect substitute for another futures contract with the same maturity. If spot and futures prices do not move exactly in parallel, hedges end up with a profit or loss. Hence,

A. Röthig, *Microeconomic Risk Management and Macroeconomic Stability*, Lecture Notes in Economics and Mathematical Systems,
DOI 10.1007/978-3-642-01565-6_1, © Springer-Verlag Berlin Heidelberg 2009

if the motive for hedging is the elimination of spot risk, spot and futures prices, not moving in parallel, prevent complete risk reduction and are therefore unfavorable.

However, differences between spot and futures price movements may provide an additional rationale for hedging activity. Working (1953) contradicts the traditional hedging literature by assuming that hedging is not solely carried out in order to reduce risk. The discrepancy between spot and futures prices can be regarded as a source of potential profit.[1] The expected return from hedging transforms the former risk reduction concept into a selective, or anticipatory, hedging concept. According to Rutledge (1972), these two concepts are quite different, since the hedging decisions are based on different variables. In the risk reduction concept the hedger chooses the hedging position that minimizes risk, while in the selective hedging concept he chooses the hedging position that maximizes expected profit. The difference between these two approaches might be considerable. Heifner (1973) notes that the optimal hedging level differs from the risk minimizing level if the expected return from the hedging position differs from zero. Compared to the risk reduction concept, the distinction between hedgers and speculators is not that clear-cut here. Ederington (1979, p. 160) notes that "in his (i.e., Working's) view hedgers functioned much like speculators, but, since they held positions in the cash market as well, they were concerned with relative not absolute price changes."

In general, regardless of whether the motive for hedging is risk minimization or the maximization of expected profit, a firm will only hedge if it benefits from hedging. As Heifner (1972) points out, if traders are expected to use futures markets for hedging, benefits from hedging must be reflected in gains or potential gains of individual traders. Therefore it is reasonable to ask why firms should hedge.

1.1.1 Why Should Firms Hedge?

In general, hedging will be a value-enhancing activity only if the expected benefits outweigh the costs. In a perfect setting without market imperfections, as proposed by the Modigliani-Miller (1958) theorem[2], firms will not hedge, since "(...) the implementation by the firm of a hedging strategy designed to eliminate the unsystematic risk will duplicate shareholders' previously achieved results at an additional set of transaction costs."[3] Following the Modigliani-Miller theorem, a vast literature emerged trying to explain why firms hedge. According to Friberg (1999), the

---

[1] For more information see e.g., Johnson (1957), Rutledge (1972) and Hirshleifer (1975, 1977).

[2] According to Allen and Gale (1994, p. 215), "(...) the MMT (i.e., Modigliani-Miller theorem) is a statement about the effect of the firm's choices." The theorem basically says that the market value of the firm is not affected by the firm's choice of its financial structure, i.e., by its debt-equity ratio. A list of the assumptions on which the Modigliani-Miller theorem is build can be found in Copeland, Weston, and Shastri (2005, p. 559). See also Jensen and Meckling (1976), MacMinn (1987) and Bauer and Ryser (2004).

[3] Fatemi and Luft (2002, p. 31–32).

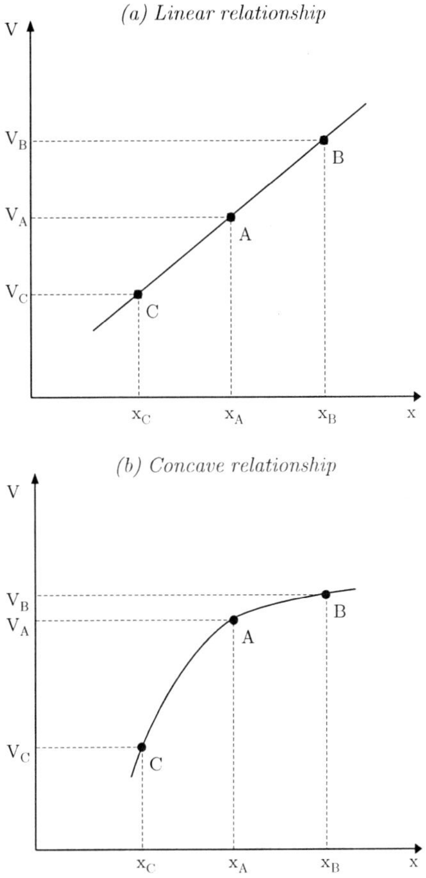

Fig. 1.1 Value of the firm and risk

main objective of large parts of the hedging literature was to find reasons why risk neutral firms should hedge their exposure. This literature can best be reviewed by inspecting Fig. 1.1.[4] Suppose the value of a firm V depends on a risky variable x in a linear fashion as depicted in Fig. 1.1a. The firm is initially at point A. The value of the firm increases by the same amount when x increases to x_B as the value decreases when x decreases to x_C. Since $V_B - V_A = V_A - V_C$, the expected value of the firm is not affected by the risky variable x. Hence, with this linear relationship between V and x hedging is irrelevant, since a hedge would not add to the value of the firm. Now suppose that V is a concave function of x, as presented in Fig. 1.1b. Here, the value of the firm increases less when x increases to x_B than it decreases when x decreases to x_C (i.e., $V_B - V_A < V_A - V_C$). The expected value of the firm is less than its initial value. Therefore, reducing the variability of V by hedging increases the expected value of

[4] See also Duffie and Singleton (2003).

the firm. A large part of the hedging literature is concerned with finding reasons why a risk neutral firm should hedge its spot exposure. In fact, this is comparable to finding reasons to transform the linear relationship between a firm's value and the risky variable, as shown in Fig. 1.1a, into a concave relationship, as presented in Fig. 1.1b. The most important findings can be broadly summarized as follows.[5]

Smith and Stulz (1985) argue that taxes provide a rationale for hedging activity. If taxes are convex in earnings, hedging is generally value-enhancing.[6] To see this, suppose the firm must pay taxes on profits but does not receive equivalent subsidies in the case of losses. Expected gains are smaller than expected losses. The firm's value is therefore a concave function although the firm is risk neutral. A further argument concerns financial distress. If bankruptcy is costly, and if bankruptcy costs increase when the firm's value shrinks, then the firm's value function is concave, as in Fig. 1.1b. Bankruptcy costs include banks being hesitant to lend money due to the worsening of credit ratings, employees demanding a risk premium for working for a firm that will probably fail, or customers losing their trust in the product of the firm. A third argument, put forth by Smith and Stulz (1985), deals with managerial compensation. If the manager's wealth is a concave function of the firm's value, then the manager will hedge perfectly in order to maximize his expected income. According to Froot et al. (1993, 1994), hedging may be useful to avoid underinvestment problems.[7] If internal funds shrink in times of financial distress, and if external funds are expensive, the firm may abstain from investing in positive net present value projects. Hedging may serve to stabilize the supply of internal funds.[8] All these arguments represent important deviations from the perfect capital market scenario, as presented in the Modigliani-Miller theorem, giving firms incentives to hedge.[9] However, this literature generally concludes that if the Modigliani-Miller theorem holds, firms do not hedge at all, while they hedge fully if the assumptions underlying the Modigliani-Miller theorem are relaxed.[10] Concerning the selective hedging

[5] For a review of the literature see Froot, Scharfstein, and Stein (1993), Nance, Smith, and Smithson (1993), Mian (1996), Géczy, Minton, and Schrand (1997), Schrand and Unal (1998), Tufano (1998), Beatty (1999), Guay (1999), Brown and Toft (2002), Fatemi and Luft (2002), Albuquerque (2003), Guay and Kothari (2003), Pennings and Garcia (2004) and Lin and Smith (2005).

[6] Graham and Rogers (2002) provide empirical findings on the impact of taxes on hedging.

[7] Empirical findings concerning the underinvestment problem and hedging are provided by Gay and Nam (1998). See also Haushalter, Klasa, and Maxwell (2007).

[8] For more information on capital market imperfections, liquidity, and hedging see Myers and Majluf (1984), Stulz (1990), Mian (1996) and Mello and Parsons (2000).

[9] Interestingly, Modigliani and Miller (1958, p. 296) themselves advocate the relaxation of their theorem's restrictive assumptions: "These and other drastic simplifications have been necessary in order to come to grips with the problem at all. Having served their purpose they can now be relaxed in the direction of greater realism and relevance, a task in which we hope others interested in this area will wish to share."

[10] See e.g., Smith and Stulz (1985) and Froot et al. (1993). Since the full hedging of the spot exposure eliminates spot risk, the full hedge can be considered a perfect hedge. Hence, the terms full hedging and perfect hedging can be used interchangeably if the full hedging strategy perfectly eliminates spot risk.

concept put forth by Working (1953), this result cannot be regarded as satisfactory. A closer look at firms' optimal hedging strategies is reasonable.

One way to circumvent the discussion of why firms hedge is to assume that firms are risk averse. In this case, a firm maximizes its utility which is defined as a concave function of profit. A second possibility is to apply the mean-variance concept to hedging. Here, the objective function to be maximized by the firm depends positively on expected profit and negatively on risk, where risk is measured by the variance of profit. In both cases, reducing risk increases the firm's expected utility.[11] This strand of literature does not investigate the question of why firms hedge, but how much firms hedge under specific market conditions. The emphasis is therefore on deriving the conditions under which firms do not hedge, hedge partially, hedge fully, or overhedge. All of these approaches to risk management can be viewed as optimal hedging strategies of the firm depending on the underlying assumptions and market conditions. This approach to hedging is therefore closer to Working's (1953) idea of selective hedging.

1.1.2 How Much Do Firms Hedge?

The Commodity Futures Trading Commission's (CFTC) Commitment of Traders (COT) report provides a periodic breakdown of the composition of open interest for futures contracts. This information on trader positions is collected on each Tuesday for markets with at least 20 trader positions. The information on trader positions is divided into reporting and nonreporting traders. Nonreporting traders are small traders who hold positions below of CFTC reporting levels, whereas reporting traders are categorized as commercial and noncommercial traders. Commercial traders are considered to be hedgers who hold the futures position in conjunction with an underlying spot position. Noncommercial traders are referred to as speculators since they are not involved in a spot business.[12] Figure 1.2 presents the position data of hedgers and speculators in six currency futures contracts traded at the Chicago Mercantile Exchange: Australian Dollar (AUD), Canadian Dollar (CAD), Swiss Francs (CHF), Euro (EUR), Japanese Yen (JPY), and Mexican Peso (MXP) futures contracts. The contract sizes of the futures contracts are 100,000 AUD, 100,000 CAD, 125,000 CHF, 125,000 EUR, 12,500,000 JPY, and 500,000 MXP, respectively. The data presented in Fig. 1.2 point to an increase in trading activity of hedgers and speculators in recent years. Interestingly, in all currency

[11] For more information on these two approaches to hedging see e.g., Peck (1975), Holthausen (1979), Levy and Markowitz (1979), Feder, Just, and Schmitz (1980), Kahl (1983), Benninga, Eldor, and Zilcha (1985), Zilcha and Broll (1992), Briys and Schlesinger (1993), Lence (1995a, 1995b), Broll and Eckwert (1996, 2000), Vukina et al. (1996), Collins (1997), Adam-Müller (2000), Haigh and Holt (2000) and Broll, Chow, and Wong (2001).

[12] For more information on the CFTC's COT report, see Ederington and Lee (2002), Chatrath, Song, and Adrangi (2003), Sanders, Boris, and Manfredo (2004) and Röthig and Chiarella (2007).

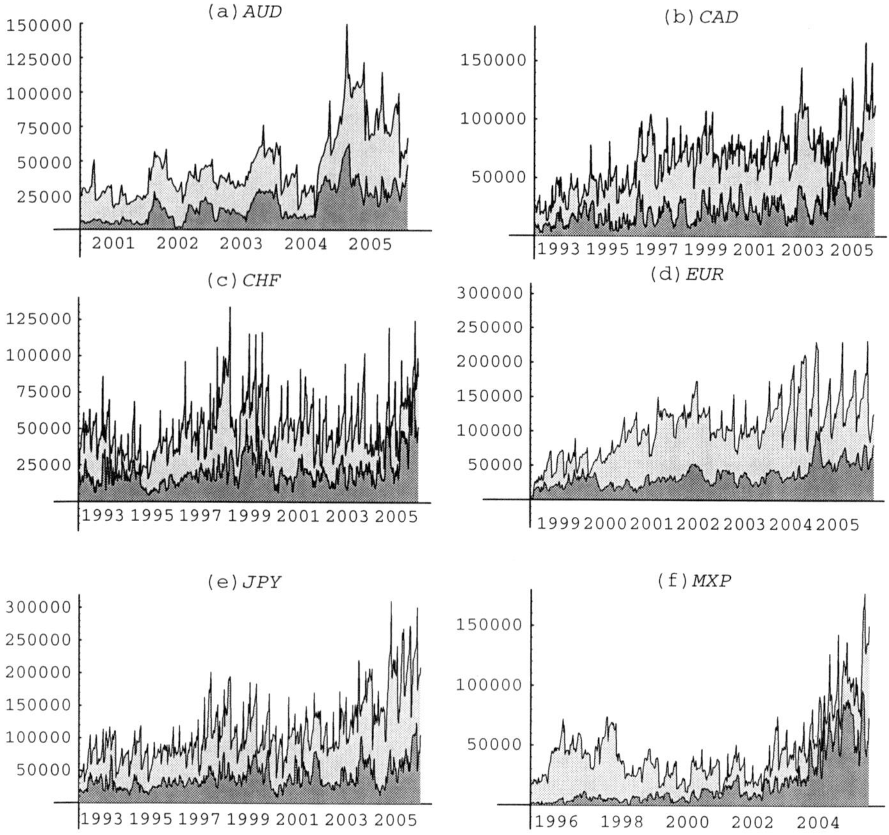

Fig. 1.2 Positions of hedgers (*light grey*) and speculators (*dark grey*) in currency futures markets as reported by the COT report

futures markets, the trading volume of hedgers exceeds the trading volume of speculators over the entire time frame. This stresses the importance of futures markets for corporate risk management. According to DeMarzo and Duffie (1995, p. 743), "(...) the demand for hedging by corporations is an important component of the explosion in financial innovation (...)." Empirical findings concerning firms' risk management strategies point to firms using financial derivatives for hedging rather than for speculation. Using survey data on derivatives usage by non-financial corporations, Bodnar, Hayt, Marston, and Smithson (1995) find that corporations use derivatives most commonly to hedge.[13] In addition, hedging is found to increase firm value.[14] Géczy, Minton, and Schrand (1997) find that derivatives may provide a

[13] See also Levich, Hayt, and Ripston (1999).

[14] See e.g., Nance, Smith, and Smithson (1993), Allayannis and Weston (2001) and Allayannis, Ihrig, and Weston (2001).

valuable benefit to firms if used rationally. According to them, rationally means using the derivatives for hedging, which they find firms to do on average. Guay (1999, p. 349) finds that "(...) new users of derivatives experience statistically and economically significant reductions in stock-return volatility, interest rate exposure, and exchange-rate exposure compared to matched samples of control firms that do not use derivatives." Additionally, hedging strategies vary across firms, indicating that they follow a selective hedging strategy. Cummins, Phillips, and Smith (1998) state that more risk loving firms have lower than average derivatives positions. Hence, more risk loving companies hedge less. According to Dolde (1993), firms hedge much, but not all exposure. Surveying a sample of Australian companies on risk management strategies, Benson and Oliver (2004) conclude that only a small number of firms hedge all their risk exposure. These findings suggest that firms' hedging strategies correspond to Working's (1953) selective hedging theory, rather than to the risk reduction concept discussed in the traditional hedging literature. Recent empirical evidence supports the selective hedging approach. Adam and Fernando (2006) examine the hedging behavior of gold mining firms and find considerable evidence of selective hedging. Knill, Minnick, and Nejadmalayeri (2006) investigate hedging strategies of oil and gas companies who use futures contracts as primary hedging instrument. Their findings suggest that these companies use futures only when their outlook is unfavorable.

Economic crises and instability are unfavorable in general. If crises are triggered by hedgeable risks like currency risk, firms can manage their vulnerability through hedging. Managing the potential impact of adverse shocks on firms, and therefore on investment, should in turn have consequences for the entire macroeconomy. In fact, Mishkin (2000) argues that the main reasons for the Asian crisis were microeconomic rather than macroeconomic. Among the microeconomic reasons, corporate risk management plays a key role. While there is a vast literature on the microeconomics of optimal corporate risk management, there is rarely any literature dealing with macroeconomic consequences. This thesis aims to fill this gap.

1.2 Outline

This thesis is subdivided into a microeconomic and a macroeconomic part, each containing two chapters. The microeconomic part basically deals with a representative firm's optimal hedging strategy. In both chapters the firm is assumed to be risk averse. Both the expected utility approach and the mean-variance concept are applied to the firm's hedging problem. The findings suggest that hedging the spot exposure fully, as suggested by the risk reduction concept, is just one possible outcome out of a number of potential optimal hedging strategies. Depending on price expectations, costs and risk aversion, it might be optimal for the firm to hedge fully, less, or more of the spot exposure. Hence, the analysis in the microeconomic part points to selective hedging strategies by firms, where underhedging, full hedging and overhedging all represent optimal hedging strategies under specific circumstances. The macroeconomic part is not concerned with optimal hedging decisions at the firm level, but with the impact of firms' hedging policies on macroeconomic stability. The effect of hedging on investment and economic activity is investigated. Again, following the selective hedging approach, all possible outcomes of optimal hedging strategies are examined. Moreover, the impact of speculation is analyzed as well. In addition, the interaction between hedging and speculation, noise trading and limits to arbitrage are examined.

Chapter 2 presents the optimal hedging problem of a representative importer exposed to currency risk. The importer's optimal hedging strategy is derived in an expected utility framework with and without hedging costs. The impact of price biases on the hedging decision are investigated and compared to findings in the literature dealing with the hedging problem of a representative exporter. The model suggests that it is optimal for the importer to overhedge (underhedge) if the futures market exhibits backwardation (contango), where backwardation (contango) is defined as the futures price being lower (higher) than the expected spot price. In general, the size of the importer's hedging position should depend positively on backwardation. The empirical part of this chapter studies the impact of backwardation on hedgers' short and long trading activity in six currency futures markets. Although the evidence, based on vector autoregressive and vector error correction models, shows that backwardation has a significant impact on hedging activity, the sign of the impact does not correspond to economic theory for all currencies.

The hedging model presented in Chap. 3 builds on the expected utility approach discussed in Chap. 2. Here, the mean-variance concept is applied to the importer's hedging problem. The optimal hedge ratio is derived and decomposed into a pure hedge component and a speculative component. It is shown that the pure hedge component equals the minimum-variance hedge ratio. This minimum-variance hedge ratio is investigated in connection with hedging effectiveness. Empirical evidence for six currency futures markets suggests that this pure hedge component is close to the "equal and opposite" hedge. The popular "equal and opposite" hedge, or "one to one" hedge respectively, represents the optimal hedge, as suggested by the risk reduction concept, where the futures position is the same size as the spot position. The importer's individual characteristics, such as the degree of risk aversion and price expectations, enter the speculative component of the hedge ratio. Hence, the speculative component can be regarded as representing the divergence between the optimal hedge ratios suggested by the selective hedging concept as opposed to the risk reduction concept. Finally, the hedger's demand for futures contracts is presented as a Marshallian-type demand function. The hedgers' surplus is derived and analyzed.

Chapter 4 deals with macroeconomic consequences of a variety of different risk management strategies. The impact of firms' hedging activities on macroeconomic stability is modeled in a Mundell–Fleming–Tobin type currency crisis model. Here, firms face exchange rate risk due to debt denominated in foreign currency. In addition to using currency futures contracts for risk management, forward contracts and options are discussed. Hence, the effect of hedging strategies with three different types of financial derivatives on investment and economic activity are at first each investigated and then compared to each other. Risk management strategies, again, include a wide range of activities from no hedging, over underhedging to full hedging, overhedging, and even speculation. In general, an increase in hedging activity decreases adverse effects of a currency depreciation and capital flight.

In Chap. 5, the interaction of different types of futures traders is investigated. First, the impact of price changes on trading activity of hedgers and speculators is examined. The empirical findings suggest that the proportion of speculators in currency futures markets increases after a price rise, and that speculators go long in futures contracts, therefore betting on further increases in prices. Further empirical investigations of nonlinearities in speculators' behavior point to positive feedback trading among speculators. Second, the interaction of hedging, speculation and arbitrage is analyzed in a cusp catastrophe model. If arbitrage pressure is reduced, positive feedback trading can increase instability, therefore leading to a deepening of mispricing after a price shock. This in turn may result in a long path back to equilibrium.

Finally, Chap. 6 surveys the results and concludes this thesis.

Part II
A Micro View: Optimal Risk Management

Chapter 2
Backwardation and Optimal Hedging Demand in an Expected Utility Hedging Model

"A theory of speculative markets under ideal conditions of certainty is Hamlet without the Prince."

Samuelson (1957, p. 205).

2.1 Introduction

Most recent models on optimal hedging deal with exporting firms facing price or exchange rate risk. In order to hedge the spot commitment, firms go short in futures contracts.[1] This hedging literature, dealing with exporting firms hedging short, unequivocally suggests a negative relation between backwardation and the size of the optimal short hedging position.[2] In sum, the literature suggests that if the

[1] See e.g., Briys, Crouhy, and Schlesinger (1993), Briys and de Varenne (1998), Briys and Schlesinger (1993), Friberg (1998), Adam-Müller (1997, 2000) and Lien and Wang (2002). For more information on the role of unbiasedness in futures markets and hedging see e.g., Benninga, Eldor, and Zilcha (1984, 1985), Broll and Eckwert (1996, 2000), Broll, Wahl, and Zilcha (1995) and Zilcha and Broll (1992).

[2] In the literature, the term backwardation is used in a variety of ways relating current and expected spot prices to futures and forward prices. Following Holthausen (1979), Briys and Schlesinger (1993) and Adam-Müller (2000), in this study, backwardation is defined as the futures price being less than the expected spot price. Explanations of backwardation include the existence of a risk premium, cost of carry, convenience yield, and capacity constraints. Note that, investigating the explanations of backwardation in more detail is beyond the scope of this chapter. Interested readers are referred to Litzenberger and Rabinowitz (1995), Frechette and Fackler (1999), Pindyck (2001), Inci and Lu (2007) and Larson (2007). In contrast to backwardation, the futures market is said to exhibit contango if the futures price exceeds the expected spot price. The literature on backwardation and contango dates back to Keynes (1930), Hicks (1939) and Kaldor (1940). There is a large literature dealing with the controversy about the Keynesian "normal backwardation" hypothesis. Some studies find backwardation to be normal while others reject the hypothesis. For a survey on the controversy, see e.g., Ehrhardt, Jordan, and Walkling (1987), Kolb (1992) and Miffre (2000). This study does not add to this controversy but rather investigates the impact of backwardation on hedgers' demand for currency futures contracts.

A. Röthig, *Microeconomic Risk Management and Macroeconomic Stability*, Lecture Notes in Economics and Mathematical Systems,
DOI 10.1007/978-3-642-01565-6_2,

futures market is characterized by backwardation (contango), it is optimal for the short hedger to underhedge (overhedge), where underhedging (overhedging) means choosing a futures position smaller (larger) than the initial spot commitment. In the absence of backwardation or contango, the firm hedges fully, and therefore chooses the futures position to be the same size as the spot position.[3] Hence, an increase in backwardation should, ceteris paribus, reduce the trading volume of hedgers in short futures contracts.

This chapter studies the impact of backwardation on hedging activity in short and long currency futures contracts.[4] First, the optimal hedging strategy of a representative importer is derived. The importing firm expects delivery of a certain amount of a good at a futures date at the then prevailing random exchange rate. To hedge the spot exposure the importer can go long in currency futures markets. Second, hedging costs are introduced into the model. Third, the impact of backwardation on long and short hedging activity in six currency futures markets is investigated empirically. To the best of our knowledge, there is rarely any literature dealing with importers hedging long. Among the few exceptions are Haigh and Holt (2000) and Jin and Koo (2006). Haigh and Holt (2000) use a model in which hedgers are simultaneously long and short in different futures markets. Jin and Koo (2006) examine the hedging problem of a Japanese grain importer facing multiple risks. However, Haigh and Holt (2000) and Jin and Koo (2006) do not investigate the role of backwardation and contango on optimal hedging. In addition the model in this chapter is related to the expected utility framework laid out by Holthausen (1979) and Briys and Schlesinger (1993), whereas Haigh and Holt (2000) and Jin and Koo (2006), both employ the mean-variance concept. Holthausen (1979) and Briys and Schlesinger (1993) investigate the impact of backwardation on the optimal hedging decisions of exporting firms. The model presented in this chapter extends these investigations to importers. In addition, the impact of hedging costs on the importer's optimal hedging strategy are investigated.

The model of the importer's hedging problem introduced in this chapter leads to the conclusion that it is optimal for long hedgers to overhedge (underhedge) if the futures market is characterized by backwardation (contango). The firm hedges fully in the absence of backwardation or contango. However, this result is altered by introducing hedging costs. In fact, the existence of hedging costs provides a rationale for backwardation to be normal. In the presence of hedging costs, the importing firm hedges fully if, and only if, the futures market exhibits backwardation. The firm tends to overhedge if the amount of backwardation exceeds hedging costs. The firm hedges fully if the extent of backwardation equals hedging costs. If hedging costs exceed the amount of backwardation, or if the futures market is unbiased or exhibits contango, the optimal hedge is a partial hedge. However, irrespective of the existence of hedging costs, an increase in backwardation should, ceteris paribus, increase the trading volume of hedgers in long futures contracts.

[3] See e.g., Briys, Crouhy and Schlesinger (1990, 1993), Briys and de Varenne (1998) and Broll and Wong (2002).

[4] A previous version of this chapter has been published as Röthig (2008).

Although there is a large literature dealing with backwardation and firms' optimal hedging strategies in the theory of the firm, few attempts have been made to approach the impact of backwardation on hedgers' demand for futures contracts empirically. The empirical part of this study analyzes the impact of backwardation on hedgers' demand for short and long currency futures contracts in six currency futures markets. Following Litzenberger and Rabinowitz (1995) and Pindyck (2001), two measures of backwardation (i.e., weak and strong backwardation) are employed. Using vector autoregressive (VAR) and vector error correction (VECM) models, the results of this study show that backwardation has a significant impact on hedgers' trading volume in currency futures markets. However, the sign of the impact does not correspond to economic theory for all currencies. The results therefore offer little support for the hypothesis that short (long) hedging activity depends negatively (positively) on backwardation.

In Sect. 2.2 the model is presented and the firm's optimal hedging strategy is derived. The impact of backwardation and contango on the optimal hedge are analyzed and hedging costs are introduced into the model. Section 2.3 presents the empirical results based on VAR and VECM models. Section 2.4 concludes.

2.2 The Expected Utility Hedging Model

2.2.1 *Optimal Long Hedging*

Suppose there is a representative importer in country A who is obliged to buy a known quantity x of a good from country B at period $t = 1$ at a certain price level p.[5] Having made the decision to import the quantity x, the firm faces exchange rate risk between the period the decision is made (i.e., $t = 0$) and the spot commitment date $t = 1$. The expected return of the spot position depends on the random exchange rate $\tilde{e}_1$ as follows:

$$E(R_S) = -\tilde{e}_1 px. \tag{2.1}$$

Since the price level p is non-stochastic and known at period $t = 0$, p is set equal to one for simplicity. In addition to the spot commitment, the importer can trade long futures contracts in the currency futures market. Let f_0 be the futures price

[5] It is important to stress that the quantity x of imports is given. Since the firm in this model is not deciding about the optimal production level, and therefore not choosing the optimal amount of imports, this model can be interpreted as concerned with the short run. Moreover, the price level p is fixed, also pointing to a short run model. According to Sandmo (1971) this approach may be considered a weakness but also a strength. The weakness concerns the separation of production policy and strategies for financing and investment. A strength of dealing with short run profits is that the model stays relatively simple and is not based on too many assumptions. Moreover it is more realistic and applicable since hedging is generally concerned with single cash flows and hedging vehicles like futures are generally available only for the short run.

at time $t = 0$ for delivery of a certain amount of foreign currency in $t = 1$. In this model the importer holds the futures position until delivery at period $t = 1$, that is, until the spot commitment date. At futures delivery date, the random futures delivery price is $\tilde{f}_1$. Suppose that, due to arbitrage relations, the random spot price and the random futures price coincide at spot commitment date (futures delivery date, respectively). Then, since basis risk is absent, the expected return of the long futures position $\tilde{f}_1 - f_0$ equals $\tilde{e}_1 - f_0$ per contract h.[6] If the term $\tilde{e}_1 - f_0$ is zero (not zero), the futures market is said to be unbiased (biased). If the futures price is less than the expected spot price (i.e., $\tilde{e}_1 - f_0 > 0$), the futures market exhibits backwardation. The futures market exhibits contango if the futures price exceeds the expected spot price (i.e., $\tilde{e}_1 - f_0 < 0$). The expected profit of the hedged portfolio is the sum of the expected return of the spot position plus the long futures position:

$$E(\Pi) = -\tilde{e}_1 x + (\tilde{e}_1 - f_0)h. \tag{2.2}$$

It can easily be seen that the long futures position can be used to offset (i.e., to hedge) the existing spot exchange rate exposure. If the importer chooses the amount of futures contracts traded h to equal the spot commitment x, then the expected profit of the hedged portfolio is non-stochastic. This hedging strategy is widely known as the "equal and opposite" or "one to one" hedge. However, although potential losses in the spot position are offset by the futures position, potential gains in the spot position due to a decrease in the exchange rate are offset as well by losses in the futures position.

The importer's decision problem is to choose a futures position h to maximize expected utility. The importing firm maximizes its expected utility of profit at date $t = 1$ where U is a concave, continuous and differentiable utility function defined over profit Π.

$$\underset{h}{Max}\, EU[\Pi] = U[-\tilde{e}_1 x + (\tilde{e}_1 - f_0)h]. \tag{2.3}$$

The firm is assumed to be risk averse, so that $U'[\Pi] > 0$, $U''[\Pi] < 0$.[7] Following Briys and Schlesinger (1993) the first-order condition is calculated:

$$\frac{\delta EU[\Pi]}{\delta h} = EU'[-\tilde{e}_1 x + (\tilde{e}_1 - f_0)h](\tilde{e}_1 - f_0) = 0. \tag{2.4}$$

Using the representation of profit presented in (2.2) the first-order condition can be rewritten as

$$\frac{\delta EU[\Pi]}{\delta h} = EU'[\Pi](\tilde{e}_1 - f_0) = 0. \tag{2.5}$$

[6] The difference between the random variables $\tilde{e}_1$ and $\tilde{f}_1$ in the delivery period is known as the basis (or, basis risk, respectively). See e.g., Peck (1975) and Lapan and Moschini (1994).

[7] For more information on similar utility functions and risk aversion see e.g., Pratt (1964), Baron (1970), Rothschild and Stiglitz (1970), Sandmo (1971), Diamond and Stiglitz (1974), Ishii (1977) and Kimball (1990, 1993).

The second-order condition for a maximum is assumed to hold given risk aversion.[8] Using the covariance operator *Cov*, (2.5) can be written as[9]

$$\frac{dEU[\Pi]}{dh} = EU'[\Pi]E(\tilde{e}_1 - f_0) + Cov[U'[\Pi], \tilde{e}_1] = 0. \tag{2.6}$$

The covariance term $Cov[U'[\Pi], \tilde{e}_1]$ is crucial in the subsequent analysis of the relationship between hedging activity and backwardation. Equation (2.6) can be used to determine the conditions under which the risk-averse firm hedges fully (i.e., $h = x$), hedges partially (i.e., $0 < h < x$), or overhedges (i.e., $h > x$). Note that (2.6) consists of three terms. $U'[\Pi]$ is positive for any Π by definition. The second term, $E(\tilde{e}_1 - f_0)$, is zero if the futures market is unbiased (i.e., $\tilde{e}_1 = f_0$). Suppose the second term is zero, then (2.6) reduces to $Cov[U'[\Pi], \tilde{e}_1] = 0$.

In order to analyze the covariance term in more detail, recall that profit at date 1 is given by $E(\Pi) = -\tilde{e}_1 x + (\tilde{e}_1 - f_0)h$. As previously mentioned, profit is independent of the exchange rate if $h = x$, and hence the covariance is zero. If the firm hedges less than full (i.e., $h < x$) the covariance is positive and if the firm overhedges (i.e., $h > x$) the covariance is negative.[10]

---

[8] The second partial derivative of the utility function with respect to h is

$$\frac{\delta^2 EU[\Pi]}{\delta h^2} = EU''[\Pi](\tilde{e}_1 - f_0)^2.$$

The equation is negative since $U'[\Pi] > 0$, $U''[\Pi] < 0$ by definition. Therefore a maximum exists. However, as Holthausen (1979, p. 989) points out, this is not the case for risk-neutral ($U''[\Pi] = 0$) or risk-loving firms ($U''[\Pi] > 0$).

[9] To see this, recall that $E(XY) = E(X)E(Y) + Cov(X,Y)$ (see e.g., Cochrane, 2001, p. 15). Equation (2.5) can therefore be rewritten as

$$EU'[\Pi](\tilde{e}_1 - f_0) = EU'[\Pi]E(\tilde{e}_1 - f_0) + Cov[U'[\Pi], (\tilde{e}_1 - f_0)] = 0,$$

which in turn, using $Cov(X+Y,Z) = Cov(X,Z) + Cov(Y,Z)$, can be formulated as

$$EU'[\Pi]E(\tilde{e}_1 - f_0) + Cov[U'[\Pi], \tilde{e}_1] + Cov[U'[\Pi], -f_0] = 0.$$

Since f_0 is non-stochastic, and using $Cov(1,X) = 0$, the equation can be simplified to

$$EU'[\Pi]E(\tilde{e}_1 - f_0) + Cov[U'[\Pi], \tilde{e}_1] = 0.$$

[10] Note that the covariance is defined as

$$Cov(X,Y) = E((X - E(X))(Y - E(Y)).$$

Suppose that $X = U'[\Pi]$ and $Y = \tilde{e}_1$. If the firm underhedges (i.e., $h < x$), the futures position is smaller than the spot position and profit therefore depends negatively on the random exchange rate. An increase in $\tilde{e}_1$ decreases Π and, due to concavity, increases $U'[\Pi]$. Hence, $(X - E(X)) > 0$. In addition, an increase in $\tilde{e}_1$ leads to $(Y - E(Y)) > 0$. The covariance is therefore positive.

However, if the firm overhedges (i.e., $h > x$), the futures position is larger than the spot position. Since the futures position yields profits when $\tilde{e}_1$ increases, profit depends positively on the exchange rate. Hence, an increase in $\tilde{e}_1$ increases Π and decreases $U'[\Pi]$, again, due to concavity. Therefore $(X - E(X)) < 0$. Since, everything else is equal, the covariance is negative.

Now, if the futures market is unbiased, the term $\tilde{e}_1 - f_0$ in (2.6) is zero. Therefore, the covariance must be zero as well for (2.6) to hold. For the covariance to be zero, which is achieved if profit is independent of exchange rate changes, the firm must hedge fully. Hence, firms hedge fully when the futures market is unbiased. If the futures market exhibits backwardation (i.e., $\tilde{e}_1 > f_0$), the second term in (2.6) is positive. The covariance in (2.6) must therefore be negative for the condition that the first-order-condition equals zero to hold. This implies that $h > x$. The resulting futures position is an overhedge. Now suppose that the futures market exhibits contango (i.e. $\tilde{e}_1 < f_0$). In this case, the covariance in (2.6) must be positive, since the first term in the equation is negative, for the condition that the first-order-condition equals zero to hold. This implies that $h < x$. The resulting futures position is a partial hedge.

2.2.2 Hedging Costs and Optimal Hedging

In this section hedging costs are introduced into the model. The expected utility of profit with hedging costs is

$$EU[\Pi] = U[-\tilde{e}_1 x + (\tilde{e}_1 - f_0 - c)h]. \tag{2.7}$$

Again, profit is independent of the exchange rate if the firm hedges fully (i.e., $h = x$). In this case, spot exposure is completely offset and therefore perfectly hedged by the futures position. Maximizing expected utility of profit with respect to h yields

$$\frac{dEU[\Pi]}{dh} = EU'[-\tilde{e}_1 x + (\tilde{e}_1 - f_0 - c)h](\tilde{e}_1 - f_0 - c) = 0. \tag{2.8}$$

Using covariances, the first-order condition can be rewritten as

$$\frac{dEU[\Pi]}{dh} = EU'[\Pi]E(\tilde{e}_1 - f_0 - c) + Cov[U'[\Pi], \tilde{e}_1] = 0. \tag{2.9}$$

Equation (2.9) consists of three terms. Again, $U'[\Pi]$ is positive for any Π by definition. The second term $E(\tilde{e}_1 - f_0 - c)$ is zero if hedging costs equal the amount of backwardation (i.e., $c = \tilde{e}_1 - f_0$). Suppose the second term is zero, then (2.9) reduces to $Cov[U'[\Pi], \tilde{e}_1] = 0$, which holds true if firms hedge fully. If $c > 0$, the term $E(\tilde{e}_1 - f_0 - c)$ in (2.9) is zero if $E(\tilde{e}_1 - f_0) > 0$, or more precisely if $E(\tilde{e}_1 - f_0) = c$. Hence, firms hedge fully if, and only if, futures markets are biased, i.e., exhibit backwardation ($E(\tilde{e}_1) > f_0$). If the amount of backwardation exceeds trading costs c (i.e., $E(\tilde{e}_1 - f_0) > c$), the second term in (2.9) is positive. The covariance in (2.9) must therefore be negative for the condition that the first-order-condition equals zero to hold. This implies that $h > x$. The resulting futures position is an overhedge. In the case of an unbiased futures market (i.e., $E(\tilde{e}_1) = f_0$), or if the futures market exhibits contango (i.e., $E(\tilde{e}_1) < f_0$), the covariance in (2.9) therefore must be positive for the condition that the first-order-condition equals zero to hold. This implies that $h < x$. The resulting futures position is a partial hedge.

2.3 Empirical Investigation

In this section the impact of backwardation on short and long hedging activity is empirically investigated. Regarding short hedging, again, the literature suggests that in the case of backwardation (contango) it is optimal to underhedge (overhedge). The theoretical model in this study dealing with a representative importer's long hedging problem suggests that it is optimal to overhedge (underhedge) if the futures market is characterized by backwardation (contango). Hence, ceteris paribus, the hedging models predict a negative effect of backwardation on short hedging activity as well as a positive effect on long hedging activity.

2.3.1 Data and Summary Statistics

The empirical investigation uses weekly data on spot and futures prices and hedgers' positions for six currency futures contracts traded at the Chicago Mercantile Exchange. Australian Dollar (AUD), Canadian Dollar (CAD), Swiss Francs (CHF), Euro (EUR), Japanese Yen (JPY), and Mexican Peso (MXP) futures contracts are investigated. The hedgers' position data come from the Commodity Futures Trading Commission's (CFTC) Commitments of Traders (COT) report and the price data come from Datastream.[11]

Following Litzenberger and Rabinowitz (1995) and Pindyck (2001), two measures of backwardation are employed. Futures markets exhibit strong backwardation if futures prices are below spot prices (i.e., $\tilde{e}_t > \tilde{f}_t$). Weak backwardation is defined as a situation where discounted futures prices are below spot prices (i.e., $\tilde{e}_t > exp(-r_t * (3/12))\tilde{f}_t$ where r_t is the three month LIBOR rate).

The summary statistics are presented in Table 2.1. With regard to the measure of weak backwardation, backwardation appears to be normal as proposed by Keynes (1930). All currency futures markets investigated exhibit weak backwardation at least 95% of the time. The results for strong backwardation are mixed. While some currency futures prices were on average strongly backwarded (i.e., the AUD and MXP series over 90% of the time), some exhibit backwardation and contango from time to time (i.e., CAD and EUR), and some exhibit contango most of the time (i.e., CHF and JPY).

[11] For more information on the COT report, see e.g., Ederington and Lee (2002), Chatrath et al. (2003) and Röthig and Chiarella (2007).

Table 2.1 Summary statistics for backwardation and hedging activity

Futures contract	AUD		CAD		CHF		EUR		JPY		MXP	
Sample	02 Jan 2001 to 31 Jan 2006		06 Oct 1992 to 31 Jan 2006		06 Oct 1992 to 31 Jan 2006		12 Jan 1999 to 31 Jan 2006		06 Oct 1992 to 31 Jan 2006		26 Mar 1996 31 Jan 2006	
Observations	252		696		694		369		696		515	
Panel A: Weak and strong backwardation												
	BW	BS	BW	BS	BW	BS	BW	BS	BW	BS	BW	BS
Mean	0.0101	0.0030	0.0101	0.0001	0.0075	−0.0023	0.0121	−0.0004	0.0000	−0.0000	0.0032	0.0018
Minimum	0.0027	−0.0040	0.0048	−0.0056	−0.0004	−0.0094	−0.0039	−0.0180	−0.0000	−0.0001	−0.0017	−0.0028
Maximum	0.0178	0.0106	0.0245	0.0091	0.0230	0.0129	0.0224	0.0115	0.0002	0.0000	0.0119	0.0101
Standard error	0.0028	0.0024	0.0026	0.0019	0.0030	0.0030	0.0030	0.0037	0.0000	0.0000	0.0023	0.0020
% in backwardation	100	92.46	100	53.01	99.85	21.32	99.72	50.13	96.40	6.75	99.61	98.83
Panel B: Short hedging activity												
	Short		Short		Short		Short		Short		Short	
Mean	35,539.88		39,196.21		22,124.58		65,122.91		47,972.39		27,602.20	
Minimum	4,910.00		4,945.00		1,932.00		2,984.00		7,440.00		1,306.00	
Maximum	114,073.00		111,552.00		86,565.00		148,495.00		184,367.00		127,620.00	
Standard error	19,312.65		21,500.59		14,244.79		28,653.69		30,963.11		23,741.40	
Panel C: Long hedging activity												
	Long		Long		Long		Long		Long		Long	
Mean	12,569.76		27,201.43		28,371.87		39,115.23		62,162.80		17,977.66	
Minimum	1,294.00		1,360.00		1,558.00		1,647.00		10,111.00		1,752.00	
Maximum	51,749.00		63,398.00		87,271.00		125,244.00		188,591.00		54,741.00	
Standard error	9,973.88		13,125.70		17,377.14		20,266.04		28,854.10		9,804.78	

Note: The summary statistics are computed using weekly data. The price data are obtained from Datastream. Strong backwardation is defined by $BS_t = \tilde{e}_t - \tilde{f}_t$ where $\tilde{e}_t$ is the spot price and $\tilde{f}_t$ is the futures price in t. Weak backwardation is defined by $BW_t = \tilde{e}_t - exp(-r_t * (3/12))\tilde{f}_t$ where r_t is the three month LIBOR rate. Data on hedging activity are obtained by the Commodity Futures Trading Commission's (CFTC) Commitments of Traders (COT) report. Short hedging activity is defined by $Short_t = Comm\_Positions\_Short\_All_t$, and long hedging activity is defined by $Long_t = Comm\_Positions\_Long\_All_t$

Interestingly, with regard to the measure of strong backwardation, in the markets where futures prices exhibit contango, hedgers are on average net long (i.e., the mean of long hedging activity exceeds the mean of short hedging activity in Table 2.1). Miffre (2000) points out that the idea that backwardation and contango depend on hedgers' net positions is consistent with the Keynesian hypothesis. According to this hypothesis, futures prices should be backwarded if hedgers are net short, and futures prices should exhibit contango if hedgers are net long. The inequality between hedgers' long and short positions requires the existence of speculators to fill the gap and restore equilibrium.[12] Since backwardation and contango can be regarded as a risk premium earned by speculators, backwardation (contango) attracts speculators to go long (short).[13] However, with regard to the hedging literature and in line with the model in the previous section, in addition to speculators, hedgers are motivated to hedge long (short) if futures prices exhibit backwardation (contango), as well. Hence, the causality may not run in one, but in both directions: Backwardation influences hedging activity, which in turn has an impact on backwardation. If the causality runs in both directions, the assumption underlying the ordinary least squares (OLS) method, that the explanatory variables (i.e., backwardation) are non-stochastic, does not hold. In fact, this assumption is likely to be violated since hedgers and speculators, as the main traders in futures markets, jointly determine the degree of backwardation. The simplest way to circumvent this problem, associated with OLS, is to employ a dynamic model where all variables are endogenous. In this study, vector autoregressive (VAR) and vector error correction (VECM) models are chosen for the empirical analysis. The flexible VAR and VECM models are dynamic in nature, and allow for a simple interpretation of the results. Applying VAR and VECM models to the analysis at hand may provide insights into the dynamics of hedgers' demand for futures contracts. Further reasons to employ dynamic models that allow for lagged values include the following. First, backwardation may not affect hedgers' demand immediately. It may take several time periods to adjust risk management strategies to a change in backwardation. It is reasonable to assume that trading activity reacts more slowly to changes in prices than prices react to changes in trading activity. The speed and extent of traders' reactions to price changes may depend on psychological, technological, and institutional factors. Second, hedging demand might initially overreact to changes in backwardation. The VAR and VECM models are able to capture these dynamics.

---

[12] Samuelson (1957, p. 194) points out that "(...) the total long position (of hedgers and speculators) must be exactly matched, at the equilibrium pattern, by the total short position (of hedgers and speculators)." See also Danthine (1978), Anderson and Danthine (1983) and Fort and Quirk (1988) for more information on backwardation and speculation.

[13] Note that, in addition of representing a risk premium, there are several alternative explanations of backwardation including the cost of carry, convenience yield, and capacity constraints. In fact, while the "(...) risk premium is unobserved (...)" (Inci and Lu, 2007, p. 181; see also Longstaff, 2000), "backwardation is an observable statistic (...)" (Frechette and Fackler, 1999, p. 761). Therefore it may be misleading to use the terms backwardation and risk premium interchangeably.

2.3.2 Vector Autoregression and Vector Error Correction Analysis

In order to check the stationarity properties of the series, augmented Dickey Fuller (ADF) tests with one lag and Kwiatowski, Phillips, Schmidt and Shin (KPSS) tests are carried out. The results indicate that several series, especially $AUD - Short$, $AUD - BW$, $EUR - Short$, $EUR - BW$, and $MXP - Short$ are integrated of order one (i.e., $I(1)$). Table 2.2 presents the results of the ADF and KPSS tests for the levels of the series and for the corresponding first differences (i.e., ADF-$I(1)$ and KPSS-$I(1)$). The levels of at least some of the variables are non-stationary, while taking first differences of the variables induces stationarity. The ADF-$I(1)$ and KPSS-$I(1)$ tests clearly suggest that all series are stationary.

Because at least some of the variables are integrated of order one, the next step in the analysis is to determine the cointegration properties of the variables. Table 2.3 presents the results of Johansen trace tests. The number of cointegrating ranks is determined sequentially. If the hypothesis that there are no cointegrating ranks ($r = 0$) is rejected, the analysis proceeds by testing for a cointegrating rank of one ($r = 1$). According to Lütkepohl (2004), the following decision rules apply: Choose a VAR model in first differences if the first null hypothesis ($r = 0$) cannot be

Table 2.2 Unit root tests

	ADF	KPSS	ADF-$I(1)$	KPSS-$I(1)$		ADF	KPSS	ADF-$I(1)$	KPSS-$I(1)$
					AUD				
Short	−0.9648	5.8098	−5.8886	0.0179	*BW*	−1.0887	5.8227	−15.2805	0.0089
Long	−1.8793	4.5654	−13.6720	0.0200	*BS*	−3.2506	2.0713	−15.4664	0.0109
					CAD				
Short	−1.7217	15.8062	−21.2685	0.0103	*BW*	−2.1031	14.9800	−23.7622	0.0735
Long	−2.9445	5.2036	−20.4193	0.0056	*BS*	−6.7597	3.2904	−24.7462	0.0195
					CHF				
Short	−3.7598	3.4793	−21.2730	0.0054	*BW*	−3.1524	13.1601	−24.2683	0.0308
Long	−2.9107	1.3423	−20.6706	0.0080	*BS*	−5.4092	3.5265	−24.3232	0.0118
					EUR				
Short	−1.4393	8.8683	−16.0090	0.0151	*BW*	−1.5966	3.0126	−20.7061	0.0063
Long	−1.9690	8.4793	−15.5425	0.0175	*BS*	−5.6774	4.0669	−20.9346	0.0099
					JPY				
Short	−2.6556	15.8938	−20.7894	0.0062	*BW*	−4.2248	9.1204	−22.8943	0.0120
Long	−1.9274	8.2294	−21.4288	0.0096	*BS*	−4.8501	3.1897	−22.8242	0.0081
					MXP				
Short	−1.1841	8.1529	−15.2272	0.0724	*BW*	−3.3479	18.8028	−19.0308	0.0284
Long	−1.7611	2.7243	−18.7324	0.0213	*BS*	−4.7321	15.8992	−18.9982	0.0273

Note: ADF and KPSS are the test statistics of the augmented Dickey Fuller and the Kwiatowski, Phillips, Schmidt and Shin test. The ADF test rejects the null hypothesis of nonstationarity if the test statistic is negative and the absolute value of the test statistic exceeds the critical value of the respective significance level: 1%: −2.56; 5%: −1.94; 10%: −1.62. The KPSS test rejects the null hypothesis of stationarity if the test statistic exceeds the critical value of the respective significance level: 1%: 0.739; 5%: 0.463; 10%: 0.347. For more information on the test statistics, see Lütkepohl and Krätzig (2004)

Table 2.3 Tests for cointegrating rank

		Short						*Long*					
		Lags	H0	LR	pval	90%	95%	Lags	H0	LR	pval	90%	95%
AUD	*BW*	2	0	35.73	0.0001	17.98	20.16	3	0	27.20	0.0038	17.98	20.16
			1	7.41	0.1085	7.60	9.14		1	8.08	0.0810	7.60	9.14
	BS	2	0	42.39	0.0000	17.98	20.16	2	0	56.57	0.0000	17.98	20.16
			1	7.42	0.1084	7.60	9.14		1	9.49	0.0426	7.60	9.14
CAD	*BW*	2	0	71.67	0.0000	17.98	20.16	2	0	97.99	0.0000	17.98	20.16
			1	20.01	0.0002	7.60	9.14		1	34.77	0.0000	7.60	9.14
	BS	2	0	65.27	0.0000	17.98	20.16	2	0	105.25	0.0000	17.98	20.16
			1	19.82	0.0002	7.60	9.14		1	36.24	0.0000	7.60	9.14
CHF	*BW*	3	0	99.04	0.0000	17.98	20.16	3	0	85.04	0.0000	17.98	20.16
			1	41.14	0.0000	7.60	9.14		1	30.03	0.0000	7.60	9.14
	BS	3	0	92.56	0.0000	17.98	20.16	3	0	81.80	0.0000	17.98	20.16
			1	39.08	0.0000	7.60	9.14		1	25.51	0.0000	7.60	9.14
EUR	*BW*	2	0	91.58	0.0000	17.98	20.16	3	0	64.80	0.0000	17.98	20.16
			1	19.29	0.0003	7.60	9.14		1	21.52	0.0001	7.60	9.14
	BS	3	0	51.20	0.0000	17.98	20.16	3	0	43.53	0.0000	17.98	20.16
			1	12.61	0.0096	7.60	9.14		1	19.80	0.0002	7.60	9.14
JPY	*BW*	3	0	94.57	0.0000	17.98	20.16	3	0	109.54	0.0000	17.98	20.16
			1	23.01	0.0000	7.60	9.14		1	21.59	0.0001	7.60	9.14
	BS	3	0	88.39	0.0000	17.98	20.16	3	0	84.69	0.0000	17.98	20.16
			1	25.32	0.0000	7.60	9.14		1	22.33	0.0001	7.60	9.14
MXP	*BW*	1	0	43.77	0.0000	17.98	20.16	3	0	41.18	0.0000	17.98	20.16
			1	5.61	0.2310	7.60	9.14		1	15.26	0.0026	7.60	9.14
	BS	1	0	55.88	0.0000	17.98	20.16	3	0	50.38	0.0000	17.98	20.16
			1	5.57	0.2349	7.60	9.14		1	15.58	0.0022	7.60	9.14

Note: In each case the lag length is chosen using the Akaike, Hannan-Quinn, and Schwartz information criteria. H0 represents the null hypothesis that the cointegrating rank r is 0 or 1, respectively. LR is the test statistics and pval is the p-value. 90% and 95% are the corresponding critical values

rejected. If $r = 0$ can be rejected but $r = 1$ cannot, a VECM model should be considered. If, however, all null hypothesis can be rejected, choose a VAR model in levels. Regarding the test results for the AUD and the $MXP - Short$ series, the Johansen trace tests reject the first null hypothesis ($r = 0$) of no cointegration whereas the null of $r = 1$ cannot be rejected. Therefore, following the decision rules, VECM models are chosen for the AUD and the $MXP - Short$ series. For the remaining series, VAR models in levels are chosen since all null hypotheses are rejected.

Table 2.4 presents the selected models, lag order, and Granger causality test results. The results of the Granger causality tests point to a significant impact of both weak and strong backwardation on short and long hedging activity. Most of the p-values are smaller than 0.05, indicating causal relations between backwardation and hedging activity. For 18 out of the total of 24 investigations, using a 5% significance level, the noncausality null hypothesis can be rejected. The next step in the analysis is to check whether the empirical results are consistent with economic theory.

Table 2.4 Lags and Granger causality test

		Short				*Long*			
		Model	Lags	Test value	p-value	Model	Lags	Test value	p-value
AUD	*BW*	VECM	1	1.9156	0.1484	VECM	3	8.0633	0.0000
	BS	VECM	1	2.3132	0.1000	VECM	1	13.9600	0.0000
CAD	*BW*	VAR	2	4.2170	0.0149	VAR	2	12.4582	0.0000
	BS	VAR	2	0.0112	0.9889	VAR	2	0.0812	0.9220
CHF	*BW*	VAR	3	21.3415	0.0000	VAR	3	21.6060	0.0000
	BS	VAR	3	13.3164	0.0000	VAR	3	16.0179	0.0000
EUR	*BW*	VAR	2	12.4326	0.0000	VAR	3	8.4114	0.0000
	BS	VAR	2	0.8242	0.4390	VAR	2	0.7981	0.4506
JPY	*BW*	VAR	3	36.8745	0.0000	VAR	3	45.7324	0.0000
	BS	VAR	3	32.2219	0.0000	VAR	3	41.7792	0.0000
MXP	*BW*	VECM	10	1.9845	0.0269	VAR	3	13.1686	0.0000
	BS	VECM	10	1.9911	0.0263	VAR	3	12.7187	0.0000

Note: In each case the lag length is chosen using the Akaike, Hannan-Quinn, and Schwartz information criteria

Figures 2.1 and 2.2 present the responses of short and long hedging activity to shocks in weak and strong backwardation. Again, economic theory suggests that, with growing backwardation, hedgers' demand for short futures contracts should be reduced and hedgers' demand for long futures contracts should increase. The impulse response functions reveal whether changes in weak and strong backwardation have a positive or negative effect on short and long hedging activity.

Considering the signs of the responses presented in Figs. 2.1 and 2.2, the empirical results do not unambiguously support the negative relation between backwardation and the trading volume of hedgers in short futures contracts as discussed in the theoretical hedging literature. Regarding the impact of weak backwardation on short hedging activity, the *AUD*, *CAD*, *CHF*, and *EUR* series show a positive response. The response of the *JPY* series reveals positive overshooting before turning negative after about 12 periods. Only the *MXP* series shows a negative effect of weak backwardation on short hedging activity, after an initial small positive reaction.

In contrast, the results for strong backwardation and short hedging activity are more significant. Here, four out of six responses (*AUD*, *CHF*, *JPY*, and *MXP*) indicate a negative impact of strong backwardation on short hedging activity after an initial overshooting. Moreover, for the remaining two series (*CAD* and *EUR*) the null hypothesis of no Granger causality cannot be rejected.

The results for long hedging activity and weak backwardation undoubtedly indicate a positive influence and, therefore, support the relation suggested by economic theory, even though two series (*AUD* and *MXP*) reveal initial negative overshooting. However, the results concerning strong backwardation and long hedging activity cannot support these findings. Only the *EUR* and *MXP* series show a positive response in the long run.

Summing up, six out of 12 responses of short hedging and eight out of 12 responses of long hedging are consistent with economic theory. Although the

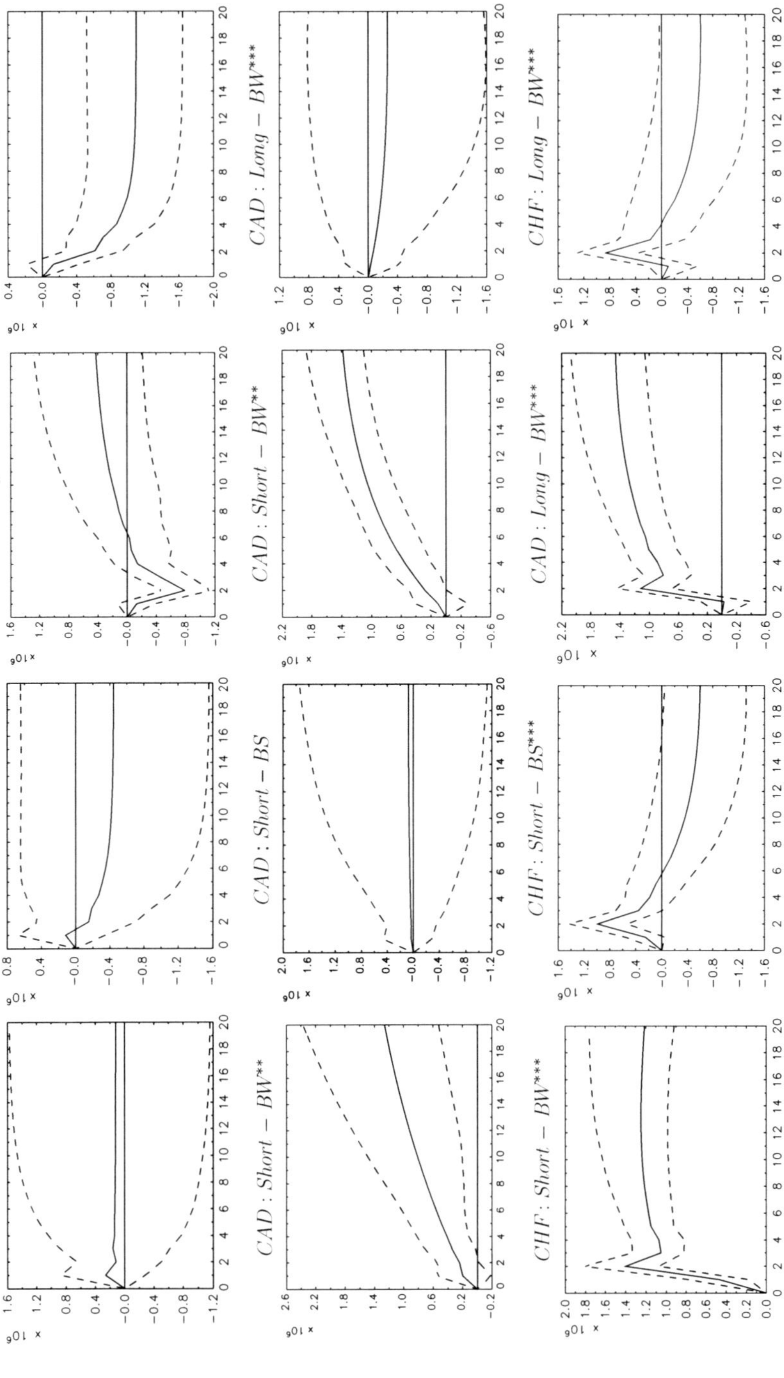

Fig. 2.1 Impulse response functions: Effects of weak (*BW*) and strong (*BS*) backwardation on short (*Short*) and long (*Long*) hedging activity. *Asterisks* *, **, and *** indicate that the null hypothesis of no Granger causality can be rejected on the 10%, 5%, and 1% levels, respectively

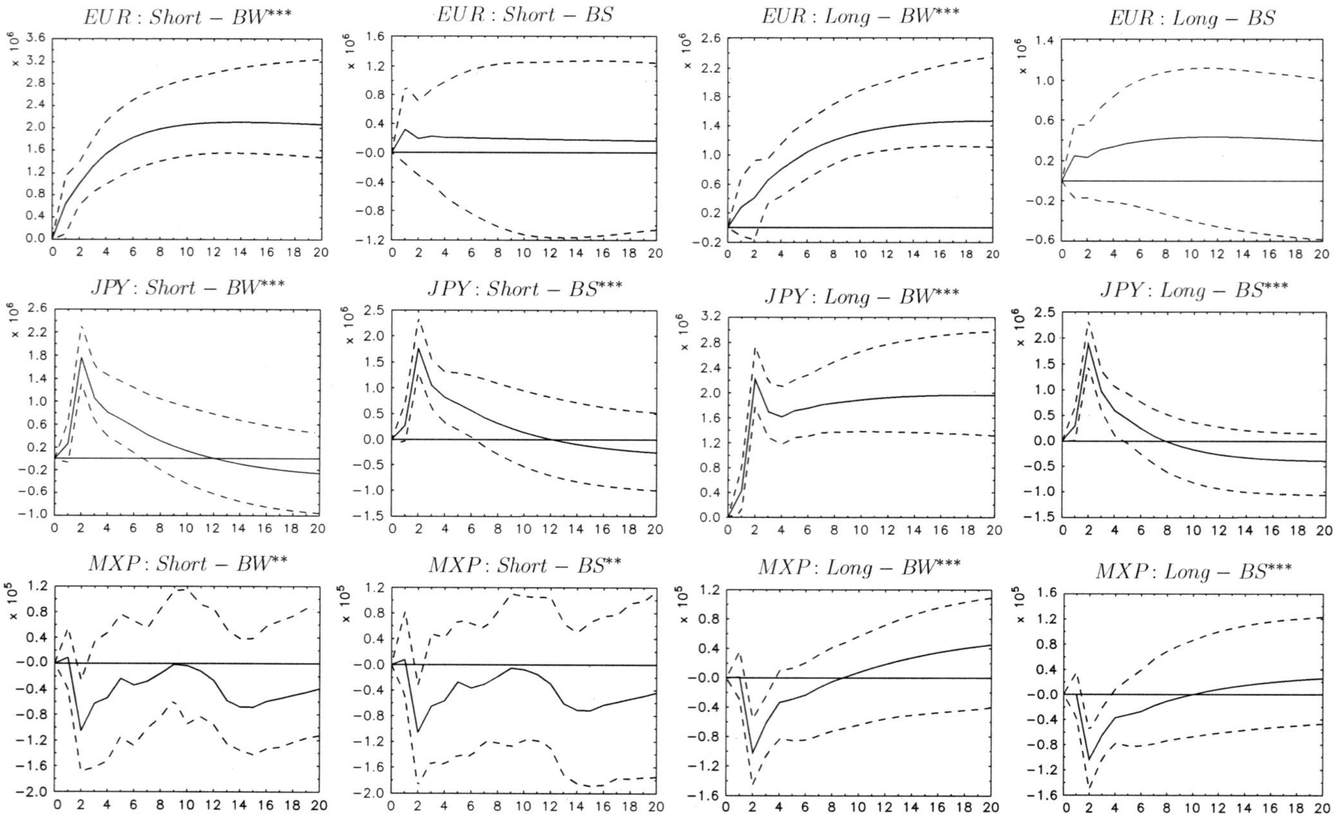

Fig. 2.2 Impulse response functions (continued): Effects of weak (*BW*) and strong (*BS*) backwardation on short (*Short*) and long (*Long*) hedging activity. *Asterisks* *, **, and *** indicate that the null hypothesis of no Granger causality can be rejected on the 10%, 5%, and 1% levels, respectively

Table 2.5 Diagnostic tests

		Short				*Long*			
		Port	LM	ARCH-LM	LJB	Port	LM	ARCH-LM	LJB
AUD	*BW*	0.3609	0.3767	0.2188	0.0000	0.1714	0.2105	0.1330	0.0000
	BS	0.2680	0.5542	0.5880	0.0000	0.0000	0.0035	0.0280	0.0000
CAD	*BW*	0.0001	0.0000	0.0000	0.0000	0.0008	0.0011	0.0429	0.0000
	BS	0.0336	0.0002	0.0000	0.0000	0.0131	0.0002	0.0350	0.0000
CHF	*BW*	0.0001	0.2331	0.0000	0.0000	0.0000	0.0000	0.0000	0.0000
	BS	0.0416	0.4304	0.0000	0.0000	0.0155	0.0066	0.0000	0.0000
EUR	*BW*	0.0524	0.0001	0.7007	0.0000	0.0700	0.0000	0.4392	0.0000
	BS	0.0349	0.0003	0.6213	0.0000	0.0578	0.0035	0.6277	0.0000
JPY	*BW*	0.0000	0.0465	0.0000	0.0000	0.0000	0.0077	0.0000	0.0000
	BS	0.0021	0.0158	0.0001	0.0000	0.0043	0.0013	0.0226	0.0000
MXP	*BW*	0.0000	0.0000	0.0020	0.0000	0.1972	0.3772	0.0524	0.0000
	BS	0.0000	0.0000	0.0028	0.0000	0.6040	0.5719	0.0639	0.0000

Note: Port and LM are the Portmanteau (10 lags) and Breusch–Godfrey Lagrange Multiplier tests (2 lags) for autocorrelation. ARCH-LM is the multivariate ARCH-LM test (5 lags). LJB is the Lomnicki–Jarque–Bera test for nonnormality

empirical results for long hedging are better than the results for short hedging, this empirical investigation offers little support for the hypotheses suggested by economic theory.

A series of diagnostic tests for autocorrelation, nonnormality, and ARCH effects in the residuals are conducted and the p-values of the tests are presented in Table 2.5. The results of the diagnostic tests are not all fully satisfactory. For example, the results for $CAD - Short$, $CAD - Long$, $CHF - Long$, $JPY - Short$, $JPY - Long$, and $MXP - Short$, all reject the respective null hypotheses of no autocorrelation, no ARCH and normality. The problem of autocorrelation in the residuals might be solved by using a model in first differences rather than in levels. However, this would contradict the decision rules applied in the context of the Johansen trace test. A second potential solution is to include more lags into the analysis. This, however, may result in imprecise coefficient estimates if the lag order is chosen too large.[14] Moreover, the lag structure is chosen by employing the Akaike, Hannan-Quinn, and Schwartz information criteria and should therefore not be altered.[15] According to Lütkepohl (2004, p. 131), the remaining ARCH found in several residuals may not be a big problem "(...) if the linear dependencies are of major concern (...)". The rejection of normality may be caused by few very extreme residuals. Because of the large sample sizes in this study the violation of the normality assumption should

[14] See e.g., Lütkepohl (1990).

[15] Note that a number of specifications of VAR and VECM models have been applied to the data, yielding results similar to the ones presented in the text. For more information on residual autocorrelation, VARs, and VECMs, see e.g., Brüggemann (2006) and Brüggemann, Lütkepohl, and Saikkonen (2006).

be inconsequential due to a central limit theorem.[16] Since the main purpose of this chapter is to investigate the sign of the impact of backwardation on hedging activity, the empirical results are still sufficient. With respect to diagnostic tests, Ericsson (1999, p. 42) argues that the "(...) rejection of the null does not imply the alternative. Even so, test rejections are informative by demonstrating that the model can be improved." However, finding potential directions of improvement will be left for future research.

2.4 Discussion

This chapter investigates the impact of backwardation on long and short hedging activity in currency futures markets. First, the optimal long hedging strategy of an importer exposed to currency risk is derived in an expected utility framework with and without hedging costs. The model suggests that it is optimal for the long hedging importer to overhedge (underhedge) if the futures market exhibits backwardation (contango). The importing firm hedges fully if the futures market is unbiased. However, in the presence of hedging costs, the firm hedges fully if the futures market is characterized by backwardation. Therefore, hedging costs provide a rationale for backwardation to exist. Irrespective of whether hedging costs are introduced into the model, backwardation has a positive impact on the size of the firm's optimal long hedging position.

The empirical part of this chapter investigates the relationship between backwardation and hedgers' demand for six currency futures contracts, using vector autoregressive and vector error correction models. The summary statistics suggest that backwardation and contango are indeed normal in currency futures markets, as proposed by Keynes (1930). However, the hypothesis of a negative (positive) impact of backwardation on short (long) hedging activity cannot be supported.

The contribution of this chapter is threefold. First, the hedging problem of the representative exporter, examined by Holthausen (1979) and Briys and Schlesinger (1993), is extended to the hedging problem of an importer. Second, hedging costs are found to provide a rationale for backwardation to be normal. Finally, the impact of backwardation on long and short hedgers' trading volume in currency futures markets is investigated empirically. To the best of our knowledge, this is the first study to directly regress hedgers' position data from the Commitments of Traders (COT) report on two measures of backwardation. However, the results offer little support for the hypotheses suggested by economic theory.

[16] See e.g., Brooks (2002) for a detailed discussion on how to deal with autocorrelation, heteroscedasticity, and nonnormality.

Chapter 3
Mean-Variance Versus Minimum-Variance Hedging

"One gains the impression that hedging, like a hitchhiker, seized the chance for a ride since speculation presented the opportunity. But as statistics have been accumulated that give appropriate quantitative information on futures markets, year in and year out, hedging begins to look like the driver, and speculation in futures like a companion going where hedging gives it opportunity to go."

Working (1953, p. 318).

3.1 Introduction

The hedging model introduced in this chapter is an extension of the expected utility approach in Chap. 2 The importing firm's hedging problem here is almost identical to the one before. The only difference is that this model allows for basis risk. This is important with regard to the definition of backwardation applied. While in the previous chapter backwardation is defined as the difference between the expected spot price and the current futures price (i.e., $\tilde{e}_1 - f_0$), here, backwardation is defined as the difference between the expected futures price and the current futures price (i.e., $\tilde{f}_1 - f_0$). Note that these two definitions of backwardation are equal in the absence of basis risk (i.e., if $\tilde{e}_1 = \tilde{f}_1$). However, aside from basis risk, the model framework is quite different, since the analysis in this chapter is based on the mean-variance concept. Nevertheless, this approach can be regarded as an extension, since mean-variance models are generally not in conflict with expected utility models.[1] On the contrary, mean-variance models have several attractive properties that may add additional insights.

One of these attractive properties is that the impact of risk aversion on the importer's optimal hedging strategy can be modeled explicitly. Moreover, the role of hedging costs and backwardation, which were already investigated in the previous

[1] See e.g., Battermann, Broll, and Wahl (2002) and Broll, Wahl, and Wong (2006).

A. Röthig, *Microeconomic Risk Management and Macroeconomic Stability*,
Lecture Notes in Economics and Mathematical Systems,
DOI 10.1007/978-3-642-01565-6_3,

chapter, can be modeled in more detail. In this chapter, the impact of risk aversion, hedging costs and backwardation on the optimal hedging strategy are investigated empirically by applying data for the Australian Dollar (AUD), Canadian Dollar (CAD), Swiss Francs (CHF), Euro (EUR), Japanese Yen (JPY), and Mexican Peso (MXP) futures contracts to the model.

Another interesting property of this modeling approach is that the derived optimal hedge ratio can be analyzed in more detail. The optimal hedge can be decomposed into a pure hedge component and a speculative component. Overhedging and underhedging can be regarded a consequence of speculative demand, affecting the hedging decision, where the pure hedge can be viewed as the full hedge or "equal and opposite" hedge, respectively. In fact, it is shown in this chapter that the pure hedge is close to the "equal and opposite" hedge for the data applied. Based on the optimal hedging demand, and following Frechette (2000), futures demand can be illustrated as a stylized Marshallian-type demand curve. Assuming futures supply to be independent of costs, a stylized futures market is constructed. Using this representation of the futures market, the hedgers' surplus is analyzed graphically and analytically. Moreover, the effect of risk aversion and hedging costs on the hedgers' surplus are examined.

A further important property of the mean-variance approach is that it can be easily compared to the minimum-variance approach, which is very popular in the field of theoretical and applied finance. The minimum-variance approach can be regarded a fraction of the mean-variance analysis, leading to the pure, risk-minimizing hedge, which neglects the hedger's expectations, hedging costs and risk aversion. Hence, the speculative component is nonexistent in the minimum-variance approach. This approach is derived in this chapter and applied to the data. Moreover, the effectiveness of this hedging strategy is discussed and its relation to the so-called statistical hedging using regression analysis is investigated.

Section 3.2 presents the mean-variance approach. The optimal hedge is derived and the impact of risk aversion, hedging costs and price expectations on optimal hedging are investigated. Moreover, the optimal hedge ratio is decomposed into the pure hedge and the speculative demand, and the hedgers' surplus is investigated. Section 3.3 deals with minimum-variance hedging, hedging effectiveness and empirical hedging using regression analysis. Section 3.4 concludes.

3.2 The Mean-Variance Approach to Hedging

3.2.1 The Model

The importer's expected profit is identical to the expected profit in the previous chapter. However, the model framework used in this chapter is quite different to the one used before. In contrast to the expected utility approach in the previous chapter, here, mean-variance analysis is conducted. Again, the starting point of the model is the representative importer's expected profit[2]

$$E(\Pi) = -\tilde{e}_1 x + (\tilde{f}_1 - f_0 - c)h, \tag{3.1}$$

which depends negatively on the random exchange rate $\tilde{e}_1$. In order to hedge the spot exposure, the importer can go long in currency futures markets, where c again represents hedging costs. The variance of profit is

$$\begin{aligned} V(\Pi) &= V(-\tilde{e}_1 x + (\tilde{f}_1 - f_0 - c)h) \\ &= V(-\tilde{e}_1 x + \tilde{f}_1 h - f_0 h - ch). \end{aligned} \tag{3.2}$$

Using $V(X+Y) = V(X) + V(Y) + 2Cov(X,Y)$, and the fact that the current futures price f_0 and hedging costs c are non-stochastic, yields:[3]

$$V(\Pi) = V(-\tilde{e}_1 x) + V(\tilde{f}_1 h) + 2Cov(-\tilde{e}_1 x, \tilde{f}_1 h). \tag{3.3}$$

Further simplification by using $V(\lambda X) = \lambda^2 V(X)$, $Cov(\lambda X, Y) = \lambda Cov(X,Y)$, and $V(Const) = 0$ leads to:

$$V(\Pi) = x^2 V(\tilde{e}_1) + h^2 V(\tilde{f}_1) - 2xhCov(\tilde{e}_1, \tilde{f}_1). \tag{3.4}$$

The objective function to be maximized is

$$\underset{h}{Max}\,\Omega = E(\Pi) - \lambda V(\Pi), \tag{3.5}$$

where λ represents risk aversion. Inserting for expected profit and the variance of profit in (3.5) yields:

$$\underset{h}{Max}\,\Omega = -\tilde{e}_1 x + (\tilde{f}_1 - f_0 - c)h - \lambda(x^2 V(\tilde{e}_1) + h^2 V(\tilde{f}_1) - 2xhCov(\tilde{e}_1, \tilde{f}_1)). \tag{3.6}$$

3.2.2 *Optimal Hedging*

Since the level of spot commitment x is given, the optimal hedge can be determined by differentiating the objective function in (3.6) with respect to the amount of futures traded h:[4]

$$\frac{\delta\Omega}{\delta h} = \tilde{f}_1 - f_0 - c - 2\lambda hV(\tilde{f}_1) + 2\lambda xCov(\tilde{e}_1, \tilde{f}_1). \tag{3.7}$$

---

[2] Note that the only difference to the model in the previous chapter is that basis risk is not absent. Hence, $\tilde{e}_1 \neq \tilde{f}_1$.

[3] For more information on the properties of expectations operators, variances, and covariances, see e.g., Pindyck and Rubinfeld (1998).

[4] See e.g., Kahl (1983).

Solving for h gives the optimal hedge:[5]

$$\begin{aligned} h &= \frac{\tilde{f}_1 - f_0 - c + 2\lambda x Cov(\tilde{e}_1, \tilde{f}_1)}{2\lambda V(\tilde{f}_1)} \\ &= \frac{\tilde{f}_1 - f_0 - c}{2\lambda V(\tilde{f}_1)} + \frac{x Cov(\tilde{e}_1, \tilde{f}_1)}{V(\tilde{f}_1)}. \end{aligned} \tag{3.8}$$

Solving for the optimal hedge ratio h/x yields:

$$\frac{h}{x} = \frac{\tilde{f}_1 - f_0 - c}{2\lambda V(\tilde{f}_1)} \frac{1}{x} + \frac{Cov(\tilde{e}_1, \tilde{f}_1)}{V(\tilde{f}_1)}. \tag{3.9}$$

Since the hedge ratio represents a quantity of futures contracts demanded, standardized by the size of the spot commitment, and since hedging costs c can be regarded the price for hedging, the optimal hedge ratio presented in (3.9) is equivalent to the demand curve for hedging.[6] Figure 3.1 presents the optimal hedge ratio depending on hedging costs c for the AUD, CAD, CHF, EUR, JPY, and MXP series.

The values of the respective variance and covariance terms, used in Fig. 3.1 and in the following graphical representations, are given in Table 3.1. It is assumed that the futures market is unbiased (i.e., $\tilde{f}_1 = f_0 = 1$). The size of the spot commitment is set to $x = 1$ and the risk aversion variable is chosen to be $\lambda = 3$. Following Lence (1995a, 1996), this level of λ reflects moderate risk aversion. Increasing hedging costs reduces the demand for futures contracts and therefore the optimal hedge ratio, as shown in Fig. 3.1. The demand for futures contracts is a linear downward sloping function of hedging costs. If hedging costs are zero, the optimal hedge ratio is close to one for all currencies investigated. Hence, in the absence of hedging costs, the firm chooses the size of the futures position to equal the size of the spot commitment. The optimal hedge is the well known "equal and opposite" hedge. Note that only the MXP series shows a larger deviation from the "equal and opposite" hedge when hedging costs are absent. Here, the optimal hedging strategy is to overhedge. The firm therefore chooses a futures position larger than the initial spot exposure. This is because in the case of the MXP series the covariance term is larger than the variance term $V(\tilde{f}_1)$. The term $Cov(\tilde{e}_1, \tilde{f}_1)/V(\tilde{f}_1)$, accordingly, exceeds one.

Figure 3.2 presents the effect of risk aversion on the optimal hedge ratio. Again, the futures market is assumed to be unbiased (i.e., $\tilde{f}_1 = f_0 = 1$) and the size of the spot commitment is $x = 1$. Since $\tilde{f}_1 - f_0 = 0$, risk aversion has an impact on hedging activity only if hedging costs c are not zero. Hedging costs are therefore

---

[5] The condition for a maximum

$$\frac{\delta^2 \Omega}{\delta h^2} = -2V(\tilde{f}_1)\lambda < 0$$

is fulfilled given risk aversion (i.e., $\lambda > 0$).

[6] See e.g., Frechette (2000) and Jin and Koo (2006).

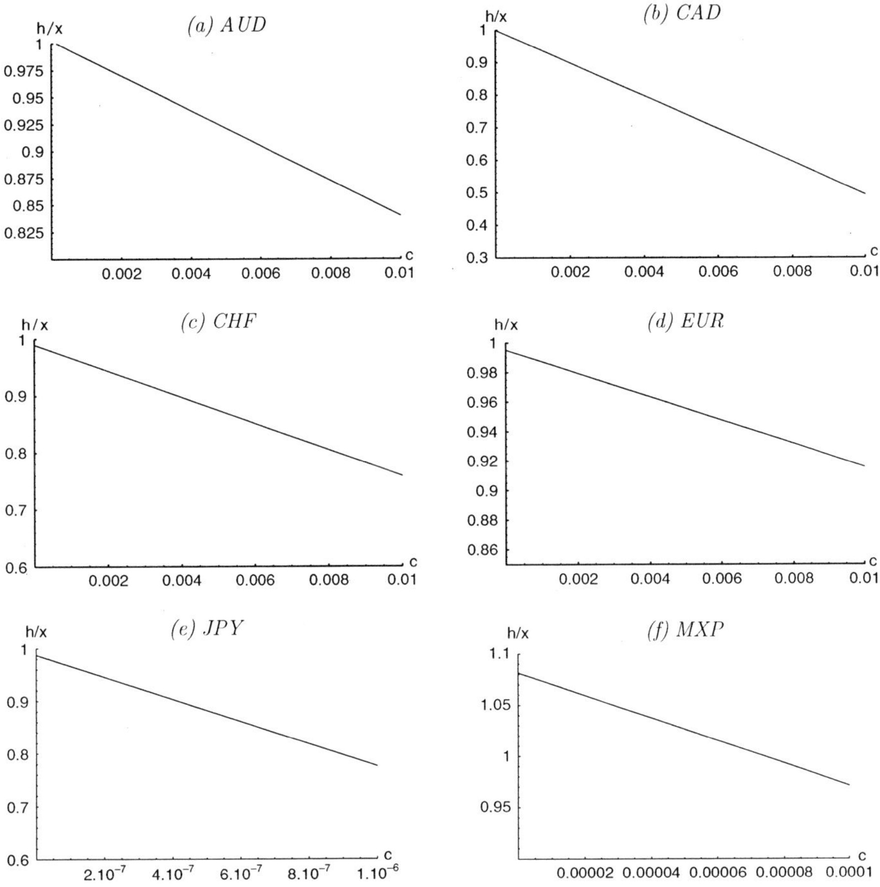

Fig. 3.1 Hedging costs and the optimal hedge ratio

Table 3.1 Variances and covariances

	AUD	CAD	CHF	EUR	JPY	MXP
Sample	01/02/2001–01/31/2006	10/06/1992–01/31/2006	10/06/1992–01/31/2006	01/12/1999–01/31/2006	10/06/1992–01/31/2006	03/26/1996–01/31/2006
$V(\tilde{e})$	0.01040773	0.00330530	0.00709616	0.02094100	0.0000007719	0.00018025
$V(\tilde{f})$	0.01026839	0.00329519	0.00721265	0.02101602	0.0000007876	0.00015096
Cov	0.01029400	0.00329353	0.00713953	0.02091480	0.0000007778	0.00016326

chosen to be $c = 0.001$ for the *AUD*, *CAD*, *CHF*, and *EUR* series, $c = 0.000001$ for the *JPY* series and $c = 0.0001$ for the *MXP* series. Increasing risk aversion increases the demand for hedging instruments. The graphical representations for the *AUD*, *CAD*, *CHF*, *EUR*, *JPY*, and *MXP* series show concave functions. Risk aversion affects hedging activity strongest at its low and moderate levels. Lence

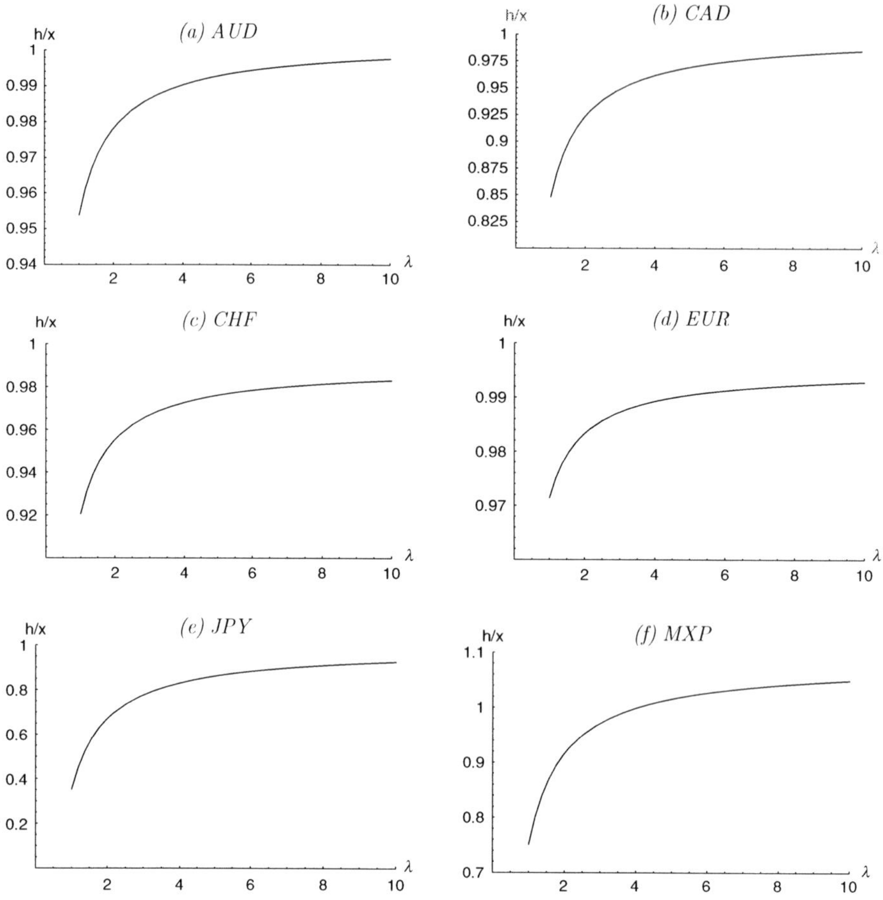

Fig. 3.2 Risk aversion and the optimal hedge ratio

(1995a, 1996) defines levels of risk aversion to be low if $\lambda = 1$, moderate if $\lambda = 3$, and high if $\lambda = 10$. In fact, Lence (1995a, p. 357) labels the level of risk aversion of $\lambda = 10$ "extremely high". According to him, this extremely high level of risk aversion is not plausible and results based on $\lambda = 10$ should therefore be interpreted with care. In the following calculations and graphical illustrations, a moderate risk aversion level of $\lambda = 3$ will be chosen. However, as risk aversion approaches infinity, the optimal hedge ratio presented in Fig. 3.2 converges to the "equal and opposite" hedge position.

It was shown in the previous chapter that hedgers' demand for long futures contracts depends positively on the extend of backwardation. Using a different definition of backwardation in this chapter, one which allows for basis risk, the effect of backwardation on hedgers' demand for long futures contracts can be investigated. Again, note that while in the previous chapter in the absence of basis risk

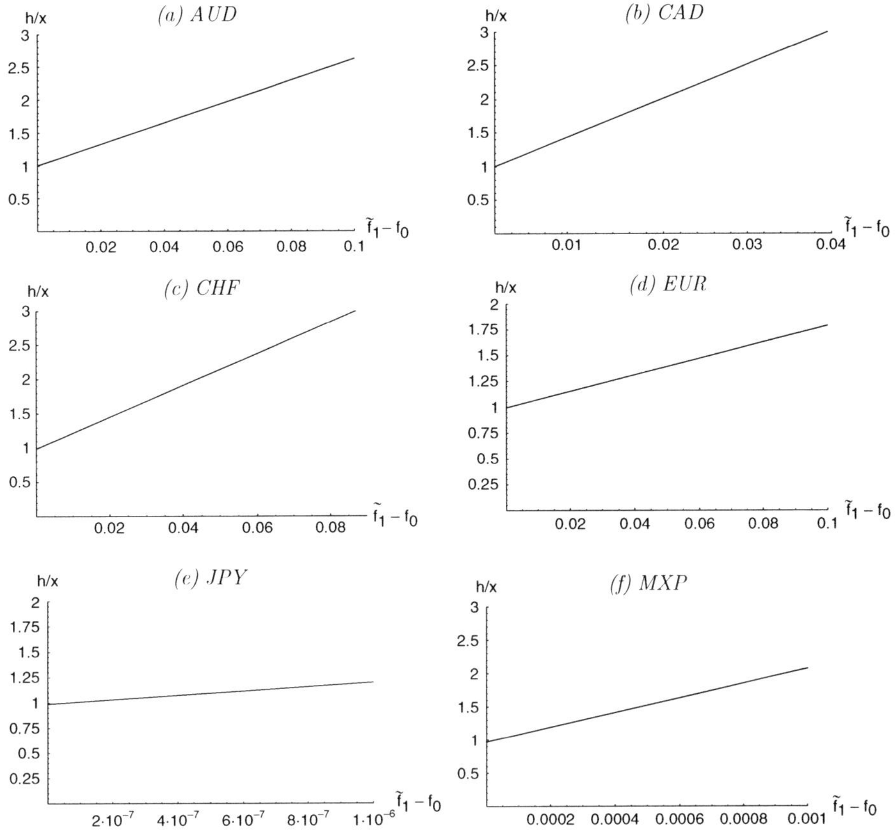

Fig. 3.3 Backwardation and the optimal hedge ratio

backwardation was defined as the difference between the expected spot price and the current futures price (i.e., $\tilde{e}_1 - f_0$), here, backwardation is defined as the difference between the expected futures price and the current futures price (i.e., $\tilde{f}_1 - f_0$).[7] In the literature, this latter definition of backwardation is often referred to as expected return of the futures position. Figure 3.3 shows a positive impact of backwardation on the size of the optimal hedge position. Hedging costs, risk aversion and the size of the spot commitment are set to $c = 0$, $\lambda = 3$, and $x = 1$, respectively. Since the futures position promises additional payoffs in the presence of backwardation, the firm overhedges the spot exposure. Hence, the futures position is larger than the spot commitment. As shown in Fig. 3.3, the hedge ratio h/x exceeds one if $\tilde{f}_1 - f_0$ is positive for all currencies investigated.

[7] Again, these definitions of backwardation are equal if basis risk is absent (i.e., if $\tilde{e}_1 = \tilde{f}_1$).

3.2.3 Pure Hedging and Speculative Demand

The role of expectations for the firm's hedging strategy is very important. Suppose the firm expects $\tilde{f}_1 - f_0$ to be positive and therefore overhedges. In this case, expected profits, as presented in (3.1), depend positively on exchange rate changes if the extent of basis risk is small (i.e., if $\tilde{e}_1 \approx \tilde{f}_1$), since $h > x$. This overhedge can be regarded as speculation, since the firm does not minimize the existing spot risk, but takes on additional risk in the futures market. In this context, Hawtrey (1940, p. 205) writes that:

> "If all hedging traders are supposed to have expectations, they are all potential speculators, and they will be more likely to abstain from incurring some probable loss on hedging if they are very confident that the expected price will be realised."

This may lead to some confusion and hence make it difficult to clearly differentiate between hedgers and speculators, since a speculator can be defined as an agent with an open position (i.e., an agent who does not fully hedge). Pure or full hedging deals with minimizing existing spot exposure and is therefore not concerned with earning profits with the futures position. As depicted in Figs. 3.1, 3.2, and 3.3, costs, risk aversion, and expectations about potential gains in the futures position may lead hedgers to not hedge fully but to underhedge or overhedge. In order to analyze these effects on the firm's hedging strategy in more detail, the optimal hedge ratio presented in (3.9) can be decomposed into a pure hedge component and a speculative component:[8]

- Pure hedging demand:

$$HD = \frac{Cov(\tilde{e}_1, \tilde{f}_1)}{V(\tilde{f}_1)}. \tag{3.10}$$

- Speculative demand:

$$SD = \frac{\tilde{f}_1 - f_0 - c}{2\lambda V(\tilde{f}_1)} \frac{1}{x}. \tag{3.11}$$

Expected futures returns, costs, and risk aversion affect the speculative demand. In accordance with Heifner (1972, 1973), the speculative demand is zero if hedging costs are absent and the futures market is unbiased (i.e., $\tilde{f}_1 - f_0 = 0$). In addition, the speculative demand approaches zero as risk aversion approaches infinity. The representations of pure hedging and speculative demand will be used to examine the relation between expected returns, costs and hedging activity in what follows. The parameter for risk aversion is therefore set to $\lambda = 3$ and the size of the spot position is set to $x = 1$.

It is important to note that the pure hedge shown in (3.10) is not affected by costs, risk aversion and expectations about prices. Concerning the graphical representation in Fig. 3.4a–f, the pure hedges are represented by the horizontal gray lines. For all currency futures markets investigated in this study, the pure hedging ratio is close to

---

[8] See e.g., Briys and Schlesinger (1993), Briys et al. (1993) and Duffie (1989).

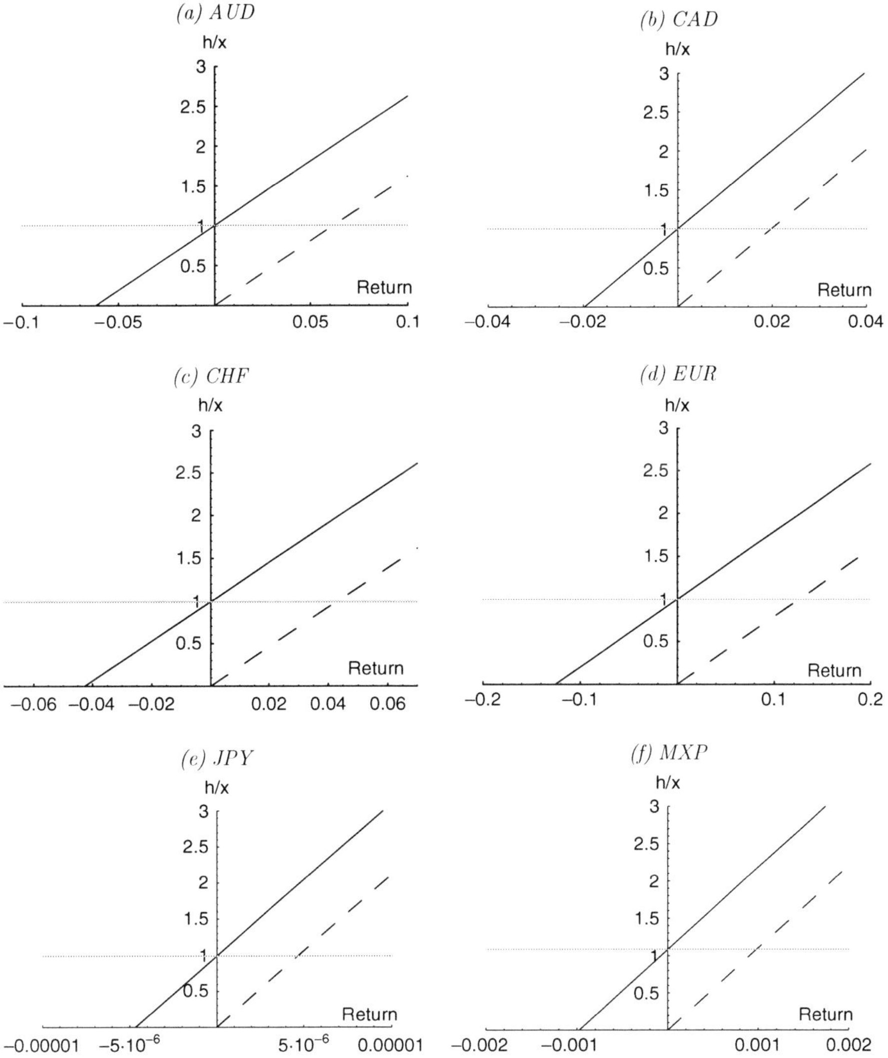

Fig. 3.4 Speculative and pure hedging demand. The optimal hedge ratio h/x is the *straight black line*. Return is defined as $\tilde{f}_1 - f_0 - c$. The speculative demand is the *dashed line* and the pure hedging demand is the *straight gray line*

one. This means that the futures position is about the same size as the spot position. Hence, the pure hedge is approximately the "equal and opposite" or "one to one" hedge ratio.

All deviations from this "equal and opposite" hedge ratio are caused by the speculative demand. Let the pure hedge represent the "equal and opposite" hedge where the futures position equals the spot position. Then this pure hedging strategy can be labelled as full hedging strategy. Since the firm hedges fully if speculative demand is zero, deviations in speculative demand cause the firm to underhedge or overhedge, respectively. The optimal hedge ratio is positive as long as

$$c < \tilde{f}_1 - f_0 + 2\lambda x Cov(\tilde{e}_1, \tilde{f}_1). \tag{3.12}$$

The firm underhedges if the hedge ratio is positive but smaller than the full hedge. As shown in Table 3.2, this is the case if the speculative demand is negative, which in turn is due to the hedging costs outweighing expected returns of the futures position. Regarding Fig. 3.4, this is the case where h/x is left of the y-axis and above the x-axis.

If hedging costs are zero and the futures market is unbiased, or, if hedging costs are positive and equal to the futures market bias, the speculative demand is zero and the optimal hedge ratio therefore reduces to the pure hedge. This full hedging strategy is represented by the intersection of the hedge ratio with the $HD - line$ and the y-axis in Fig. 3.4. At this point, speculative demand is zero and therefore the dashed $SD - line$ intersects the x-axis. With growing expected returns, the firm demands more futures contracts than necessary to reduce risk. Since the speculative demand increases, the futures position is larger than the spot position. The firm therefore overhedges its spot exposure. In Fig. 3.4 the $SD - line$ represents the extra demand for futures contracts that adds to the pure hedge $HD - line$. The overall

Table 3.2 Full, over-, and underhedging

Costs	Speculative demand	Hedging strategy	Hedge ratio
$c > \tilde{f}_1 - f_0$	$SD < 0$	Underhedging	$h/x < HD$
$c = \tilde{f}_1 - f_0$	$SD = 0$	Full hedging	$h/x = HD$
$c < \tilde{f}_1 - f_0$	$SD > 0$	Overhedging	$h/x > HD$

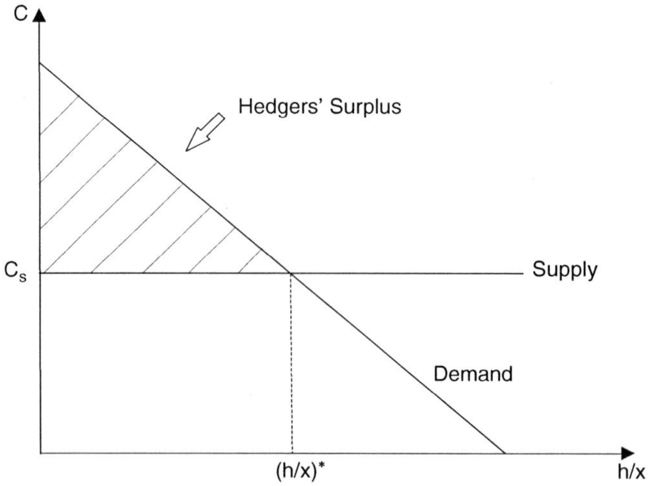

Fig. 3.5 The hedgers' surplus

hedge ratio, which is the sum of pure hedge and speculative demand, therefore, exceeds the full hedge. Hence, the firm overhedges.

3.2.4 *The Value of the Futures Market*

Since the hedge ratio is analogous to the quantity of futures contracts per spot position demanded by the hedger, and the hedging cost is the price for hedging, (3.9) can be regarded as the demand curve for hedging. The empirical results presented in Fig. 3.1 point to a linear, negative relation between hedging costs and the demand for futures contracts. The stylized Marshallian-type demand curve presented in Fig. 3.5 is therefore linear and downward sloping as well.[9] Following Frechette (2000), the supply curve is a horizontal line, where c_s represents the price for hedging demanded by the hedger's broker. The hedgers' surplus is the area above the horizontal supply line and left of the demand curve.[10]

According to Frechette (2000), the hedgers' surplus measures the value of the futures market for the hedging firm. The hedgers' surplus can be calculated as[11]

$$HS = \Omega H - \Omega 0, \tag{3.13}$$

where ΩH and $\Omega 0$ is the objective function presented in (3.5) with and without hedging, respectively:

$$\Omega H = -\tilde{e}_1 x + (\tilde{f}_1 - f_0 - c_s)h - \lambda(x^2 V(\tilde{e}_1) + h^2 V(\tilde{f}_1) - 2xhCov(\tilde{e}_1, \tilde{f}_1)), \tag{3.14}$$

$$\begin{aligned} \Omega 0 &= -\tilde{e}_1 x + (\tilde{f}_1 - f_0 - c_s)0 - \lambda(x^2 V(\tilde{e}_1) + 0^2 V(\tilde{f}_1) - 2x0Cov(\tilde{e}_1, \tilde{f}_1)) \\ &= -\tilde{e}_1 x - \lambda(x^2 V(\tilde{e}_1)). \end{aligned} \tag{3.15}$$

Let, for simplicity, the spot commitment be standardized to $x = 1$. Inserting for ΩH and $\Omega 0$ in (3.13) yields

$$\begin{aligned} HS &= -\tilde{e}_1 + (\tilde{f}_1 - f_0 - c_s)h - \lambda(V(\tilde{e}_1) + h^2 V(\tilde{f}_1) \\ &\quad - 2hCov(\tilde{e}_1, \tilde{f}_1)) - (-\tilde{e}_1 - \lambda(V(\tilde{e}_1))) \\ &= (\tilde{f}_1 - f_0 - c_s)h - \lambda(h^2 V(\tilde{f}_1) - 2hCov(\tilde{e}_1, \tilde{f}_1)). \end{aligned} \tag{3.16}$$

---

[9] For a similar graphical representation of demand curves for hedging goods, see Frechette (2000) and Jin and Koo (2006).

[10] The graphical representation of the hedgers' surplus resembles the standard consumers' surplus in economic theory.

[11] An alternative derivation of the hedgers' surplus is presented in the appendix.

The next step is to solve the optimal hedge ratio given in (3.9) for the covariance term

$$Cov(\tilde{e}_1, \tilde{f}_1) = \frac{-\tilde{f}_1 + f_0 + c_s + 2\lambda h V(\tilde{f}_1)}{2\lambda}, \tag{3.17}$$

and inserting in (3.16) yields

$$\begin{aligned} HS &= (\tilde{f}_1 - f_0 - c_s)h - \lambda(h^2 V(\tilde{f}_1) - 2h(\frac{-\tilde{f}_1 + f_0 + c_s + 2\lambda h V(\tilde{f}_1)}{2\lambda})) \\ &= \lambda h^2 V(\tilde{f}_1), \end{aligned} \tag{3.18}$$

which is equivalent to the result obtained by Frechette (2000).

Figure 3.6 presents the hedgers' surplus as a function of risk aversion λ and hedging costs c. The empirical results for the *AUD*, *CAD*, *CHF*, *EUR*, *JPY*, and *MXP* series suggest a positive impact of risk aversion and a negative effect of hedging costs on the hedgers' surplus. Hence, the value of the futures market increases as firms become more risk averse. However, firms appreciate the futures market less as hedging costs increase.

3.3 Minimum-Variance Hedging and Hedging Effectiveness

This section presents a well known and very popular hedging method, widely used in theoretical and applied finance. Regarding the investigation in the previous sections, this minimum-variance approach can be regarded as a component of the mean-variance analysis. While the mean-variance approach is based on both the firm's expected profit and the variance of profit, the minimum-variance approach simply deals with the variance. Although this approach is very practical and popular, it will be shown that, compared to the mean-variance analysis, information is neglected.

3.3.1 Deriving the Pure Hedge

Applying the minimum-variance approach to the importer's hedging problem leads to the pure hedge presented in (3.10). To see this, recall that the variance of profits is

$$V(\Pi) = x^2 V(\tilde{e}_1) + h^2 V(\tilde{f}_1) - 2xhCov(\tilde{e}_1, \tilde{f}_1). \tag{3.19}$$

The partial derivative with respect to h is

$$\frac{V(\Pi)}{h} = 2hV(\tilde{f}_1) - 2xCov(\tilde{e}_1, \tilde{f}_1). \tag{3.20}$$

The optimal hedge ratio is then given by

$$\frac{h}{x} = \frac{Cov(\tilde{e}_1, \tilde{f}_1)}{V(\tilde{f}_1)}, \tag{3.21}$$

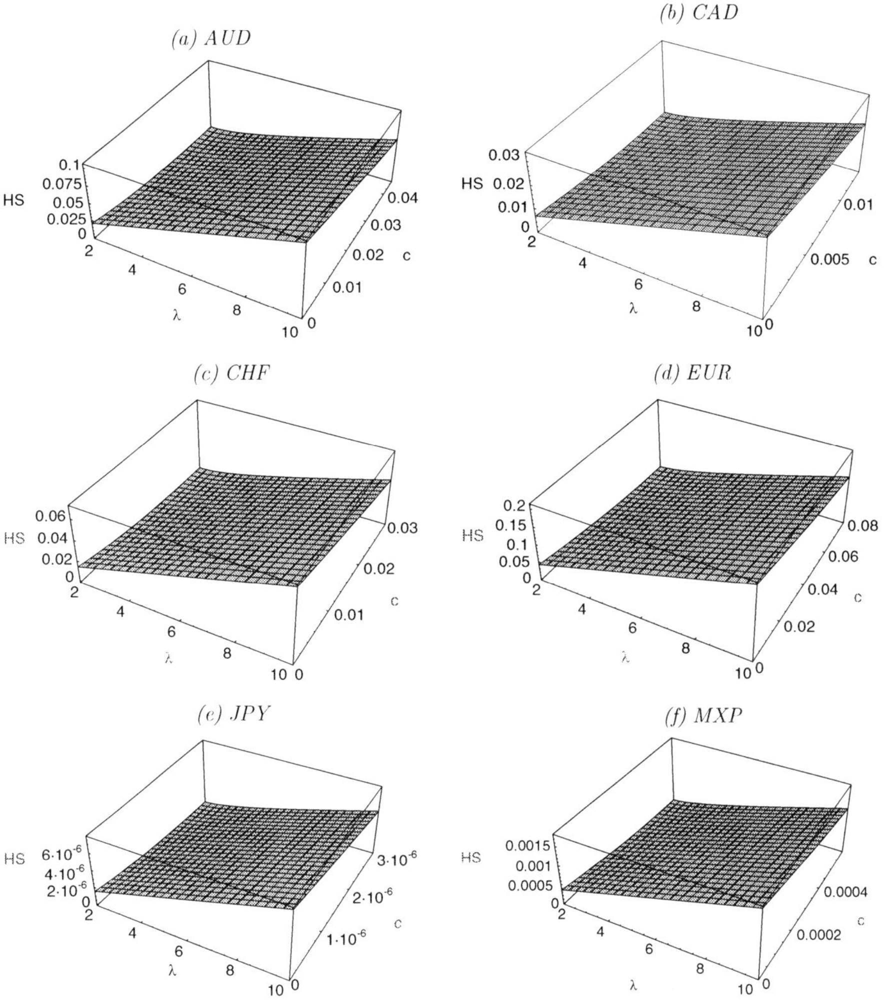

Fig. 3.6 The hedgers' surplus as a function of risk aversion and hedging costs

which is the pure hedge presented in (3.10). Hence the speculative demand is not a component of the optimal hedge ratio anymore. Therefore risk aversion, hedging costs, and price expectations do not affect the minimum-variance hedge ratio. Since this hedge is independent of the individual firm's characteristics, such as risk aversion and expectations, it is equal for all hedgers. Moreover, applying this hedging method is very simple, since hedge ratios are based solely on price data which are assumed to be available to the hedging firm.

3.3.2 Hedging Effectiveness and Correlation

Minimum-variance hedging is indeed very popular. However, this popularity is not only due to its simplicity, but also to its effectiveness with respect to reducing the spot risk exposure. Following Heifner (1972) and Ederington (1979), hedging effectiveness can be measured as the percent reduction in the variance of profits:

$$HE = 1 - \frac{Variance\ \ with\ \ hedging}{Variance\ \ without\ \ hedging}. \tag{3.22}$$

Inserting (3.19) yields:

$$\begin{aligned} HE &= 1 - \left(\frac{x^2V(\tilde{e}_1) + h^2V(\tilde{f}_1) - 2xhCov(\tilde{e}_1,\tilde{f}_1)}{x^2V(\tilde{e}_1) + 0^2V(\tilde{f}_1) - 2x0Cov(\tilde{e}_1,\tilde{f}_1)}\right) \\ &= 1 - \left(\frac{x^2V(\tilde{e}_1) + h^2V(\tilde{f}_1) - 2xhCov(\tilde{e}_1,\tilde{f}_1)}{x^2V(\tilde{e}_1)}\right) \\ &= \frac{-h^2V(\tilde{f}_1) + 2xhCov(\tilde{e}_1,\tilde{f}_1)}{x^2V(\tilde{e}_1)}. \end{aligned} \tag{3.23}$$

Further, inserting the variance minimizing hedge $h = xCov(\tilde{e}_1,\tilde{f}_1)/V(\tilde{f}_1)$ yields

$$\begin{aligned} HE &= \frac{-\left(\frac{xCov(\tilde{e}_1,\tilde{f}_1)}{V(\tilde{f}_1)}\right)^2 V(\tilde{f}_1) + 2x\left(\frac{xCov(\tilde{e}_1,\tilde{f}_1)}{V(\tilde{f}_1)}\right)Cov(\tilde{e}_1,\tilde{f}_1)}{x^2V(\tilde{e}_1)} \\ &= \frac{-\left(\frac{x^2Cov(\tilde{e}_1,\tilde{f}_1)^2}{V(\tilde{f}_1)}\right) + 2\left(\frac{x^2Cov(\tilde{e}_1,\tilde{f}_1)^2}{V(\tilde{f}_1)}\right)}{x^2V(\tilde{e}_1)} \\ &= \frac{Cov(\tilde{e}_1,\tilde{f}_1)^2}{V(\tilde{f}_1)V(\tilde{e}_1)} \end{aligned} \tag{3.24}$$

which is in fact the squared correlation coefficient, since the correlation coefficient is defined as

$$\rho = \frac{Cov(\tilde{e}_1,\tilde{f}_1)}{std(\tilde{f}_1)std(\tilde{e}_1)} \tag{3.25}$$

with $std(.)$ the standard deviation. Hence, the higher the correlation, the more effective the hedge is.[12] If spot and futures prices are perfectly correlated (i.e., if $\rho = 1$), $Cov(\tilde{e}_1,\tilde{f}_1) = std(\tilde{f}_1)std(\tilde{e}_1) = V(\tilde{f}_1)$, since $std(\tilde{f}_1) = std(\tilde{e}_1)$, and the optimal hedge ratio is

$$\frac{h}{x} = \frac{Cov(\tilde{e}_1,\tilde{f}_1)}{V(\tilde{f}_1)} = \frac{V(\tilde{f}_1)}{V(\tilde{f}_1)} = 1, \tag{3.26}$$

[12] For similar findings see e.g., Franckle (1980), Johnson (1960), McKinnon (1967), and Vukina, Li, and Holthausen (1996).

which is the "equal and opposite" hedge ratio.[13] Hence, the futures position is the same size as the spot position, and, since spot and futures prices are perfectly correlated, the spot risk is eliminated. With perfect correlation, the "equal and opposite" hedge ratio is optimal.

3.3.3 Optimal Hedge Ratios by Linear Regression

In the previous section, the squared correlation coefficient ρ^2 was derived as a measure of hedging effectiveness. With respect to empirical research, ρ^2 can be referred to as the coefficient of determination R^2. In fact, according to Brooks (2002, p. 134), "one way to define R^2 is to say that it is the square of the correlation coefficient (...)." Ederington (1979) stresses that the coefficient of determination R^2 is widely used as a measure of hedging effectiveness.[14] In general, R^2 is the most common goodness of fit measure in linear regression analysis. Regarding hedging effectiveness, R^2 can be computed by regressing the spot price series on the futures price series. Moreover, the optimal hedge ratio can be obtained by this regression:[15]

$$\tilde{e}_t = \alpha + \beta \tilde{f}_t + \hat{\varepsilon}_t. \tag{3.27}$$

The estimated slope coefficient β gives the optimal hedge ratio. The regression results as well as the coefficient of determination R^2 for the six currency futures markets are shown in Fig. 3.7.

Note that the estimated betas are very close to the optimal hedge ratios, presented in Table 3.3. In addition, squaring the correlation coefficients in Table 3.1 yields results very similar to the R^2, as shown in Fig. 3.7. The slight differences between the values presented in Table 3.3 and the estimated hedge ratios in Fig. 3.7 are due to the intercept in the regression analysis and due to rounding errors. The high hedging effectiveness, and hence the high correlation, becomes clear by inspecting the scatterplots presented in Fig. 3.7. For all currency markets investigated, there is a strong positive linear relationship between spot prices $\tilde{e}_t$ and futures prices $\tilde{f}_t$. In some cases, such as in the case of the *CHF* series, the approximation of the relationship through a linear regression line is so good that the regression line is almost invisible or, in fact, covered by the single data points, respectively. In general, the

[13] To make this point clearer, note that the optimal hedge ratio can be rewritten as

$$\frac{h}{x} = \frac{Cov(\tilde{e}_1, \tilde{f}_1)}{V(\tilde{f}_1)} = \frac{Cov(\tilde{e}_1, \tilde{f}_1)}{std(\tilde{f}_1)^2} = \rho \frac{std(\tilde{e}_1)}{std(\tilde{f}_1)}.$$

If spot and futures prices are perfectly correlated (i.e., $\rho = 1$) and share the same standard deviation (i.e., $\frac{std(\tilde{e}_1)}{std(\tilde{f}_1)} = 1$), the "equal and opposite" hedging strategy is optimal. See Haigh and Holt (2000) for more information.

[14] For additional information see Hauser and Neff (1993).

[15] See e.g., Brooks (2002) and Lence and Hayes (1994).

(a) AUD

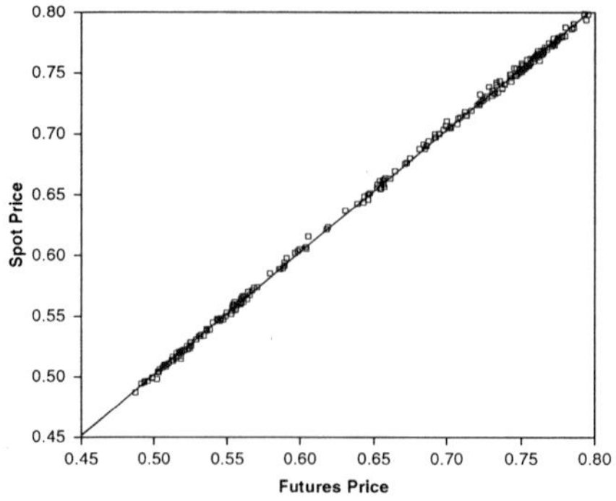

$$\tilde{e}_t = -0.0011 + 1.0064\tilde{f}_t + \hat{\varepsilon}_t;\ R^2 = 0.99.$$

(b) CAD

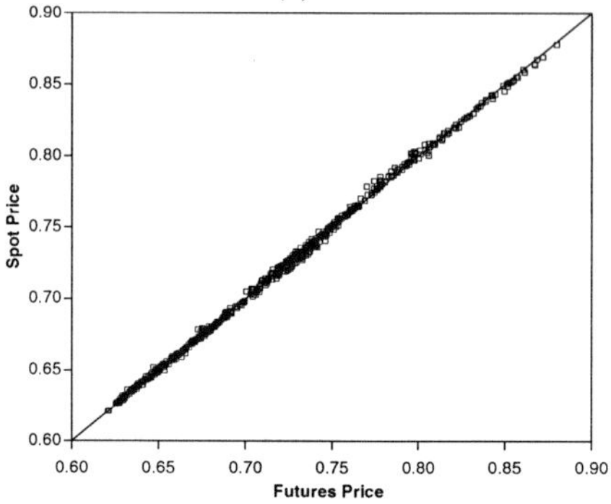

$$\tilde{e}_t = -0.0004 + 1.0009\tilde{f}_t + \hat{\varepsilon}_t;\ R^2 = 0.99.$$

(c) CHF

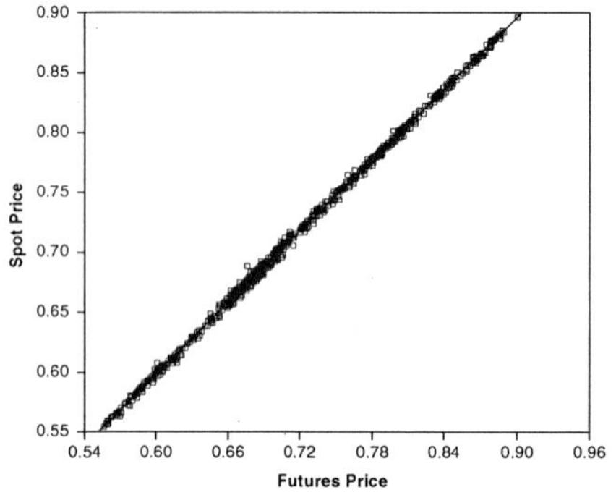

$$\tilde{e}_t = 0.0039 + 0.9912\tilde{f}_t + \hat{\varepsilon}_t;\ R^2 = 0.99.$$

(d) EUR

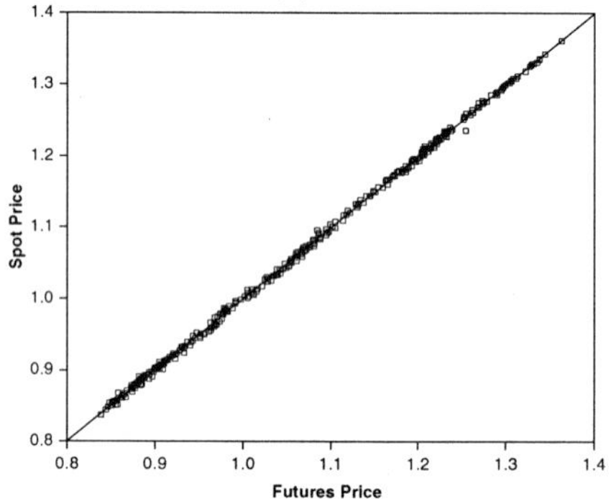

$$\tilde{e}_t = 0.0018 + 0.9978\tilde{f}_t + \hat{\varepsilon}_t;\ R^2 = 0.99.$$

(e) JPY

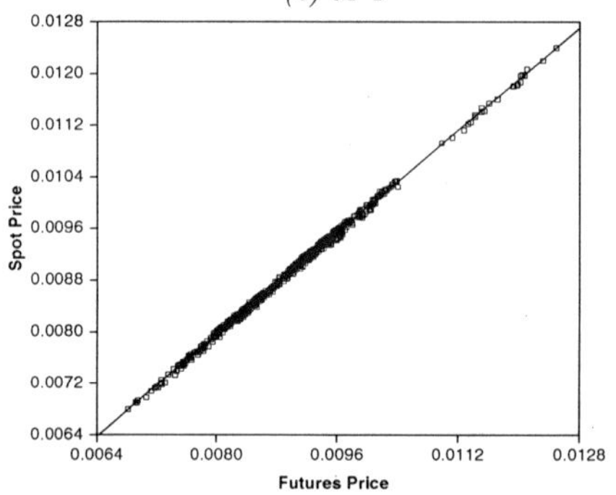

$$\tilde{e}_t = 0.0000 + 0.9888\tilde{f}_t + \hat{\varepsilon}_t;\ R^2 = 0.99.$$

(f) MXP

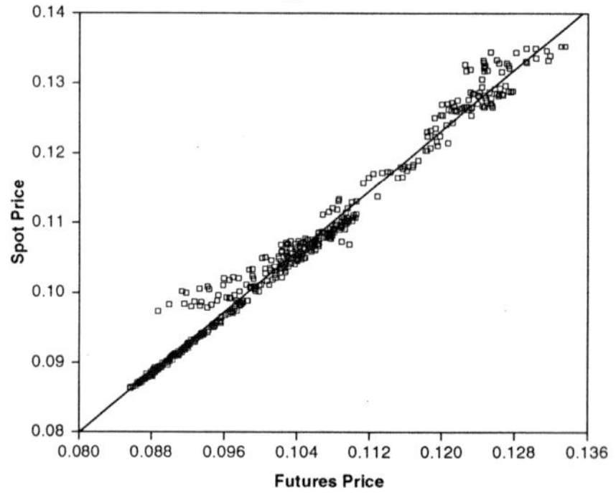

$$\tilde{e}_t = -0.0067 + 1.0835\tilde{f}_t + \hat{\varepsilon}_t;\ R^2 = 0.98.$$

Fig. 3.7 Estimated hedging regression lines and data

Table 3.3 Correlation and pure hedge ratios

	AUD	CAD	CHF	EUR	JPY	MXP
Sample	01/02/2001–01/31/2006	10/06/1992–01/31/2006	10/06/1992–01/31/2006	01/12/1999–01/31/2006	10/06/1992–01/31/2006	03/26/1996–01/31/2006
ρ	0.99576506	0.99940376	0.99939293	0.99967398	0.99891762	0.99161999
h/x	1.00249871	0.99949748	0.98986114	0.99518384	0.98746539	1.08144143

R^2 as well as the betas are close to one for all series, suggesting an "equal and opposite" hedging strategy to be optimal. The worst fit of the linear regression model in this investigation is the case of Mexico. This is the only case where one can see larger deviations of data points from the regression line in the scatterplot. However, even in this case the R^2 is 0.9833 and therefore very close to one. As already mentioned, the optimal pure hedge is a slight overhedge. The optimal futures position is therefore larger than the spot position. This finding corresponds to the previous graphical representations. Regarding the usefulness and applicability of regression analysis for hedging, Benninga, Eldor, and Zilcha (1984, p. 158) note:

> "The strength of the result derives from its generality (it is free from assumptions about utility functions) and from the ease of its applicability (it requires only a regression analysis to derive the optimal hedge ratio)."

However, its generality may also be considered its weakness since the hedge ratio derived by linear regression may not represent the optimal hedge ratio with respect to the firm's utility function. It must be clear that information on the firm's risk aversion, expectations, and hedging costs are not taken into account using this method.

3.4 Discussion

This chapter applies mean-variance and minimum-variance concepts to the hedging problem of a representative importer facing exchange rate risk. Since the importer's problem is chosen to be almost identical to the importer's problem in the previous chapter, this chapter can be regarded as an extension of the previously applied expected utility framework. However, this extension and the consequential results are quite considerable.

First, the mean-variance approach adds to the expected utility framework by allowing a more detailed analysis of the effects of costs and expectations on the optimal hedging decision. Using this method and price data, it is possible to quantify these effects without the necessity of defining the firm's utility function. In addition, the effect of risk aversion can be modeled in detail. Hence, this approach offers diverse insights into the individual firm's characteristics and attitudes towards risk, price expectations, and costs.

Second, the optimal hedge ratio can be decomposed into the pure hedge component and the speculative component. It is in fact very important and interesting to differentiate between these two components, since the speculative component is unique for each individual firm, while the pure hedge component is the same for all firms. Hence, this analysis can be used to investigate why one firm hedges more or less than another firm. Or, put differently, it can be used to approach the question why single firms overhedge or underhedge instead of just minimizing or even eliminating the existing spot exposure.

Third, this chapter briefly shows how to construct the equilibrium of futures demand and futures supply in the futures market. The stylized Marshallian-type demand curve is derived from the representative firm's optimal hedging demand, while futures supply is set constant for simplicity. Based on this basic representation of the futures market, the hedgers' surplus is derived graphically and analytically. The hedgers' surplus can be considered the value of the futures market for the hedging firm. It is shown in this chapter that the perceived value of the futures market increases as risk aversion increases and hedging costs decrease.

The fourth contribution of this chapter leads back to the original problem of the importing firm. Neglecting a single firm's unique attitudes towards risk and price expectations, and therefore neglecting the speculative component, minimum-variance hedging is introduced as a simple and straightforward way to derive the pure hedge. The only difference between the mean-variance and the minimum-variance approach is the speculative component. Nevertheless, this method adds some interesting insights into the analysis. Suppose the only interest of the hedging firm is to minimize the existing spot risk and therefore the variance of profit, which would correspond to the risk reduction approach to hedging, as discussed in Chap. 1. Then, the minimum-variance concept does not only tell the hedger how many futures contracts to purchase, but also the expected effectiveness of the hedging strategy. That is, this hedging method gives the hedger the expected percent reduction in risk, based on historical data. Since the measure for hedging effectiveness is the squared coefficient of correlation between spot and futures prices, it is very simple for the hedger to forecast the expected effectiveness of a single hedging strategy and to compare different hedging strategies. This, together with the fact that optimal hedge ratios can be obtained by simple linear regressions, explains the popularity of this method. However, it is important to stress that this perceived strength of the minimum-variance concept may also be considered a weakness. Neglecting firm specific features and characteristics, such as risk aversion and expectations, may lead to a suboptimal hedging strategy although the risk is technically minimized.

Part III
A Macro View: Economic Stability

Chapter 4
Corporate Risk Management in Balance-Sheet Triggered Currency Crises

> *"In fact, the very distinction between hedging and speculation is fuzzy; when the trader takes market positions on the basis of expectations concerning relative price changes, he is speculating insofar as he is not betting on a 'sure thing'."*
>
> Johnson (1960, p. 142).

4.1 Introduction

This chapter deals with the role of corporate risk management for macroeconomic stability. Firms' balance sheets and the financing-investment relationship are at the center of this study. The interrelation of firms' balance sheets and investment has been extensively investigated in connection with monetary policy transmission and, in particular, in connection with the balance sheet channel. Bernanke and Gertler (1990, 1995), Bernanke and Lown (1991), Calomiris and Hubbard (1990), Gertler and Gilchrist (1994), and Onliner and Rudebusch (1996) model investment as being sensitive to current cash flows and net worth.[1] A decrease in a firm's cash flow and, hence, in a firm's net worth will decrease its ability to borrow. This leads to investment contraction. An initial monetary shock, which worsens credit market conditions, can therefore result in large cycles as described by the financial accelerator.[2] The role of balance sheets in currency and financial crises are also well recognized.[3] Mishkin (1998, p. 13) for example states that:

> "(...), there is another factor affecting balance sheets that can be extremely important in precipitating financial instability in emerging market countries that is not operational in most

---

[1] Fazzari, Hubbard, and Petersen (1988) provide empirical evidence on the interdependence of firm cash flow and investment. For more recent empirical facts, see e.g., Hu and Schiantarelli (1998), Bond, Elston, Mairesse, and Mulkay (2003) and Mizen and Vermeulen (2005).

[2] See Bernanke, Gertler, and Gilchrist (1996, 1999).

[3] See e.g., Aghion, Bacchetta, and Bannerjee (2000a, 2000b, 2004), Céspedes, Chang, and Velasco (2000) and Jeanne and Zettelmeyer (2005).

A. Röthig, *Microeconomic Risk Management and Macroeconomic Stability*, Lecture Notes in Economics and Mathematical Systems,
DOI 10.1007/978-3-642-01565-6_4,

industrialized countries: unanticipated exchange rate depreciation or devaluation. Because of uncertainty about the future value of the domestic currency, many nonfinancial firms, banks and governments in emerging market countries find it much easier to issue debt if the debt is denominated in foreign currency. (...) With debt contracts denominated in foreign currency, when there is an unanticipated depreciation or devaluation of the domestic currency, the debt burden of domestic firms increases."

This increased debt burden worsens firms' balance sheets and therefore leads to a decline in investment and economic activity. There are several empirical studies that investigate balance sheet effects on investment induced by domestic currency depreciation. Pratap, Lobato, and Somuano (2003) study the role of balance sheet effects in the Mexican crisis in 1994. They find strong negative effects of foreign currency denominated debt on investment during episodes of exchange rate depreciations. Echeverry, Fergusson, Steiner, and Aguilar (2003) find negative balance sheet effects on firms' profitability in Colombia. Additionally, Carranza, Cayo, and Galdón-Sánchez (2003) find negative effects of exchange rate depreciation on investment in Peru. However, Benavente, Johnson, and Morandé (2003) do not observe balance sheet effects in Chile. In addition, Bonomo, Martins, and Pinto (2003) do not find empirical evidence on effects of foreign currency denominated debt on investment in Brazil. They argue that the main reason for this is that large firms in Brazil hedge against exchange rate variations where the government is the net provider of hedging opportunities. Moreover, Gruben and Welch (2001, p. 12) note that "(...) Brazilian private sector foreign liabilities were largely hedged in ways that shifted the impact of the devaluation from the private to the public sector."[4]

With respect to crisis prevention, Krugman (2000, p. 90) notes that proposals for reducing the risk of crisis involve doing something that will diminish the vulnerability of countries to capital flight and the vulnerability of firms' balance sheets to exchange rate changes. Mishkin (2000) stresses that the underlying reasons for the Asian crisis are microeconomic rather than macroeconomic, and points to the key role played by financial and nonfinancial balance sheets. In fact, the Asian crisis was largely unanticipated because most warning signals were based on macroeconomic variables which were generally sound.[5] Concerning the microeconomic reasons for the Asian crisis, Harvey and Roper (1999, p. 114) note:

"Although Asian corporate managers did not initiate the crisis, deficiencies in their risk management practices greatly exacerbated it. The decline of many corporations can be tied directly to their failure to manage and control risk."

With regard to currency and financial crises in Latin America, Galindo, Panizza, and Schiantarelli (2003) point out that corporate hedging could serve to reduce

[4] For more information on the conflict between government guarantees and private hedging activity, see e.g., Burnside, Eichenbaum, and Rebelo (2001), Martinez and Werner (2002) and Galiani, Yeyati, and Schargrodsky (2003).

[5] See e.g., Corsetti, Pesenti, and Roubini (1998a, 1998b, 1998c) and Radelet and Sachs (2000).

balance sheet problems.[6] Moreover, the differences in the responses of investment in Mexico and Brazil to exchange rate changes might be due to risk management.

This chapter builds on Röthig, Semmler, and Flaschel (2007), and proposes corporate risk management as the adequate tool to approach the balance sheet and the capital flight problem. Corporate risk management directly influences firms' exposure to specific risks and therefore investment's sensitivity to cash flow variability. Several different corporate risk management strategies and their effects on investment and output are discussed and compared. This chapter shows that corporate hedging also serves to decrease the vulnerability of economies to capital flight.

Section 4.2 presents the basic Mundell–Fleming–Tobin (MFT) model introduced by Rødseth (2000) and further developed by Flaschel and Semmler (2006). Section 4.3 introduces linear risk management strategies. Based on simulation results, the impact of hedging activity and speculation on economic stability are discussed. The role of derivatives trading costs, as the main discrepancy between exchange traded linear futures contracts and over-the-counter traded linear forwards contracts, is investigated. In Sect. 4.4, nonlinear hedging strategies with currency options are introduced into the model and compared to the linear hedging strategies. Section 4.5 discusses implications for economic stability of the different hedging strategies. Moreover, the effects of a capital flight in these hedging scenarios are investigated. Finally, Sect. 4.6 concludes this chapter.

4.2 The Basic Mundell–Fleming–Tobin Model

4.2.1 The Goods Market

The basic model consists of the goods market equilibrium curve (IS curve) and the financial markets equilibrium curve (AA curve). The equilibrium in the goods market is characterized by the condition that production Y equals aggregate demand Y^d (i.e., the sum of consumption C, investment I, government expenditure G, and net exports NX):

$$Y = C(Y - \delta\bar{K} - \bar{T}) + I(e) + \bar{G} + NX(Y, \bar{Y}^*, e). \tag{4.1}$$

Following Flaschel and Semmler (2006) and Röthig et al., (2007), the domestic and foreign price levels are normalized to one for reasons of simplicity. Therefore, real interest rates and real exchange rates need not be considered. Moreover, effects

[6] Corporate hedging as a potential approach to solving balance sheet problems is not only discussed with regard to currency and financial crises, but also with regard to monetary policy transmission. Fender (2000a) investigates the impact of corporate risk management on the broad credit channel of monetary policy and finds that corporate hedging strategies enable firms to diminish the impact of monetary policy measures. For more information on the effects of financial derivatives on monetary policy transmission, see Vrolijk (1997).

of wealth and interest rates on consumption and investment are not modelled. The basic model prefers to concentrate on the necessary variables and interrelations for investigating the balance sheet driven crisis considered by Krugman (1999, 2000).[7] Because of this, consumption depends only on disposable income. The capital stock $\bar{K}$, the rate of depreciation δ, and the lump-sum tax $\bar{T}$ are given. Government expenditure $\bar{G}$ is given as well. Nevertheless, the definitions of investment and net exports need some explanation. In this model the exchange rate has an impact on net exports and on investment. As usual, net exports depend negatively on domestic output Y, positively on foreign output $\bar{Y}^*$, and positively on the exchange rate e. A depreciation of the domestic currency (i.e., an increase in e) makes domestic goods more competitive and therefore leads to an increase in net exports ($NX_e > 0$). If this was the only effect on the goods market, the IS curve would be upward sloping in the output – exchange rate phase space.

Assume that investment depends on the exchange rate as well. Firms finance their investment merely through foreign currency denominated debt. This definition of investment is based on Krugman (2000), who introduces an investment function where investment is constrained by firms' net wealth.[8] A sharp depreciation of the domestic currency will increase firms' debt measured in domestic currency and therefore decrease their net worth shown in the balance sheet. This has negative effects on the creditworthiness of the borrowing firm. The balance sheet problems reduce the ability of firms to finance current investment, as described by the financial accelerator, and therefore lead firms to cut back investment ($I_e < 0$).[9]

The investment function shown in Fig. 4.1 is downward sloping and nonlinear. The nonlinearity is due to the assumption that exchange rate changes affect investment most strongly at intermediate values of e around steady state investment $I(e_0)$. For low values of e, firms are not wealth constrained and investment is high. In this situation balance sheet effects induced by exchange rate changes are rather weak. On the other hand, if e is large and investment is already very depressed, additional changes of the exchange rate do not have such a strong impact on the balance sheet and therefore on investment. Flaschel and Semmler (2006) present further arguments for the nonlinearity of the investment function. They note that for low values of e and subsequent high investment demand, investment might be limited by supply bottlenecks. In contrast, if e is high and investment is very depressed, there will still be some investment projects that can be carried out, despite the reduced creditworthiness of firms. Therefore, for very high and very low values of e, changes of the exchange rate do not have such a strong impact on investment.

---

[7] For more information on the model, see Flaschel and Semmler (2006) and Proaño, Flaschel, and Semmler (2005).

[8] See also Goodhart (2000).

[9] With regard to the link between a firm's net worth and investment, Bernanke et al. (1996, p. 2) write that "(...) a fall in the borrower's net worth, by raising the premium on external finance and increasing the amount of external finance required, reduces the borrower's spending and production."

Fig. 4.1 The Krugman type investment function

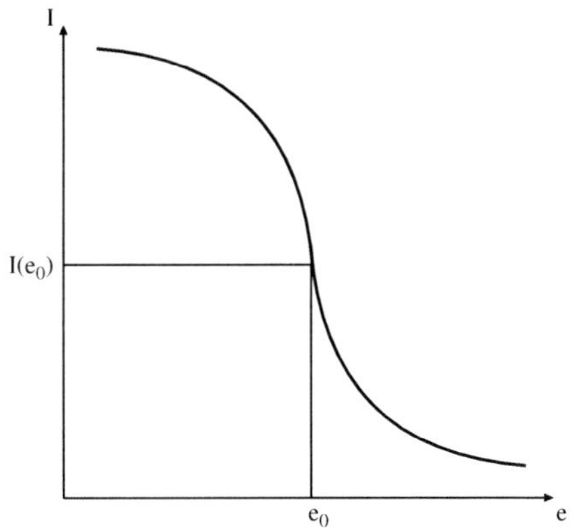

This nonlinear investment function is the key element in the balance sheet driven crisis model. The slope of the IS curve depends on the effects of e on Y. However, the sign of this effect is ambiguous. At mid-range values of e, where investment reacts strongly to exchange rate changes, these negative balance sheet effects may dominate the positive competitiveness effects ($I_e > NX_e$). This will cause the goods market curve to bend backwards. In case of extraordinarily high or low values of e where investment is not that sensitive to changes in the exchange rate, the competitiveness effects outweighs the balance sheet effects ($NX_e > I_e$). In this case the goods market curve is upward sloping.

The adjustment process in the goods market is:[10]

$$\dot{Y} = \beta_Y(Y^d - Y) = \beta_Y[C(Y - \delta\bar{K} - \bar{T}) + I(e) + \bar{G} + NX(Y, \bar{Y}^*, e) - Y]. \tag{4.2}$$

Using the implicit function theorem, the slope of the IS curve can be derived:

$$Y'(e) = -\frac{I_e + NX_e}{C_Y + NX_Y - 1}. \tag{4.3}$$

It is assumed that $C_Y + NX_Y < 1$. Therefore, the denominator in (4.3) is negative. The sign of the numerator is ambiguous. It depends on whether competitiveness effects outweigh negative effects on investment ($NX_e > I_e$), or whether exchange rate effects on investment dominate the competitiveness effects ($I_e > NX_e$). If $NX_e > I_e$, then the numerator is positive and the IS curve slopes upward ($Y'(e) > 0$). If $I_e > NX_e$, then the numerator is negative and $Y'(e) < 0$. Hence, the IS curve is upward sloping if $NX_e > I_e$ and backward bending otherwise.

[10] For a similar formulation, see Blanchard and Fischer (1989, p. 540).

4.2.2 The Financial Markets

The financial sector in this model is represented by the financial markets equilibrium curve (AA curve). The AA curve consists of the following equations:

Private wealth:	$W_p = M_0 + B_0 + eF_{p0}$.		(AA1)
LM curve:	$M = m(Y,r)$,	$m_Y > 0, m_r < 0$.	(AA2)
Demand for foreign bonds:	$eF_p = g(\xi, W_p)$,	$g_\xi < 0, g_{W_p} \in (0,1)$.	(AA3)
Demand for domestic bonds:	$B = W_p - m(Y,r) - g(\xi, W_p)$.		(AA4)
Expected depreciation:	$\varepsilon = \beta_\varepsilon(\frac{e_0}{e} - 1)$,	$\varepsilon_e \leq 0$.	(AA5)
Risk premium:	$\xi = r - \bar{r^*} - \varepsilon$.		(AA6)
Foreign exchange market:	$\bar{F^*} = F_p + F_c$.		(AA7)

Private sector wealth is presented in (AA1). It is defined as a portfolio of domestic money M_0, foreign bonds eF_{p0}, and domestic bonds B_0. The respective demand functions for money, foreign bonds, and domestic bonds are presented in (AA2), (AA3), and (AA4). Money demand depends positively on output Y and negatively on the interest rate r, as commonly assumed in the LM-relation. The demand for foreign bonds depends negatively on the risk premium ξ and positively on private sector wealth W_p, where the partial derivative of eF_p with respect to private sector wealth g_{W_p} cannot exceed unity. The demand for domestic bonds is then defined as the difference between private wealth and the demands for money and foreign bonds. The expected rate of domestic currency depreciation is defined in (AA5). This definition is a representation of the standard regressive expectations mechanism, as it is extensively used in Rødseth (2000). Note that $\varepsilon(e_0) = 0$, where e_0 is the steady state exchange rate level. Economic agents have perfect knowledge of the equilibrium exchange rate and, therefore, expect the actual exchange rate to adjust to the steady state value after the occurrence of a shock. Flaschel and Semmler (2006) call these expectations asymptotically rational because they allow agents to behave forward looking. Moreover, this assumption ensures that the instability in the model is not caused by the expectations formation process. The risk premium ξ presented in (AA6) is defined as the difference between the domestic and the foreign interest rate, minus the expected rate of currency depreciation. Equation (AA7) is the equilibrium condition for the foreign exchange market where the total amount of foreign bonds held in the domestic economy $\bar{F^*}$ equals domestic private foreign bond holdings eF_p plus the central bank's foreign bond holdings F_c. The financial markets equilibrium curve (AA curve) can be derived by inserting (AA1) and (AA6) into (AA3):

$$eF_p = g(r(Y, M_0) - \bar{r^*} - \beta_\varepsilon(\frac{e_0}{e} - 1), M_0 + B_0 + eF_{p0}). \tag{4.4}$$

The dynamics in the financial markets are the following:

$$\dot{e} = \beta_e[g(r(Y, M_0) - \bar{r^*} - \beta_\varepsilon(\frac{e_0}{e} - 1), M_0 + B_0 + eF_{p0}) - eF_{p0}]. \tag{4.5}$$

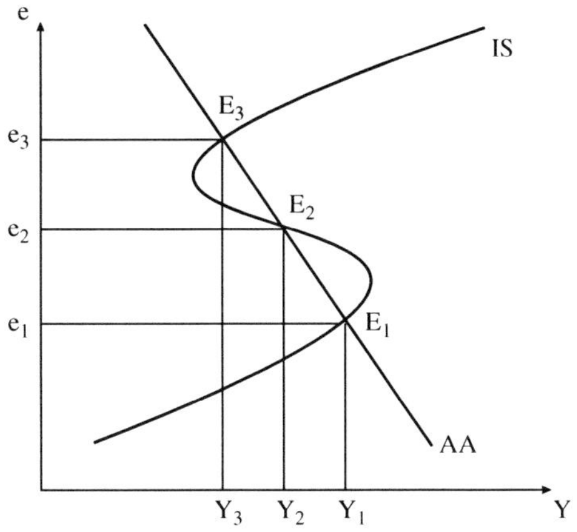

Fig. 4.2 The IS-AA model

The slope of the AA curve is determined by the implicit function theorem:

$$e'(Y) = -\frac{g_\xi * r_Y}{-g_\xi * \varepsilon_e + (gw_p - 1) * F_{p0}} < 0. \tag{4.6}$$

The numerator in (4.6) is negative since $g_\xi < 0$ and $r_Y > 0$. The denominator is negative as well, since $\varepsilon_e \leq 0$, $gw_p \in (0,1)$, and $F_{p0} \geq 0$. Therefore, the AA curve is downward sloping (i.e., $e'(Y) < 0$). In the following sections, the AA curve will be assumed to be linear to ease graphical expositions.

4.2.3 The Multiple Equilibria MFT Model

Figure 4.2 shows the graphical representation of the IS-AA model. Due to the different reactions of Y to e, depending on I_e and NX_e, the IS curve is S-shaped. This nonlinear IS curve and the strictly downward sloping AA curve have three equilibria.[11] Two equilibria are situated on the upward sloping segments of the IS curve (E_1 and E_3) and one equilibrium is on the backward bending segment of the IS curve (E_2). Hence, in equilibria E_1 and E_3 the competitiveness effect dominates the balance sheet effects ($NX_e > I_e$), for which reason the overall effect of the exchange rate on output is positive (i.e., $Y'(e) > 0$). However in equilibrium E_2, balance sheet effects outweigh competitiveness effects ($I_e > NX_e$). Therefore, the effect of e on Y is negative (i.e., $Y'(e) < 0$), and the IS curve bends backward.

The three equilibria presented in Fig. 4.2 represent three different states of the economy. Equilibrium E_1 represents the stable "good equilibrium" with high output

[11] Note that the AA curve needs to be sufficiently steep for the model to have three equilibria. The higher the elasticity of substitution between domestic and foreign bonds, the steeper the AA curve is, as measured by g_ξ. According to Flaschel and Semmler (2006), g_ξ is a measure of capital mobility. For a representation of the IS-AA model with one equilibrium, see Flaschel and Semmler.

Table 4.1 Competitiveness vs. balance sheet effects and output

Competitiveness vs. balance sheet effects	The effect of e on Y	Stability of equilibrium
$NX_e > I_e$	Positive ($Y'(e) > 0$)	Stable
$NX_e < I_e$	Negative ($Y'(e) < 0$)	Unstable

and a low exchange rate. E_2 represents the "fragile intermediate equilibrium," and E_3 is the stable "crisis equilibrium" with low output and a high exchange rate.[12] The impact of the exchange rate on output, depending on competitiveness and balance sheet effects, and the stability of the respective equilibria are given in Table 4.1.

Now suppose the economy is initially in the fragile intermediate equilibrium E_2. In this situation a depreciation of the domestic currency (i.e., an increase in e) leads the economy to the crisis equilibrium E_3. The result is high output loss, from Y_2 to Y_3 in Fig. 4.2. In contrast, if the domestic currency appreciates, the economy moves into a boom situation (E_1) with output expansion from Y_2 to Y_1. In this fragile situation (E_2), firms are given the opportunity to directly manage their exposure to currency risk (i.e., I_e), which indirectly impacts the fragility of the entire economy.

4.3 Linear Hedging and Speculation in the MFT Model

4.3.1 The Hedging Methodology and the Investment Function

In this section firms can trade linear financial derivatives (i.e., futures and forwards) to influence their investment's sensitivity to the exchange rate.[13] A depreciation of the domestic currency (i.e., an increase in e) increases the value of foreign currency denominated debt in terms of the domestic currency. Therefore, the depreciation negatively affects the balance sheet of firms. Since a balance sheet mirrors the net worth of a firm and therefore its credit worthiness, this may lead to credit rationing in cases where large depreciations occur.[14] In contrast, if the domestic currency appreciates, the value of the debt of firms is reduced, which in turn leads to an increase in their credit worthiness.

In general, a depreciation induces a loss on the firms if the debt has to be settled or if specific debt payments occur after the depreciation. Figure 4.3 presents the value of a single payment depending on the exchange rate. Now suppose that firms

[12] The stability properties of the equilibria are derived in Appendix B.

[13] Derivative securities may be grouped into linear and nonlinear instruments. Futures and forwards are linear instruments since these contracts obligate the holder to buy or sell an underlying asset on a known future date at a specific price. Nonlinear instruments like options, in contrast, give the holder the right, but not the obligation, to buy or sell an asset on a known future date at a certain price. For more information, see e.g., Chew (1996), Hull (2000) and Neftci (2000).

[14] Mishkin (1998, p. 10) writes that "net worth performs a similar role to collateral."

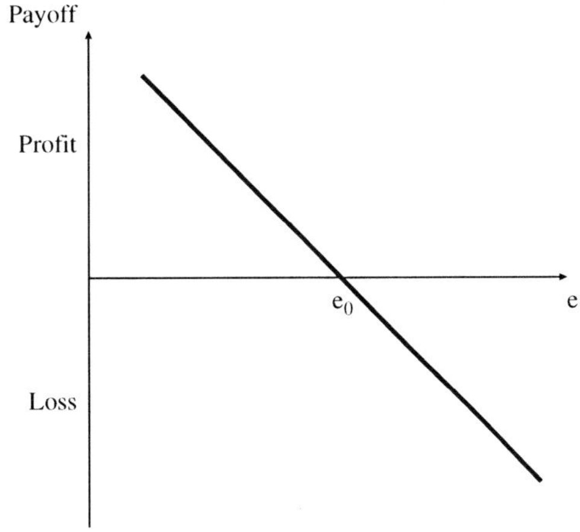

Fig. 4.3 Firm's payoff depending on e

have the possibility of entering into linear futures contracts to either hedge (i.e., reduce the existing spot risk) or speculate (i.e., take on risk). In this model, futures trading activity h_{fut} impacts the investment function $I(e, h_{fut})$ as follows:

$$I(e, h_{fut}) = I(e_0) - (ArcTan(e) - h_{fut} * ArcTan(e)) - c_{fut} * h_{fut}, \tag{4.7}$$

with the costs associated with futures trading given by c_{fut}. It is assumed that futures demand h^d_{fut} equals futures supply h^s_{fut}:

$$h^d_{fut} = h^s_{fut} = h_{fut}. \tag{4.8}$$

Assume that firms want to trade futures to hedge their spot currency risk. This spot risk is represented by the $ArcTan(e)$–term in (4.7). If this risk is to be reduced, then the second term in the brackets $h_{fut} * ArcTan(e)$ must at least partially offset this spot risk term. Hence, h_{fut} must take a value between zero and one ($0 \leq h_{fut} \leq 1$). If $h_{fut} = 0$, there is no demand for futures and therefore no hedging activity. In this case the investment function is:

$$I(e, h_{fut}) = I(e_0) - ArcTan(e), \tag{4.9}$$

which corresponds to the graphical representation of the Krugman (2000) investment function, presented in Fig. 4.1.

With increasing hedging activity, the risk term in the brackets in (4.7) decreases. Hence, for values of h_{fut} between 0 and 1, the futures position partly offsets the spot exposure to currency risk. If $h_{fut} = 1$, the firm is perfectly hedged, since negative effects of e on investment are completely offset by positive effects of e on the futures position (i.e., $ArcTan(e) - h_{fut} * ArcTan(e) = 0$ in (4.7)).

The assumption that perfect hedges and, therefore, the potential to eliminate existing spot risks exist may at first appear unrealistic. However, it has been shown in Chap. 3 that hedging strategies using linear regression are highly effective in reducing exchange rate risk.[15] Moreover, the assumption that perfect hedging is possible is widely used in the literature. Benninga et al. (1985), Kawai and Zilcha (1986), and Zilcha and Broll (1992), among others, base the "full-hedging theorem" and the "Separation theorem" on the assumption that unbiased derivatives markets exist. These derivatives are perfectly correlated to the underlying spot position and therefore allow for perfect hedging. These authors conclude that if perfect hedging is possible, then firms will tend to fully hedge their spot exposure (i.e., the "full-hedging theorem" holds). This, in turn, leads to the "Separation theorem" which states that the export decision does not depend on expectations, or firm's risk behavior. Therefore, hedging promotes international trade.[16]

The model in this chapter, however, does not rely on the assumption that perfect hedging opportunities necessarily lead to the full hedging of spot risk. As discussed in Chap. 3, using the mean-variance hedging approach, a firm's optimal hedging strategy may diverge from the variance-minimizing hedge. This is due to the firm specific speculative component of the optimal hedge. The hedging approach in this chapter builds on this finding, and is therefore broader in perspective by allowing firms to partly hedge, perfectly hedge, not hedge at all, or even speculate using financial derivatives.

A perfect hedge in this model is a simple "one to one" or "equal and opposite" hedge, which corresponds to the pure hedge derived in Chap. 3.[17] Hence, if the firm hedges perfectly, the futures position is as large as the spot position (i.e., $h_{fut} = 1$). Since the spot price for foreign exchange (e_T^s) is assumed to equal the price for foreign exchange in futures markets (e_T^f) at futures delivery date, this can be easily seen by calculating the optimal hedge ratio:[18]

$$\beta = \frac{cov(e_T^f, e_T^s)}{var(e_T^f)} = \frac{var(e_T^f)}{var(e_T^f)} = 1. \qquad (4.10)$$

[15] In Sect. 3.3, the squared correlation coefficient ρ^2 and the coefficient of determination R^2, between spot and futures prices, are derived as measures of hedging effectiveness. For all currency futures markets investigated, ρ^2 and R^2 are close to one. A minimum-variance hedging strategy would therefore almost eliminate the existing spot exposure.

[16] For more information on the "full-hedging theorem" and the "Separation theorem" see Broll and Wahl (1992), Broll et al. (1995), Broll and Eckwert (1998, 2000), and Zilcha and Broll (1992). Broll and Eckwert (1996) build on the assumption of perfect hedging and model perfect cross hedging. Cross hedging is important if derivatives markets do not exist for the spot position. Here, derivatives on other assets that are correlated with the spot position should be used. Broll (1997) points out that the two assets involved have to behave similar for the cross hedge to be successful. If the correlation between the assets is perfect, then perfect hedging is possible. For more information on cross hedging, see Anderson and Danthine (1981) and Eaker and Grant (1987).

[17] Since, in this setting, a full hedge eliminates spot risk, the terms full hedge and perfect hedge can be used interchangeably.

[18] See Sect. 3.3. See also Duffie (1989, p. 207) and Röthig, Semmler and Flaschel (2009) for simple numerical examples of linear hedging strategies.

Hence, the optimal hedge ratio equals the "equal and opposite" hedge (i.e., $\beta = h_{fut} = 1$). This similarity between the naive hedge and the optimal hedge, based on the assumption that $e_T^s = e_T^f$, has some empirical foundation. Fung and Leung (1991) find empirical evidence that the naive "equal and opposite" hedging strategy performs similar to optimal hedge ratios. Irrespective of how the perfect hedge ratio is calculated, if firms are perfectly hedged, investment is not exposed to currency risk anymore. Therefore, investment remains on its steady state level $I(e_0)$ minus the hedging costs c_{fut}:

$$I(e, h_{fut}) = I(e_0) - c_{fut}. \tag{4.11}$$

Table 4.2 summarizes the investment functions depending on the hedging strategy. For a graphical representation on how this linear hedging strategy works, see Fig. 4.4. Here, the spot risk of a single payment, as presented in Fig. 4.3, is perfectly hedged. Since the spot position generates losses if e increases, the futures position must generate profits if e increases. Hence, the futures position must be long in the exchange rate e. The illustrated perfect "equal and opposite" linear hedging strategy (i.e., $h_{fut} = 1$), with balanced gains and losses from spot and futures positions, always yields a zero payoff.

It is important to note that with this linear hedging strategy the firms do not benefit if the domestic currency appreciates. If the spot position generates profits due to an appreciation, the futures position will generate losses. Hence, the payoff

Table 4.2 Linear hedging and the investment function

Hedging strategy	Investment function
No hedge	$I(e, h_{fut}) = I(e_0) - ArcTan(e)$
Partial hedge	$I(e, h_{fut}) = I(e_0) - (ArcTan(e) - h_{fut} * ArcTan(e)) - c_{fut} * h_{fut}$
Full hedge	$I(e, h_{fut}) = I(e_0) - c_{fut}$

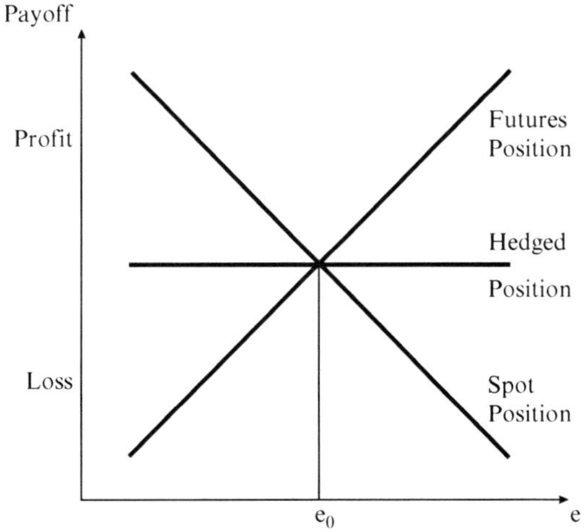

Fig. 4.4 Firm's perfectly hedged payoff

of this perfect linear hedging strategy is again zero. If all single payments of firms are perfectly hedged in this way, the investment function is independent of exchange rate changes.

4.3.2 Speculation and the Investment Function

Now suppose that firms want to trade futures contracts not to reduce spot risk, but to take on more risk. In this case, the second term in the brackets in (4.7) has to add to the first term in the brackets, which represents spot risk. Therefore, in order to analyze speculation h_{fut} must take negative values (i.e., speculation is assumed to be negative hedging). Assume that, for example, $h_{fut} = -0.5$. Then the investment function is:

$$\begin{aligned} I(e,h_{fut}) &= I(e_0) - (ArcTan(e) - (-0.5) * ArcTan(e)) - c_{fut} * |-0.5| \\ &= I(e_0) - 1.5 * ArcTan(e) - 0.5 * c_{fut}. \end{aligned} \quad (4.12)$$

Note that the trading costs c_{fut} have been multiplied with the absolute value of h_{fut} in order to guarantee that the costs affect investment negatively. The futures position in (4.12) adds to the already existing spot exposure. Hence, the sensitivity of investment to exchange rate changes is increased. Figure 4.5 presents this risk-taking strategy. The slope of the speculative position is steeper than the slope of the original spot position. This makes clear the increased sensitivity of the cash flow to exchange rate changes. Note however that not only potential losses in the case of a depreciation are increased. Potential profits in the case of an appreciation are increased as well. Therefore, speculation can make sense if the domestic currency is expected to appreciate.

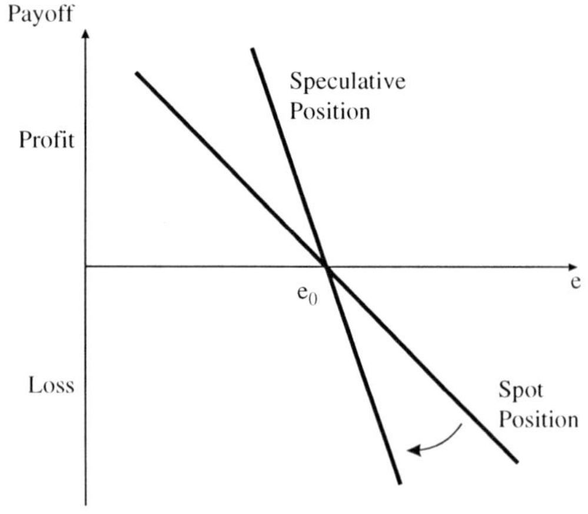

Fig. 4.5 Firm's payoff plus speculation

4.3.3 Simulation of the Basic Model

In this section the basic model without derivatives trading is simulated in order to get more insights into the mechanisms of the model. The investment function is:

$$I(e) = I(e_0) - b_1 * (ArcTan(b_2 * e) - h_{fut} * ArcTan(b_2 * e)) - c_{fut} * |h_{fut}|, \quad (4.13)$$

where $I(e_0) = 0$, $b_1 = 100$, and $b_2 = 0.1$. Figure 4.6a presents the original investment function without futures trading ($h_{fut} = 0$). This ArcTan investment function is a fairly good representation of the Krugman (2000) function shown in Fig. 4.1.

Next, this investment function is introduced into the IS curve of the model:

$$a_1 * e^3 + I(e_0) - b_1 * (ArcTan(b_2 * e) - h_{fut} * ArcTan(b_2 * e)) - c_{fut} * |h_{fut}| - Y = 0, \quad (4.14)$$

where $a_1 * e^3$ represents net exports. The focus in this IS representation is on the interaction of output Y and the exchange rate e. Other variables and relations, like consumption C and government expenditure $\bar{G}$, are set to zero for reasons of simplicity. The IS relation with $a_1 = 0.0001$ is the following:

$$0.0001 * e^3 - 100 * (ArcTan(0.1 * e) - h_{fut} * ArcTan(0.1 * e)) - c_{fut} * |h_{fut}| - Y = 0. \quad (4.15)$$

Figure 4.6b shows the IS curve without futures trading ($h_{fut} = 0$). In the mid-range of e, where e is approximately between -50 and 50, the IS curve bends backwards. Hence, the balance sheet effects outweigh competitiveness effects (i.e., $I_e > NX_e$). For values of $e < -50$ and $e > 50$, effects on net exports dominate effects on investment (i.e., $NX_e > I_e$). Therefore, the IS curve is upward sloping.

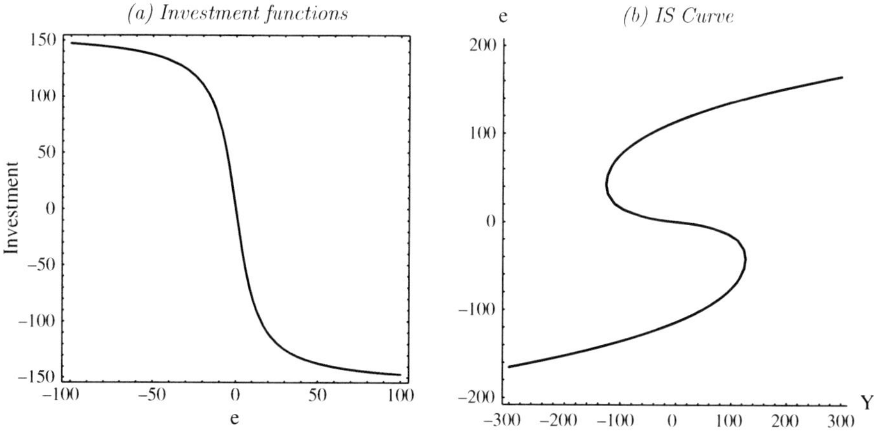

Fig. 4.6 ArcTan investment function and IS curve

4.3.4 Simulation of Hedging Activity

In this section, linear corporate hedging strategies are simulated in the model. Futures trading activity h_{fut}, therefore, ranges from 0 to 1.[19] Figure 4.7 presents the investment function and the respective IS curve with different hedging-levels ($h_{fut} = 0$, $h_{fut} = 0.5$, and $h_{fut} = 1$). With increasing hedging activity h_{fut}, the investment function linearizes, which, in turn, reduces the backward bending segment of the IS curve. Although the investment function is linear if firms are perfectly hedged ($h_{fut} = 1$), the IS curve is still nonlinear. This is due to the definition of net exports. If the investment function is perfectly hedged, the IS curve slopes strictly upwards. There is no backward bending segment and, therefore, there are no multiple equilibria. To stress this point, a very simple representation of the AA curve is introduced into the model. Again, variables and relations that do not affect the "Y−e interface" are neglected for simplicity. The AA curve is simply defined as $e + Y = 0$.

Figure 4.8 presents the IS-AA model with different levels of futures trading activity $h_{fut} = 0$, $h_{fut} = 0.5$, and $h_{fut} = 1$. If firms do not hedge ($h_{fut} = 0$), there are three equilibria. If half of the spot exposure is hedged ($h_{fut} = 0.5$), there are still three equilibria. However, the potential magnitudes of crises, as well as of booms, are reduced. This is because spot losses and futures profits (or spot profits and futures losses, respectively) are increasingly balanced with growing hedging activity h_{fut}. If investment is perfectly hedged ($h_{fut} = 1$), only the intermediate steady state equilibrium remains. Figure 4.9 presents the IS-AA model with h_{fut} ranging from 0 to 1. Again, if firms are perfectly hedged ($h_{fut} = 1$), there is only one equilibrium determined by the intersection of the AA-plane with the IS curve. With decreasing

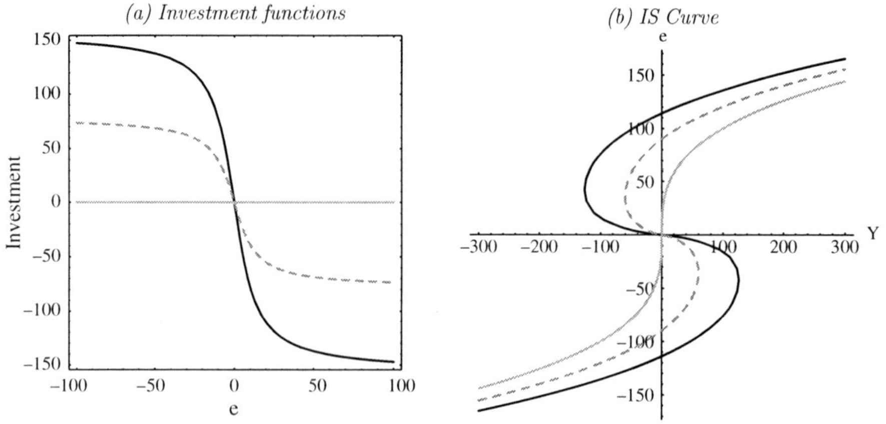

Fig. 4.7 Investment function and IS curve with linear hedging, $h_{fut} = 0$ (*black line*), $h_{fut} = 0.5$ (*dashed line*), and $h_{fut} = 1$ (*gray line*)

[19] Futures trading costs are set to zero ($c_{fut} = 0$).

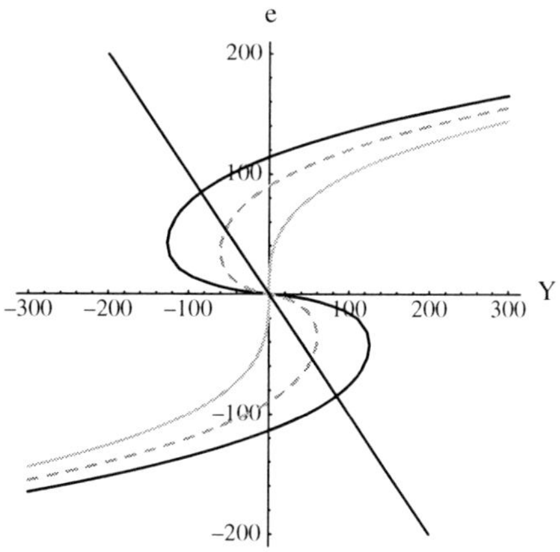

Fig. 4.8 IS-AA model with linear hedging, $h_{fut} = 0$ (*black line*), $h_{fut} = 0.5$ (*dashed line*), and $h_{fut} = 1$ (*gray line*)

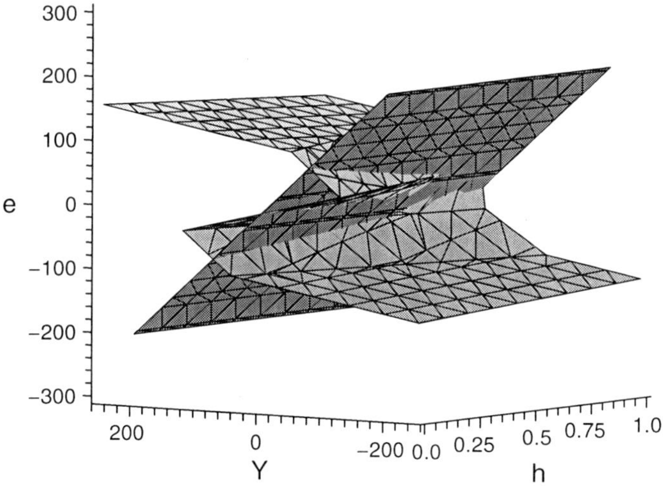

Fig. 4.9 IS-AA model with h_{fut} ranging from 0 to 1

hedging activity (i.e., h_{fut} going from 1 to 0), the backward bending segment of the IS curve increases, which leads to multiple equilibria.

4.3.5 *Simulation of Speculation*

In this section, futures trading activity h_{fut} is in the range $[-1, 0]$. Again, $h_{fut} = 0$ is the case without futures trading and therefore without speculation. If $h_{fut} = -1$,

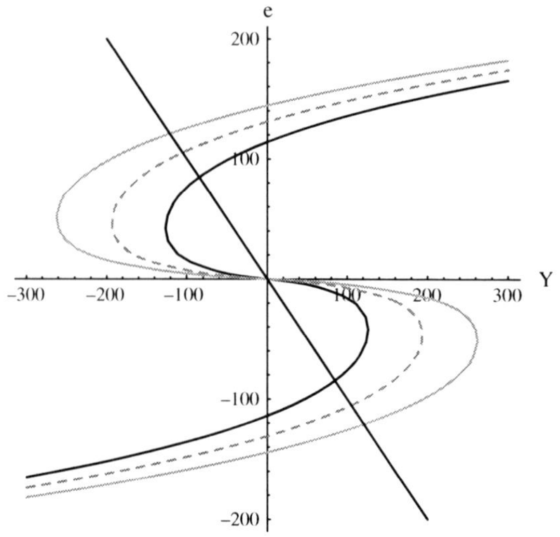

Fig. 4.10 IS-AA model with speculation, $h_{fut} = 0$ (*black line*), $h_{fut} = -0.5$ (*dashed line*), and $h_{fut} = -1$ (*gray line*)

firms double their exposure to currency risk. In general, speculation is not bound to doubling the existing spot risk. Analyzing futures trading for values $h_{fut} < -1$, however, does not yield additional insights. Therefore, this investigation is restricted to the range $-1 \leq h_{fut} \leq 0$ of futures trading activity.

Figures 4.10 and 4.11 present the effect of speculation in the IS-AA model. While the backward bending segment of the IS curve decreases if firms hedge, here, the backward bending segment increases with increasing speculation. This, in turn, leads to an increased potential magnitude of recessions and booms.[20]

4.3.6 *The Role of Trading Costs: Forwards Versus Futures*

There is one main difference and one main similarity between futures and forwards contracts. The similarity concerns the payoff functions. Both types of contracts call for future delivery of a standard amount of foreign exchange at a fixed time, place, and price. The main difference applies to the different ways these contracts are traded.[21] Forwards are traded over-the-counter (OTC). These OTC products are, in general, "custom-made" concerning timing and size of the contracts. However, since forward contracts are not standardized, these products are not available at small contract sizes. Small amounts of foreign exchange cannot be traded with these

[20] Note that, again, futures trading costs are set equal to zero. Their role will be discussed in the next section.

[21] For a brief comparison of futures and forwards, see Eiteman, Stonehill, and Moffett (2004).

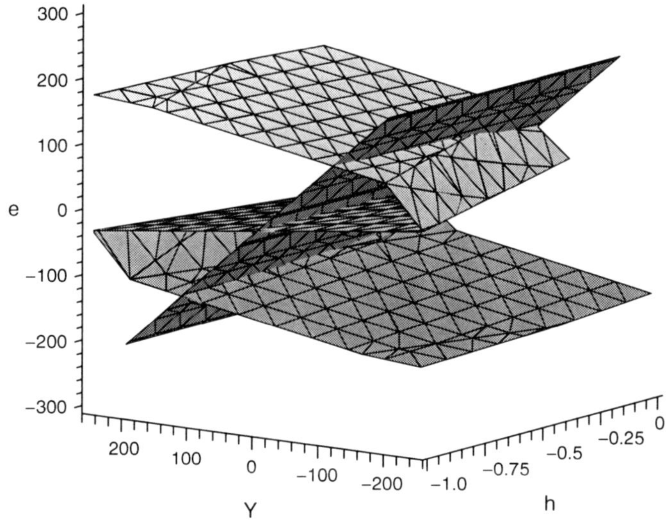

Fig. 4.11 IS-AA model with h_{fut} ranging from -1 to 0

Table 4.3 Relative OTC to CME FX futures contract size (08/04/2005)

	OTC contract size	CME contract size	OTC to CME
Australian Dollar (AUD)	1,000,000 AUD	100,000 AUD	10
British Pound (GBP)	1,000,000 GBP	62,500 GBP	16
Canadian Dollar (CAD)	1,000,000 USD	100,000 CAD	14.8588
Euro FX (EUR)	1,000,000 EUR	125,000 EUR	8
Japanese Yen (JPY)	1,000,000 USD	12,500,000 JPY	9.4517
Swiss Franc (CHF)	1,000,000 USD	125,000 CHF	11.0375

Data source: Chicago Mercantile Exchange (CME): FX position management

contracts. Table 4.3 presents a comparison between currency forwards and futures contract sizes. The large contract sizes in OTC markets may pose a barrier to small firms' hedging activities, as discussed in Röthig et al. (2009).[22] Although the size of OTC contracts may be considered a disadvantage, there is at least one demonstrative advantage compared to standardized futures contracts. OTC derivatives are "zero-sum games." That means that they are free of costs. Since there are no costs, OTC derivatives are off-balance-sheet items as long as no collateral is demanded by the market maker.[23] This, in turn, might be a disadvantage with respect to market transparency and the counterpart's default risk.[24]

[22] For more information on firms size and hedging, see Fender (2000b), Mian (1996), Géczy et al. (1997) and Pennings and Garcia (2004).

[23] See Garber (1998).

[24] For more details on this subject, see Dodd (2000, 2002).

Investigating the costs of futures trading, or futures prices respectively, is not as straightforward as the investigation of costs of their "OTC counterparts". In regard to futures prices, Duffie (1989, p. 11) notes: "A 'futures price' is something of a misnomer, for it is not a price at all." Therefore, it is reasonable to take a closer look at futures trading. Futures are traded on organized exchanges, where they are marked to market on a daily basis. Two types of clearing margin requirements can be distinguished:

1. Initial margin or collateral: The initial deposit is required when a position is opened or increased.[25] According to Clifton (1985, p. 376), the initial margin can be considered a "(...) good faith deposit to ensure that a buyer or seller of a futures contract will adhere to the terms of the contract, i.e., a performance guarantee."
2. Variation margin: The daily resettlement payments. The initial margin is adjusted on a daily basis. Since the changes of value of the futures position can be positive or negative, the related variation margin can be positive and negative as well. Therefore, the variation margin requirements cannot generally be regarded as a price or a cost.[26]

In this model, the initial margin, which has to be deposited when the futures position is opened, is regarded a cost, since it reduces the financial means of the firms and therefore the amount at their disposal for investment. The variation margin is not considered, since there are only two time periods in the model.

Table 4.4 shows initial margins and maintenance requirements for currency futures traded at the Chicago Mercantile Exchange (CME) in total value, as well as in percentage of contract size.[27] The initial margins for non-members range from 1.93% (Canadian Dollar futures contract) to 7.96% (Brazilian Real futures contract) of contract size. The initial margins for members equal the maintenance requirements and range from 1.43% (Canadian Dollar futures contract) to 5.69% (Brazilian Real futures contract) of contract size.[28]

The investment functions with the perfect linear hedging strategies are presented in Fig. 4.12. Since the payoffs of futures equal the payoffs of forwards, the only difference between these two products are the inherent costs. Therefore, the difference between the investment function, resulting from a perfect futures hedging

[25] There a several synonyms for initial margin. At the Eurex the term "additional margin" is used. The Chicago Mercantile Exchange (CME) uses the term "performance bond." Other synonyms are "original margin," "earnest money," and "good faith deposit."

[26] For more details on futures trading see e.g., Röthig (2004).

[27] The maintenance performance bond shown in Table 4.4 is the set minimum value that the trader must maintain in his account. For example, if a futures position moves against a trader and reaches the minimum maintenance value, a margin call may be required.

[28] Members are brokers or traders registered with the exchange. Initial requirements and maintenance requirements can and do change according to market action. The rates in Table 4.4 are from July 2005.

Table 4.4 CME currency futures: Performance bond requirements (07/26/2005)

Currency	*Trader*	Contract size		Initial margin		Maintenance	
		Original	*In US Dollars*	*Total* ($)	*% to contract size*	*Total* ($)	*% to contract size*
Czech Koruna (CZK)	Non-member	4,000,000 CZK	152,520	3,510	2.30	2,600	1.70
	Member	4,000,000 CZK	152,520	2,600	1.70	2,600	1.70
Hungarian Forint (HUF)	Non-member	30,000,000 HUF	144,690	3,375	2.33	2,500	1.72
	Member	30,000,000 HUF	144,690	2,500	1.72	2,500	1.72
Polish Zloty (PLN)	Non-member	500,000 PLN	130,550	3,780	2.89	2,800	2.14
	Member	500,000 PLN	130,550	2,800	2.14	2,800	2.14
Australian Dollar (AUD)	Non-member	100,000 AUD	52,820	1,418	2.68	1,050	1.98
	Member	100,000 AUD	52,820	1,050	1.98	1,050	1.98
Norwegian Krone (NOK)	Non-member	2,000,000 NOK	227,000	6,885	3.03	5,100	2.24
	Member	2,000,000 NOK	227,000	5,100	2.24	5,100	2.24
Swedish Krona (SEK)	Non-member	2,000,000 SEK	192,400	6,750	3.50	5,000	2.59
	Member	2,000,000 SEK	192,400	5,000	2.59	5,000	2.59
British Pound (GBP)	Non-member	62,500 GBP	89,775	1,755	1.95	1,300	1.44
	Member	62,500 GBP	89,775	1,300	1.44	1,300	1.44
Canadian Dollar (CAD)	Non-member	100,000 CAD	62,640	1,215	1.93	900	1.43
	Member	100,000 CAD	62,640	900	1.43	900	1.43
Euro FX (EUR)	Non-member	125,000 EUR	136,525	3,105	2.27	2,300	1.68
	Member	125,000 EUR	136,525	2,300	1.68	2,300	1.68

(continued)

Table 4.4 (continued)

Currency	*Trader*	Contract size		Initial margin		Maintenance	
		Original	*In US Dollars*	*Total ($)*	*% to contract size*	*Total ($)*	*% to contract size*
Japanese Yen (JPY)	Non-member	12,500,000 JPY	95,487.5	2,700	2.82	2,000	2.09
	Member	12,500,000 JPY	95,487.5	2,000	2.09	2,000	2.09
Swiss Franc (CHF)	Non-member	125,000 CHF	75,500	1,890	2.50	1,400	1.85
	Member	125,000 CHF	75,500	1,400	1.85	1,400	1.85
Mexican Peso (MXP)	Non-member	500,000 MXP	55,372.5	1,875	3.38	1,500	2.70
	Member	500,000 MXP	55,372.5	1,500	2.70	1,500	2.70
Brazilian Real (BRR)	Non-member	100,000 BRR	43,915	3,500	7.96	2,500	5.69
	Member	100,000 BRR	43,915	2,500	5.69	2,500	5.69
New Zealand Dollar (NED)	Non-member	100,000 NED	43,560	1,688	3.87	1,250	2.86
	Member	100,000 NED	43,560	1,250	2.86	1,250	2.86
Russian Ruble (RUR)	Non-member	2,500,000 RUR	80,100	3,000	3.74	2,000	2.49
	Member	2,500,000 RUR	80,100	2,000	2.49	2,000	2.49
South African Rand (SAR)	Non-member	500,000 SAR	68,275	3,848	5.63	2,850	4.17
	Member	500,000 SAR	68,275	2,850	4.17	2,850	4.17

Data source: Chicago Mercantile Exchange; CME SPAN minimum performance bond requirements

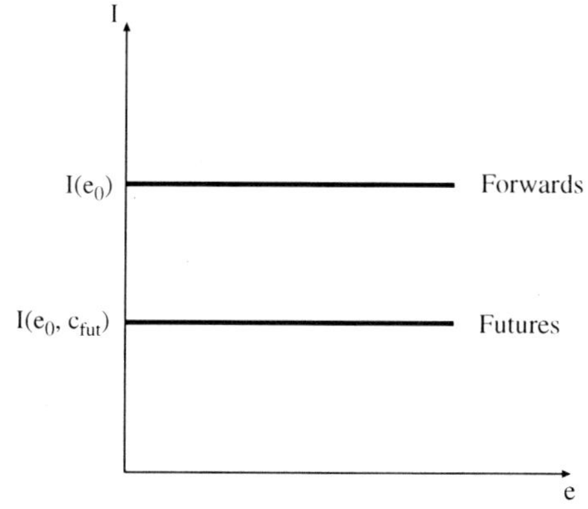

Fig. 4.12 Investment functions with linear hedging

strategy, and the investment function, with the perfect forwards hedging strategy, equals the costs of futures hedging. The payoff of a forwards hedging strategy consists of forward payoffs $\Delta Forwards$ and spot payoffs $\Delta Spot$:

$$\Delta\Pi_{Forwards} = \underbrace{h_{for} * (e_T - e_0)}_{\Delta Forwards} + \underbrace{(e_0 - e_T)}_{\Delta Spot}. \tag{4.16}$$

This strategy yields $\Delta\Pi_{Forwards} = 0$ in the case of a perfect hedge, where $h_{for} = 1$. The payoff of a futures hedging strategy, including hedging costs, must be equal to

$$\Delta\Pi_{Futures} = \underbrace{h_{fut} * (e_T - e_0 - c_{fut})}_{\Delta Futures} + \underbrace{(e_0 - e_T)}_{\Delta Spot}, \tag{4.17}$$

with the futures position $\Delta Futures$ and the spot position $\Delta Spot$. The futures strategy yields $\Delta\Pi_{Futures} = -c_{fut}$ if $h_{fut} = 1$. Therefore, the forwards hedging strategy is always superior to the futures hedging strategy, due to the fact that the only difference between these strategies are the costs of futures trading. The linearity of both hedging strategies becomes obvious, considering that the hedged payoffs of the forwards hedging strategy ($\Delta\Pi_{Forwards} = 0$) and of the futures hedging strategy ($\Delta\Pi_{Futures} = -c_{fut}$) are independent of the developments of the underlying exchange rate.

Figure 4.13 presents the perfectly hedged economy for different values of c_{fut}. Increasing costs have a negative effect on investment, leading to reduced output. Figure 4.14 compares the IS curve without hedging to a perfectly hedged IS curve with $c_{fut} = 200$. For this high value of c_{fut}, the perfectly hedged equilibrium is inferior to the crisis equilibrium in the case without hedging. However, the values of c_{fut} in Figs. 4.13 and 4.14 were chosen arbitrarily in order to stress the linkage between trading costs and output.The extremely high value of c_{fut} in Fig. 4.14

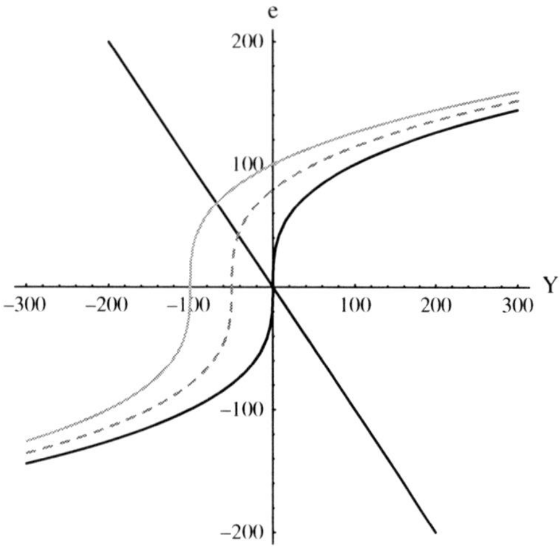

Fig. 4.13 Perfectly hedged economy with hedging costs $c_{fut} = 0$ (*black line*), $c_{fut} = 50$ (*dashed line*), and $c_{fut} = 100$ (*gray line*)

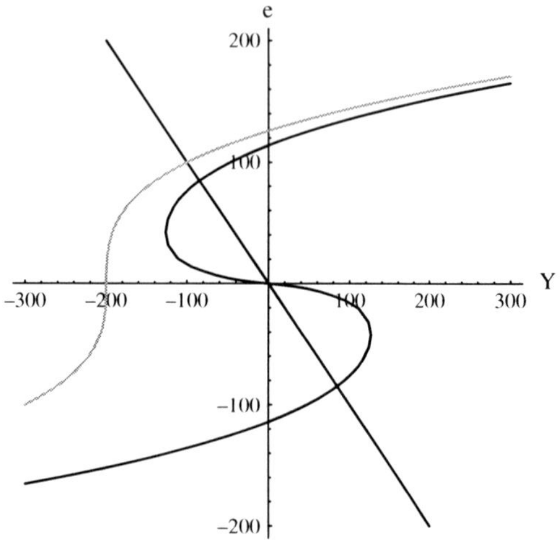

Fig. 4.14 Perfect hedge ($h_{fut} = 1$; *gray line*) with $c_{fut} = 200$ and "no hedge" ($h_{fut} = 0$; *black line*)

does not correspond to the empirical findings presented in Table 4.4. Generally speaking, trading futures on organized exchanges costs only a fraction of contract size. Therefore, in reality, futures trading costs will not have such an direct impact on output. Nevertheless, there is an indirect linkage, since firms base their risk management decision at least partly on the costs of risk management, as shown in Chaps. 2 and 3. In this way, trading costs have an impact on the risk exposure of investment and, therefore, on output.

4.4 A Nonlinear Hedging Strategy Using Options

4.4.1 Options Hedging and Investment

In this section, a nonlinear risk management strategy using options is introduced into the model. As the options position must generate profits if e increases, in order to balance losses of the spot position, the hedge must be a long call options strategy in the exchange rate e. A call option gives the holder the right, but not the obligation, to buy the underlying asset at a certain future date for a certain price.[29] In this model, and in the case of a depreciation (where $e_T > e_0$), the holder of the call option at time T has the right to purchase foreign currency at the pre-agreed strike price e_0. If he then sells the foreign currency at the spot price e_T, his profit is $e_T - e_0$. With these gains in his options position he is able to offset losses in the spot position. Now imagine the occurrence of an appreciation. Here, the purchaser of the option will not exercise the option, since it would induce losses.[30] For the privilege that there is no obligation to exercise the option, the purchaser of the option has to pay a premium to the seller of the option.

Figure 4.15 shows the payoff of the long call options hedging strategy and the relevant investment function. In this graphical representation of the payoffs, hedging

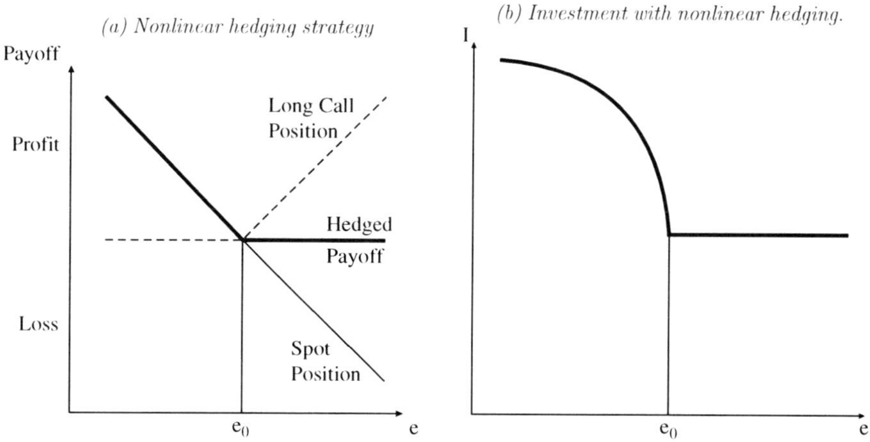

Fig. 4.15 Nonlinear hedging strategy with strike price = e_0

[29] For an introduction on options, see e.g., Hull (2000), Kolb (1991, 1996) and Neftci (2000).

[30] Here, the option would give the holder the right to buy foreign exchange at the pre-agreed price e_0. Because of the appreciation, the spot price in T is: $e_T < e_0$. If the option is exercised, the holder would pay e_0 although the price in the spot market (e_T) is lower. The payoff would therefore be $e_T - e_0 < 0$. Hence, the purchaser of the option will walk away from the deal and, therefore, restrict his losses to the premium paid upfront.

costs (i.e., the options premium) are not included.[31] The main difference between the hedged payoffs presented in Figs. 4.4 and 4.15a is that the linear hedging strategy always yields a payoff of zero, while the nonlinear hedging strategy yields a payoff of zero only in case of a depreciation of the domestic currency. In the case of an appreciation, the option is not exercised. The firm, therefore, gains a positive payoff due to profits of the spot position. Hence, the option hedge provides insurance against a depreciation of the domestic currency while still allowing the firm to participate in a capital gain associated with an appreciation of the domestic currency. The payoff of the long position in a call option including hedging costs is given by

$$\Delta Options = max\{(e_T - e_0 - c_{opt}), -c_{opt}\}, \tag{4.18}$$

with e_T the final price of the underlying asset at spot commitment date T, and e_0 the strike price. If the domestic currency appreciates ($e_T < e_0$), the firm will choose not to exercise. In this case, the payoff equals the hedging costs $-c_{opt}$. If the domestic currency depreciates ($e_T > e_0$), the long call position generates a profit under the condition that

$$e_T - e_0 > c_{opt}. \tag{4.19}$$

The break-even-point at which the firm neither gains nor loses on exercise of the option is

$$e_T - e_0 = c_{opt}. \tag{4.20}$$

However, even if $0 < e_T - e_0 < c_{opt}$, the option will be exercised, since the profits $e_T - e_0$ reduce the costs. The payoff of the hedged position, accordingly, consists of the options position $\Delta Options$ and the spot position $\Delta Spot$:

$$\Delta\Pi_{Options} = \underbrace{h_{opt} * max\{(e_T - e_0 - c_{opt}), -c_{opt}\}}_{\Delta Options} + \underbrace{(e_0 - e_T)}_{\Delta Spot}. \tag{4.21}$$

Depending on whether the domestic currency depreciates or appreciates, one obtains the following payoffs:

$$\Delta\Pi_{Options} = \begin{cases} -c_{opt} & if\ e_T > e_0\ (depreciation) \\ e_0 - e_T - c_{opt} & if\ e_T < e_0\ (appreciation), \end{cases} \tag{4.22}$$

where h_{opt} is set to unity. If the domestic currency depreciates, the option is exercised, and the profits from the options position outweigh losses in the spot position. The overall payoff equals the hedging costs $-c_{opt}$. In the case of an appreciation, the break-even-point of the options hedging strategy is given by $e_0 - e_T = c_{opt}$. This hedging strategy yields profits if the gains in the spot position connected to the appreciation $e_0 - e_T$ exceed the hedging costs c_{opt}.

[31] According to Hull (2000, p. 9), it is useful not to include the options premium into the graphical representation of the payoff.

Modelling these payoffs in the ArcTan investment function yields:[32]

$$I(e) = I(e_0) - (ArcTan(e) - h_{opt} * max\{(ArcTan(e) - c_{opt}), -c_{opt}\}). \qquad (4.23)$$

It is assumed that the demand for call options equals the supply of call options:

$$h^d_{opt} = h^s_{opt} = h_{opt}. \qquad (4.24)$$

Equation (4.23) can be written as:

$$I(e) = I(e_0) - (ArcTan(e) - h_{opt} * max\{0, ArcTan(e)\}) - c_{opt} * h_{opt}. \qquad (4.25)$$

Equations (4.23) and (4.25) represent the same investment function and can be used interchangeably. The second equation, however, will be used in the following simulation studies, since it allows for a simpler, more intuitive approach to comparisons of different hedging strategies with and without hedging costs.

If the domestic currency depreciates (i.e., $ArcTan(e)$ increases), (4.25) yields:

$$\begin{aligned} I(e) &= I(e_0) - (ArcTan(e) - h_{opt} * ArcTan(e)) - c_{opt} * h_{opt} \\ &= I(e_0) - (1 - h_{opt}) * ArcTan(e) - c_{opt} * h_{opt}. \end{aligned} \qquad (4.26)$$

In the case where all firms are perfectly hedged ($h^d_{opt} = 1$), investment is independent of exchange rate changes:

$$I(e) = I(e_0) - c_{opt}. \qquad (4.27)$$

This result is equal to the investment function with linear hedging and hedging costs, as presented in (4.11) if $c_{opt} = c_{fut}$.

If the domestic currency appreciates (i.e., $ArcTan(e)$ decreases), investment is:

$$I(e) = I(e_0) - ArcTan(e) - c_{opt} * h_{opt}. \qquad (4.28)$$

Since $ArcTan(e) < 0$ in this case, the appreciation affects investment positively.[33] The overall effect on investment is positive if

$$|ArcTan(e)| > h_{opt} * c_{opt}. \qquad (4.29)$$

[32] Note that an increase in $ArcTan(e)$ and the term $e_T > e_0$ (or $e_T - e_0 > 0$ respectively) both represent a depreciation of the domestic currency. Contrariwise, a decrease in $ArcTan(e)$ and $e_T < e_0$ (or $e_T - e_0 < 0$ respectively) both represent an appreciation. In the following these terms will be used interchangeably when discussing effects of appreciations and depreciations on investment and the IS curve.

[33] Note that deriving the effects of depreciations and appreciations from (4.23) yields the same results.

Hence, the break-even-point is

$$|ArcTan(e)| = h_{opt} * c_{opt}. \tag{4.30}$$

4.4.2 Simulation of Options Hedging

In the simulation studies, the following representation of the investment function is used:

$$I(e) = I(e_0) - b_1 * (ArcTan(b_2 * e) - h_{opt} * max\{0,\ ArcTan(b_2 * e)\}) - c_{opt} * h_{opt}, \tag{4.31}$$

with $I(e_0) = 0$, $b_1 = 100$, $b_2 = 0.1$, and $c_{opt} = 0$. Figure 4.16a presents this investment function with $h_{opt} = 0$, $h_{opt} = 0.5$, and $h_{opt} = 1$. In contrast to the linear hedging strategy shown in Fig. 4.7, the nonlinear hedging strategy always yields a positive payoff in case of an appreciation of the domestic currency. Since there are no hedging costs in this example, the payoff, which results from spot profits and the firm's decision to not exercise the option, is identical for all $h_{opt} \in [0,1]$ and, therefore, independent of the size of the hedging position. If the domestic currency depreciates, the amount of corporate hedging activity h_{opt} is very important for the shape of the investment function. A devaluation does not affect the investment curve if firms are perfectly hedged. The smaller the hedging activity, the larger the investment's sensitivity to exchange rate changes is. At this point, it is important to note that in the case of a depreciation, the investment functions with linear hedging (Fig. 4.7a) and nonlinear hedging (Fig. 4.16a) are identical if $c_{opt} = c_{fut}$. The main difference between these two hedging strategies, therefore, concerns the event of an

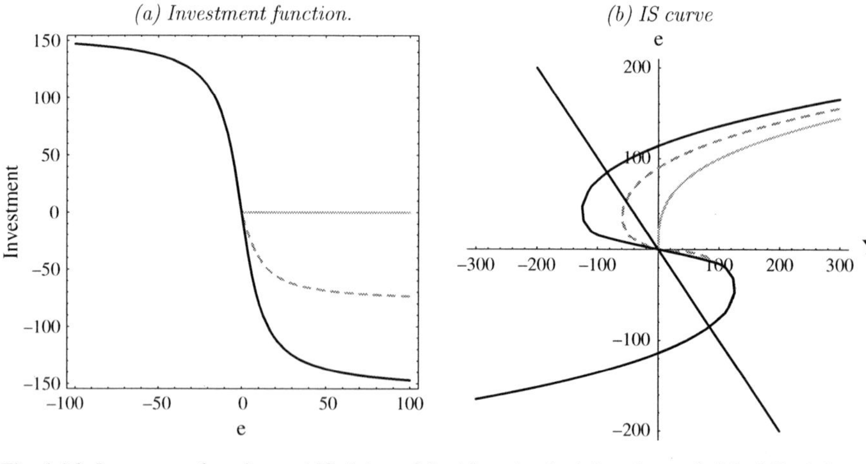

Fig. 4.16 Investment function and IS-AA model with option hedging: $h_{opt} = 0$ (*black line*), $h_{opt} = 0.5$ (*dashed line*), $h_{opt} = 1$ (*gray line*)

appreciation of the domestic currency, where option holders do not exercise their call options, whereas futures holders have to stick to their contracts, which, in turn, will lead to losses in futures markets outweighing profits in spot markets.

Introducing this investment function into the IS curve yields:

$$a_1 * e^3 + I(e_0) - b_1 * (ArcTan(b_2 * e) \; - h_{opt} * max\{0, ArcTan(b_2 * e)\}) \\ - c_{opt} * h_{opt} - Y = 0, \quad (4.32)$$

with $a_1 = 0.0001$. Figure 4.16b illustrates this IS curve for different hedging levels ($h_{opt} = 0$, $h_{opt} = 0.5$, and $h_{opt} = 1$). With growing hedging activity, the backward bending segment of the IS curve in the depreciation-range (where $e_T > e_0$) decreases. The shape of the IS curve in the appreciation-range (where $e_T < e_0$) stays unchanged and independent of hedging activity h. This graphical result corresponds to the shape of the investment function in the event of an appreciation. Compared to the linear hedging strategy presented in Fig. 4.7b, the tendency of linearization applies only to the depreciation case. The remaining nonlinearities in the range $e_T < e_0$ allow for output expansion due to spot profits of firms.

The same IS curve is also presented in Fig. 4.17. Here, h_{opt} ranges from 0 to 1. As in Fig. 4.16b, the shape of the IS-plane stresses the reduction in output loss through corporate hedging when $e_T > e_0$, while still allowing for output expansion when $e_T < e_0$. This main difference to the linear hedging strategy will be discussed in more detail in the next section.

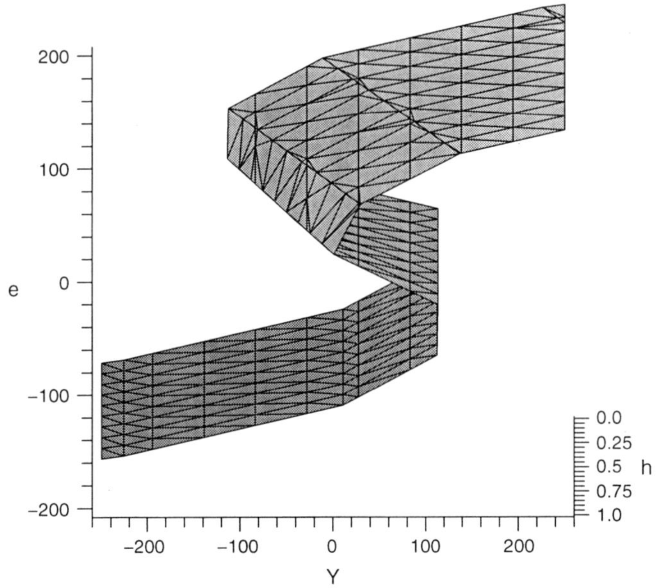

Fig. 4.17 IS curve with option hedging and h_{opt} ranging from 0 to 1

4.4.3 Linear Versus Nonlinear Hedging Strategies

In this section the call options hedging strategy is compared to the futures and forwards hedging strategies. Since the payoffs of long futures and forwards contracts are assumed to be identical, trading costs play a crucial role in determining which linear strategy is better. There are futures trading costs, whereas there are none for entering into a forward contract. However, in general, margin requirements in futures markets cannot be perceived a cost. In this model futures trading is costly as it decreases the financial means to finance investment. Since the payoffs are the same, but there are costs of futures trading while there are none for forwards trading, the forwards hedging strategy is always superior to the futures hedging strategy.

To compare the nonlinear options hedging strategy to these linear strategies is more difficult, since the structure and character of the payoffs as well as of costs differ considerably. Regarding options trading costs, options prices or premiums are costs due to be paid by the hedging firms. Option premiums have to be paid upfront and cannot be retrieved. In order to make hedging with futures and options comparable, the costs of futures and options are assumed to be identical and equal to c in this model:

$$c_{fut} = c_{opt} = c. \tag{4.33}$$

To motivate this empirically, average option premiums of foreign currency call options are presented in Table 4.5. The average premium, as percentage of contract size shown in Table 4.5, ranges from 0.65% for the Swiss Franc option to 2.62% for the Australian Dollar option. Hence, in general, the option premiums, presented in Table 4.5, are lower than the initial margins demanded from non-members at the CME, as presented in Table 4.4. However, for some currencies, the option premiums are very close to the initial margin requirements in futures markets. For example, the initial margin for the Australian Dollar futures contract (2.68% of contract size) at the CME is very close to the average option premium for the Australian Dollar call option (2.62% of contract size) demanded at the Philadelphia Stock Exchange

Table 4.5 Premiums of PHLX foreign currency call options

Currency	Contract size	Average size in US $	Cleared contracts	Total premiums ($)	Average premium per contract ($)	% to contract size
EUR	62,500 EUR	75,250	1,148	711,438	619.72	0.82
AUD	50,000 AUD	37,623	1,066	1,050,755	985.70	2.62
GBP	31,250 GBP	54,765	542	471,625	870.16	1.59
CAD	50,000 CAD	40,823	180	59,025	327.92	0.80
JPY	6,250,000 JPY	55,875	1,713	1,121,381	654.63	1.17
CHF	62,500 CHF	48,298	354	110,688	312.68	0.65

Data source: The OCC monthly statistical report for foreign currency options. Monthly totals for July, 2005. The Options Clearing Corporation, Chicago, Illinois. The currency options are traded at the Philadelphia Stock Exchange (PHLX)

Table 4.6 Payoffs of different hedging strategies

	Forwards	Futures	Options
Depreciation ($e_T > e_0$)	0	$-c$	$-c$
Appreciation ($e_T < e_0$)	0	$-c$	$e_0 - e_T - c$

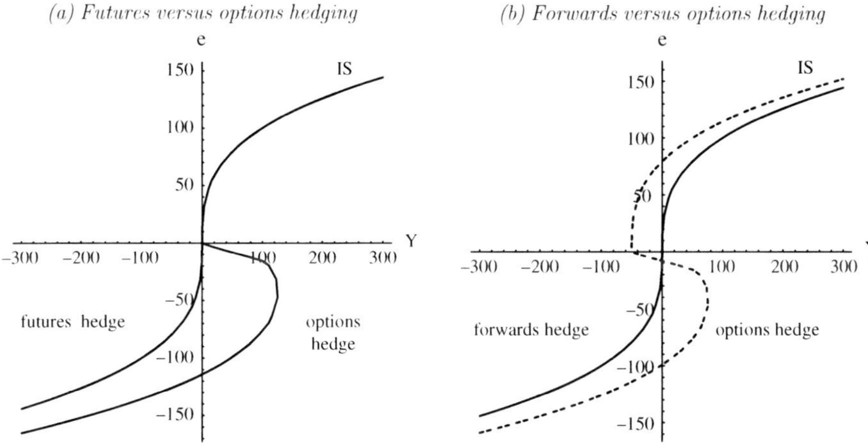

Fig. 4.18 IS curves with futures, forwards, and options hedging strategies

(PHLX). In general, and with respect to Tables 4.4 and 4.5, trading options and futures costs a small percentage of total contract size.

The payoffs of the different hedging strategies, including hedging costs, are summarized in Table 4.6. Hedging strategies using forwards are always better than futures hedging strategies, since there are no costs associated with them. The options hedging strategy and the futures hedging strategy yield equal payoffs in the case of a depreciation due to the assumption that the costs of both strategies are identical and equal to c. In the event of an appreciation, however, the payoff of the options hedging strategy increases because of profits in the spot position.

For a graphical comparison of futures and options hedging strategies see Figs. 4.18a and 4.19.[34] Figure 4.18a presents IS curves with perfect futures and options hedging (i.e., $h = 1$). As already presented in Table 4.6, the IS curves are identical if the domestic currency depreciates (i.e., if e increases). However, if e decreases, the shapes of the IS curves differ considerably. While an appreciation leads to an output loss if firms use the linear futures hedging strategy, the nonlinear options hedging strategy leads to output expansion. Figure 4.19 presents the IS-AA diagram with futures and options hedging from different viewpoints. For all

[34] Notice that in Figs. 4.18a and 4.19 hedging costs are left out because they are equal for both strategies.

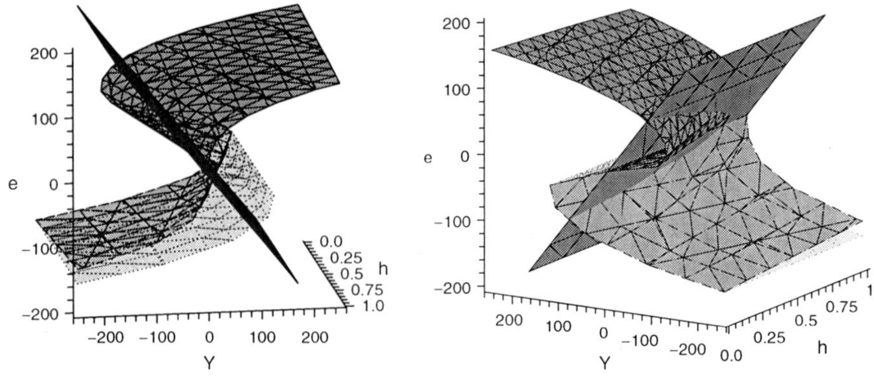

Fig. 4.19 Futures versus options hedging strategies from different viewpoints

possible values of hedging activity $h \in [0,1]$, the IS curve is the same for the futures and the options hedging strategy if the domestic currency depreciates (dark gray surface area in Fig. 4.19). For values $e_T < e_0$ (i.e., an appreciation of the domestic currency), the IS curve with futures hedging is represented by the solid gray surface and the IS curve with options hedging is represented by the dashed, light gray surface. If firms do not hedge at all ($h = 0$), the IS curves are identical, since futures and options are not traded and, therefore, do not affect the investment function. The discrepancy between the IS curves grows with increasing hedging activity h. When h approaches unity, the backward bending segments of the IS curve with futures hedging are substantially reduced. The linearly hedged IS curve slopes strictly upwards. The perfect options hedging strategy, on the other hand, only reduces the nonlinearities in the depreciation-area $e_T > e_0$ of the IS curve. The sigmoid nonlinearity in the appreciation area remains unchanged, leading to output expansion due to more investment in the event of an appreciation of the domestic currency. The options hedging strategy is therefore at least as good as the futures hedging strategy, and should be preferred.

Comparing the forwards and the options hedging strategy is more delicate. In contrast to trading forwards, trading options is costly. In the following numerical simulation, the option premium is set to $c = 50$. A graphical comparison is presented in Figs. 4.18b and 4.20. In Fig. 4.18b the IS curve with the perfect forwards hedging strategy is represented by the solid line, whereas the IS curve with the perfect options hedge including trading costs is the dashed line. In Fig. 4.20 the IS curve with forwards hedging is the dark gray surface and the IS curve with options hedging is the light gray surface. An important difference to the former comparison of futures and options is that the surfaces of the two IS curves are not identical in the case of a depreciation. This is because investment in the IS curve with options hedging is reduced by the trading costs. Therefore, the forwards hedging strategy is superior to the options strategy when $e_T > e_0$. Which strategy is to be preferred in the case of an appreciation depends on the options position's

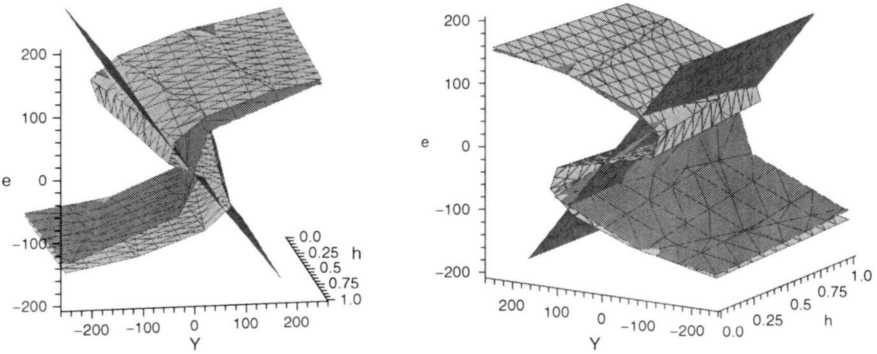

Fig. 4.20 Forwards versus options hedging strategies from different viewpoints. (Options trading costs: $c = 50$)

break-even-point. If $e_T < e_0$, the options strategy dominates the forwards strategy as soon as $e_0 - e_T > c$.[35] Otherwise, the forwards strategy is to be preferred.

4.5 Economic Implications

4.5.1 *Corporate Hedging and Economic Stability*

In the previous sections four different corporate hedging strategies were discussed: No hedging, linear hedging using futures, linear hedging using forwards, and nonlinear hedging using options. Each approach has different consequences for the investment function and, therefore, different consequences for the shape of the IS curve. Figure 4.21 presents these investment functions and the corresponding IS-AA dynamics. Figure 4.21a, b presents the investment function and IS-AA dynamics without hedging. The IS-AA diagram shows multiple equilibria with E_1, the stable "good equilibrium," E_2, the "fragile intermediate equilibrium," and E_3, the stable "crisis equilibrium."[36] The intermediate equilibrium is unstable because slight deviations from E_2 can result in an economic boom, or in a crisis. Above E_2 there is output contraction according to the IS curve. Hence, the economy converges to the "crisis equilibrium" E_3. However, below E_2 output expands and the economy converges to the "good equilibrium" E_1.

The linear hedging strategies are presented in Fig. 4.21c, d. The economy is initially in equilibrium E_2. In this situation, the firms can hedge their currency

---

[35] See Table 4.6.

[36] The stability properties of each equilibrium are derived in Appendix B. The Jacobian presented in (B.9) corresponds to equilibria E_1 and E_3. The Jacobian presented in (B.11) corresponds to equilibrium E_2.

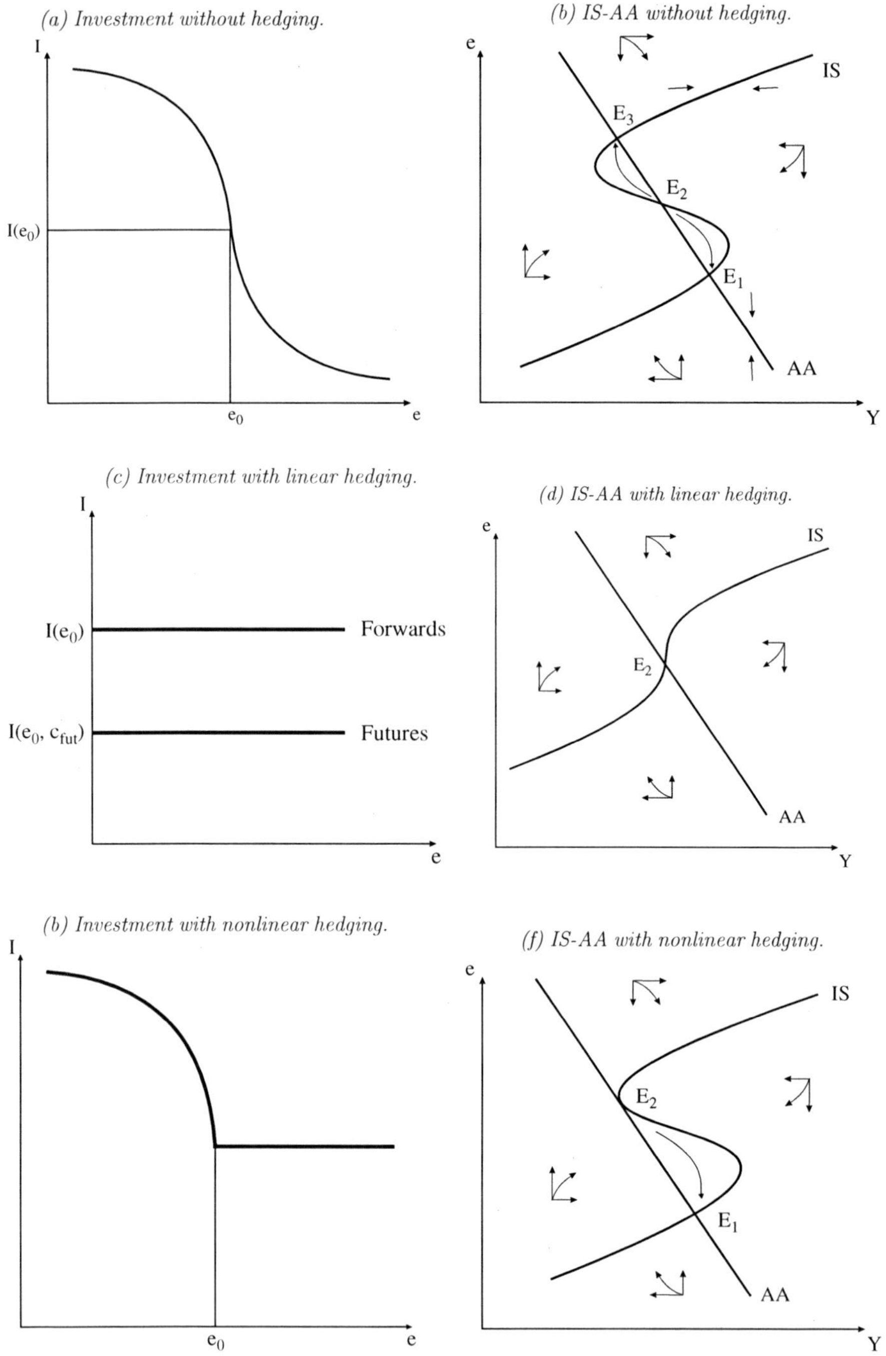

Fig. 4.21 Investment and IS-AA dynamics without hedging, with linear hedging, and with nonlinear hedging

exposure in derivatives markets. The investment function with perfect forwards and futures hedging is shown in Fig. 4.21c for the sake of completeness. However, in Fig. 4.21d only the IS curve with the perfect forwards hedging strategy (i.e., without hedging costs) is shown because of the inferiority of the futures hedging strategy. Since there is no backward bending segment of the IS curve, currency crises are ruled out. Moreover, the remaining single equilibrium E_2 is stable since $NX_e \geq I_e$.[37]

Figure 4.21e, f present the investment function and the IS-AA diagram with the nonlinear options hedging strategy. As in the case with linear hedging, here, there is no crisis equilibrium any more, due to corporate hedging activity. If the domestic currency depreciates, investment is fixed at the initial exchange rate level. However, in contrast to the linear hedging case presented in Fig. 4.21d, in addition to the intermediate equilibrium E_2, there is still the "good equilibrium" E_1. Equilibrium E_2 is unstable since the IS curve is backward bending in this point. The dynamics in the area between the two remaining equilibria, therefore, correspond to the case analyzed in the Jacobians presented in (B.9) and (B.11) where (B.9) corresponds to equilibrium E_1 and (B.9) corresponds to equilibrium E_2. In the event of an appreciation, the options are not exercised, and the firm gains profits in the spot position if $e_0 - e_T > c$. These profits in the spot position are due to reduced debt burdens and, therefore, positive balance sheet effects. This leads to output expansion. Hence, the economy moves towards the "good equilibrium" E_1. Irrespective of which hedging strategy is best, it should be emphasized that all hedging strategies avoid the occurrence of a currency crisis since there is no "crisis equilibrium" E_3 left if firms hedge perfectly.

4.5.2 *Capital Flight and Private Asset Allocation*

Up to now, this study focussed on the effects of different corporate risk management strategies on the investment function and therefore on the IS curve. This section deals with the impact of shifts of the AA curve in the model. Financial markets in general, and private asset holders in particular are at the center of this investigation. Assume that the economy is initially in the intermediate equilibrium E_2. In this situation the AA curve shifts to the right. One reason for this might be a capital flight leading to increased demand for foreign bonds. Flaschel and Semmler (2006) introduce the capital flight parameter α into the financial markets equilibrium curve:

$$eF_p = g(r(Y,M_0) - \bar{r^*} - \beta_\varepsilon(\frac{e_0}{e} - 1), M_0 + B_0 + eF_{p0}, \alpha). \tag{4.34}$$

[37] See the Jacobian matrix for $NX_e > I_e$ (B.9) and $NX_e = I_e$ (B.17) in Appendix B. Note that futures trading costs do not have implications for stability. Costs shift the IS curve to the left as illustrated in Fig. 4.13. Therefore $NX_e \geq I_e$ still holds.

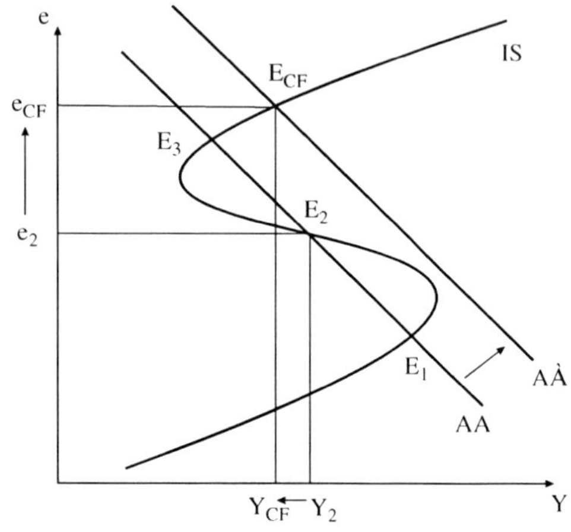

Fig. 4.22 Capital flight in the IS-AA diagram

The parameter α represents the risk of domestic private asset holders to invest in domestic bonds.[38] If agents expect the domestic currency to depreciate, this perceived risk will increase. It is assumed that households do not have access to derivatives markets to manage this risk. The only way to avoid this risk is to reallocate private asset holdings from domestic into foreign bonds. Hence, the demand for foreign bonds eF_p depends positively on α.

Figure 4.22 presents the effects of a capital flight in the model without hedging. An increase in α shifts the AA curve to the right to AA'. The AA curve in Fig. 4.22 shifts to such an extent that the "good equilibrium" E_1 and the "intermediate equilibrium" E_2 vanish. The economy moves to the new "crisis equilibrium" E_{CF}. Although the shock in the capital flight parameter which pushes the economy towards the crisis equilibrium (E_{CF}) shows up in the AA curve, the main cause of the crisis is, again, the S-shaped nonlinearity in the goods market equilibrium curve. Therefore, Fig. 4.23 presents the effect of an increase in the capital flight parameter α in the case of a perfectly hedged economy ($h = 1$) with linear hedging. Here, the capital flight leads to a depreciation of the domestic currency, but also to output expansion. This output expansion results from positive competitiveness effects which in turn lead to a trade surplus (i.e., $NX_e > 0$ and $NX_e > I_e$, since $I_e = 0$ in the perfectly hedged economy). The linear hedging strategy does not prevent the domestic currency from depreciating. However, there is no output loss but a slight output expansion. This moderate effect on output is in line with empirical facts. In regard to differing output reactions during crises, Aghion et al. (2000b, p. 3) note:

> "For example, countries with less developed financial systems are more likely to experience an output decline during a crisis. It is indeed striking that several countries that experienced a large depreciation in the ERM crisis in 92–93 had a relatively good output performance; while others, like Finland, and countries that suffered from the Mexican and Asian crises faced serious recessions."

[38] For more details, see Flaschel and Semmler (2006).

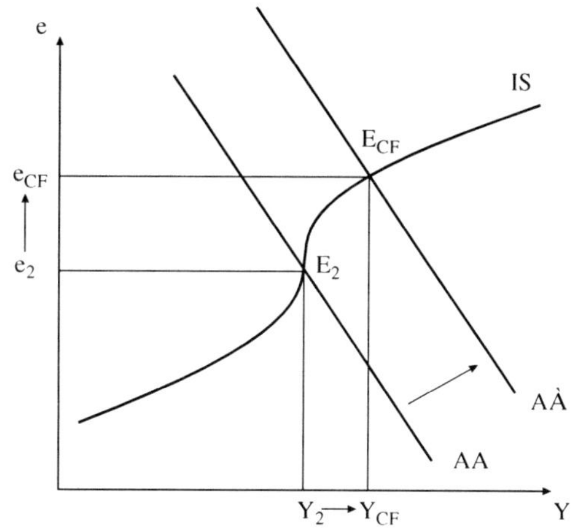

Fig. 4.23 Capital flight in the IS-AA diagram with linear hedging

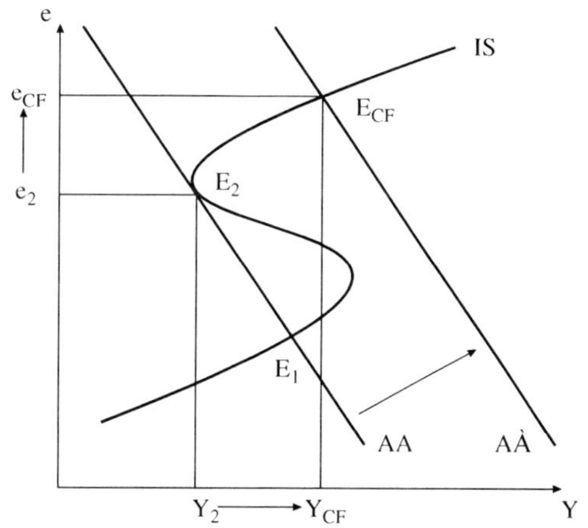

Fig. 4.24 Capital flight in the IS-AA diagram with nonlinear hedging

Suppose now, that Fig. 4.22 presents an economy with a less developed financial system (i.e., without derivatives markets), while Fig. 4.23 presents an economy with a developed financial system (i.e., with complete derivatives markets). Both economies experience a depreciation of the domestic currency. However, the effects on output are very different. Therefore, the corporate risk management approach presented in this simple model is able to capture the puzzle described in the above citation.

The findings shown in Fig. 4.23 also apply to the perfectly hedged economy with nonlinear hedging, presented in Fig. 4.24. Here the AA curve shifts to such an extend that there is only one equilibrium (E_{CF}) remaining.[39] The result therefore equals

[39] If there was a smaller shift of the AA curve again resulting in three equilibria, the results would be similar. The intermediate equilibrium was unstable and the other equilibria stable. The economy

the case with linear hedging strategies. The domestic currency depreciates without leading to output losses. Again, output expands due to positive effects on net exports. Both hedging strategies, therefore, are successful in preventing a crisis in the case of a capital flight.

4.6 Discussion

This chapter deals with the implementation of corporate risk management strategies in a Mundell–Fleming–Tobin type currency crisis model. In this model, firms are exposed to exchange rate risk due to debt denominated in foreign currency. A depreciation of the domestic currency increases the debt burden. This worsens the firms' balance sheets and, in turn, leads to investment contraction and a decline in economic activity. However, firms can trade financial derivatives in order to manage their investment's vulnerability to exchange rate shocks. Several different hedging strategies are compared and their impact on economic stability is investigated. Two contributions of this chapter are noteworthy.

First, a direct linkage between microeconomic risk management and macroeconomic stability is modelled. In this simple model a variety of different derivatives products can be analyzed. Moreover, a wide range of firms' selective hedging activities from no hedging over partial hedging to perfect hedging, as well as risk taking can be studied. Therefore, the flexibility of this model is an advantage. Corporate risk management strategies in this model are based on risk management vehicles actually traded in financial derivatives markets. By introducing payoffs of derivatives, such as futures and options, directly into the investment function, this investigation suggests a new approach on how to investigate the effects of derivatives trading in a macroeconomic setting.

Second, corporate risk management in this model is able to solve the balance sheet problem. Moreover, it is possible to simulate different outcomes of currency crises with respect to output. In this model the effect of a currency depreciation on output depends on the hedging level of the economy and ranges from output loss to output expansion. If the economy is perfectly hedged (i.e., firms in the respective economy are perfectly hedged), then a capital flight will lead to a currency depreciation, but not to an output loss. Therefore, empirical findings such as the different responses of output in Mexico and Brazil to currency crises can be sketched within this simple model.

---

would move along the new AA curve (AA') towards the new equilibrium above the intermediate one (similar to E_{CF} in Fig. 4.24). Hence, the currency would depreciate (i.e., e would increase). However, output would increase as well. Therefore, the results equal the case with only one remaining equilibrium.

Chapter 5
Arbitrage Pressure, Positive Feedback Speculation, Selective Hedging, and Economic Stability: An Empirical Analysis and Catastrophe Modelling

"It is natural to associate speculation with optimistic opinion and hedging with pessimistic opinion as to the likelihood of more and less favorable states of the world."

Hirshleifer (1975, p. 539).

5.1 Introduction

This chapter studies nonlinearities and complexity in currency futures markets. First, the impact of price changes on trading volume is empirically investigated using linear vector autoregression analysis and nonlinear logistic smooth transition regression analysis. Second, the empirical findings regarding nonlinearities in traders' behavior, together with economic theory concerning arbitrage pressure and noise trading, are modelled in a cusp catastrophe model. There is a large body of literature dealing with nonlinearities in financial markets.[1] These studies generally analyze nonlinearities in prices due to inefficient arbitrage and the existence of noise traders.[2] The empirical study in this chapter differs considerably from the one chosen in the studies mentioned above, since it focusses on nonlinearities in the responses of the quantity of trading volume to price changes. The empirical investigation follows Röthig and Chiarella (2007), and applies the logistic smooth transition regression (LSTR) model to investigate the impact of changes of currency futures settlement prices on the trading positions of futures traders. Smooth transition regression models have been widely used in a range of different fields of

[1] For a recent survey, see e.g., McMillan and Speight (2006) and Saadi, Gandhi, and Elmawazini (2006). See also Abhyankar, Copeland, and Wong (1997).

[2] Arbitrageurs may be reluctant to exploit and therefore eliminate arbitrage opportunities because of trading costs. Noise trading can make arbitrage even more costly and less efficient. In addition, due to low liquidity and infrequent trading, prices may not always adjust instantaneously to new information. See e.g., Monoyios and Sarno (2002), McMillan and Speight (2002, 2006) and Sarno and Thornton (2003).

A. Röthig, *Microeconomic Risk Management and Macroeconomic Stability*, Lecture Notes in Economics and Mathematical Systems,
DOI 10.1007/978-3-642-01565-6_5, © Springer-Verlag Berlin Heidelberg 2009

research, including stock market returns, exchange rates and interest rates[3], monetary economics[4], GDP growth[5], business cycles[6], and for modelling phenomena like El Niño.[7]

The empirical investigation is conducted for six currency futures contracts traded at the Chicago Mercantile Exchange (CME): The Australian Dollar (AUD), the Canadian Dollar (CAD), Swiss Francs (CHF), the Euro (EUR), the Japanese Yen (JPY), and the Mexican Peso (MXP) futures contracts. First, linear vector autoregressions (VARs) are used to investigate the impact of price increases on the ratio of speculators' trading volume to hedgers' trading volume. For all currencies, except the Japanese Yen, the "speculation-hedging-ratio" increases. In order to obtain more insights into the characteristics of speculation, impulse response functions (IRFs) of the ratio between long and short speculation to price shocks are analyzed. For all currencies, the responses of the "long-short-speculation-ratio" to price shocks are positive. Hence, this introductory linear analysis leads to two conclusions. First, the proportion of speculators in these futures markets increases after a price rise. And second, speculators go long. That is, they bet on further price increases. The next step of the empirical investigation is to analyze whether the reactions of speculation to price increases are linear (as suggested by the VARs) or whether there are nonlinearities in the reactions depending on the price regime. An attribute of the LSTR model is that it is possible to test for linearity and estimate a nonlinear model without the necessity of assuming specific structures of nonlinearities a priori. By allowing for distinct regimes the model is suitable for analyzing regime dependent mean behavior. The results of the LSTR analysis reject linearity in the reaction of long speculation to price changes in all currency futures markets except for the Canadian Dollar (CAD) series. In four out of the six currency futures markets the reaction of the quantity of long speculation to price increases is positive and much larger in expansion regimes than in contractions. Hence, these results for the AUD, EUR, JPY, and MXP series point to positive feedback trading. It is only for the CHF series that long speculation appears to react more moderately to price increases during expansions.

The empirical findings together with the theory concerning the interrelation between arbitrage and noise trading are then modelled in a cusp catastrophe approach. The relatively parsimonious catastrophe model is able to capture the inherent nonlinearities and complexities associated with the interaction of different types of traders. The modelling approach is closely related to Zeeman (1974), who investigates the interaction of fundamentalists and chartists in stock markets. The approach in this chapter is different because, here, three different types of traders

[3] Lundbergh and Teräsvirta (1998, 2006), McMillan (2001, 2003), Aslanidis, Osborn, and Sensier (2002, 2003), Holmes (2002) and Sensier, Osborn, and Öcal (2002).

[4] Lütkepohl, Teräsvirta, and Wolters (1999), Sarno (1999), Sarno, Taylor, and Peel (2003), Osborn and Sensier (2004) and Lundbergh and Teräsvirta (2006).

[5] Camacho (2004) and Mejia-Reyes, Osborn, and Sensier (2004).

[6] Skalin and Teräsvirta (1999), van Dijk and Franses (1999) and Arango and Melo (2006).

[7] Hall, Skalin, and Teräsvirta (2001).

are modelled: Speculators, hedgers, and arbitrageurs. In particular the role of arbitrage has not yet been investigated in a cusp catastrophe approach. It is shown that reduced arbitrage pressure leads to increased instability in the presence of positive feedback traders. Small changes in traders' sentiment and behavior can lead to sudden and radical crashes in prices.

The remainder of this chapter is organized as follows. Section 5.2 presents an overview of the theoretical arguments with regard to the band of inactivity of arbitrageurs and the role of noise traders. Section 5.3 describes the data and presents the results of the VAR analysis including Granger causality tests and impulse response functions. Section 5.4 reports the results of the LSTR analysis. Section 5.5 presents the cusp catastrophe approach, incorporating the empirical results and the theory concerning the interaction of arbitrage and noise trading. Section 5.6 concludes.

5.2 Arbitrage Pressure and Noise Trading

As noted in the introduction, the interrelation of trading costs and arbitrage offers an appealing explanation for mispricing and nonlinear dynamics of market returns. In a frictionless market without costs of arbitrage, rational arbitrageurs fully eliminate mispricing. Figure 5.1 shows the amount of mispricing as the difference between the wave-like hypothetical price path and the fair value, represented by the horizontal line.[8] In a frictionless market the price path would be congruent with the horizontal line. That is, the price would always be equal to the fair value of the asset. However, this is only the case in the absence of costs. According to Pontiff (1996), there are two types of costs affecting arbitrage: Transaction costs and holding costs.

5.2.1 *Arbitrage with Transaction Costs*

Transaction costs include brokerage fees, commissions, and bid-ask spreads.[9] These costs are incurred per transaction and directly reduce arbitrage profits. These reduced arbitrage profits will in turn decrease the arbitrageurs' willingness and ability to reduce mispricing through corrective trades.[10] Hence, assets that are more costly to trade will be subject to less corrective arbitrage. Figure 5.2 illustrates this point. Transaction costs are labelled tc and $-tc$, respectively. The two dotted horizontal lines at tc and $-tc$ represent transaction costs bounds. Within these bounds

---

[8] For a similar graphical representation see Pontiff (2006).

[9] Kawaller (1991, p. 455) presents a detailed list of arbitrage costs.

[10] Biais, Glosten, and Spatt (2005) state that high transaction costs reduce the efficiency of portfolio allocation. Tse (2001) finds empirical evidence for a positive relation between the extent of mispricing and the frequency of arbitrage trades conducted. The larger the mispricing, the stronger the tendency to return to equilibrium. See also Shleifer (2000) and McMillan (2003).

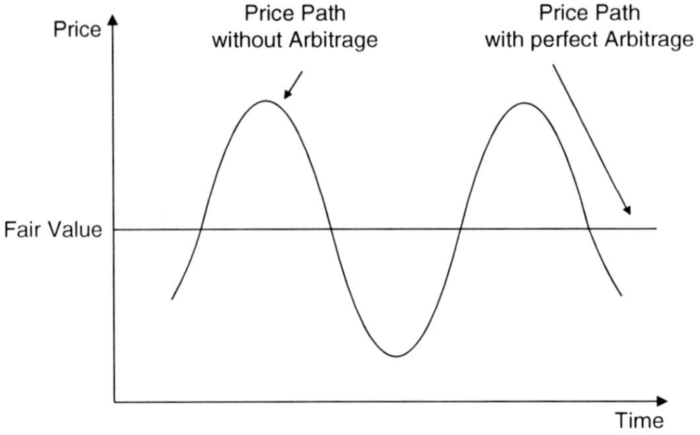

Fig. 5.1 Price path with and without arbitrage

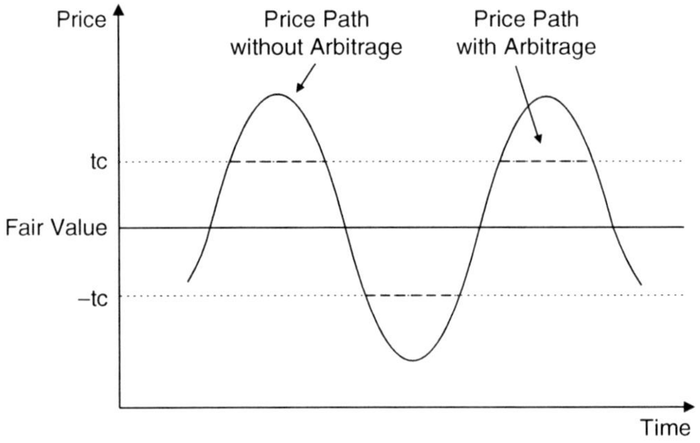

Fig. 5.2 Arbitrage with transaction costs

(i.e., this band of inactivity) arbitrage is unprofitable and, hence, prices are determined by the wave-like price path. Outside these transaction costs bounds arbitrage is profitable.[11] Hence, the price path is congruent with the horizontal lines representing the transaction costs. The potential for mispricing therefore increases with increasing transaction costs. This presentation is somehow unsatisfying, since arbitrage is not existent within the band of inactivity, whereas there is perfect arbitrage pressure outside these bounds. Therefore, in addition to transaction costs, holding costs should be considered.

[11] For an empirical approach on how to estimate the band of inactivity, see Martens, Kofman, and Vorst (1998) and Gemmill and Thomas (2002).

5.2.2 Arbitrage with Holding Costs

Holding costs include opportunity costs, borrowing costs, and risk exposure. Interest rates are an important opportunity cost. Pontiff (1996, p. 1137) states that, "(...) the average magnitude of mispricing is shown to increase when the level of interest rates increases." Borrowing costs occur if capital constrained arbitrageurs have to incur debt to exploit arbitrage opportunities. The potentially strange relationship between capital constrained arbitrage and arbitrage opportunities becomes obvious in the following citation from Shleifer and Vishny (1997, p. 37):

> "When arbitrage requires capital, arbitrageurs can become most constrained when they have the best opportunities, i.e., when the mispricing they have bet against gets even worse."

In contrast to transaction costs, opportunity costs and borrowing costs are incurred in each period in which the arbitrage position is held. The risk exposure is due to fundamental or idiosyncratic risk that is unhedgeable. This fundamental risk includes various risks. If, for example, there is uncertainty about the equilibrium price level and, therefore, about the nature and the actual amount of mispricing, arbitrageurs may be reluctant to exploit the arbitrage opportunity.[12] This is in particular the case if it is unclear whether potential gains outweigh the inherent costs. Even if arbitrageurs learn about the distribution of their expected arbitrage returns, arbitrage opportunities may not be exploited, because arbitrageurs still learn how to best exploit them.[13] Tse (2001, p. 1833) notes that arbitrageurs "(...) may skip small mispricings to wait for larger ones."

Even in the case with full information about the equilibrium price level and certain convergence to this level, arbitrage might be risky. This is because the length of the path of convergence is unknown. Increasing the length of the time interval reduces the return of the arbitrageur.[14] Mitchell, Pulvino, and Stafford (2002) note that, in addition to this horizon risk, the path of convergence itself might be a source of risk if prices do not converge monotonically to equilibrium, but temporarily diverge from this optimal path. If the path to the equilibrium price level is very volatile, conducting arbitrage might become more costly, or even impossible. Additional costs can result from margin calls if the arbitrageur has to post additional collateral in response to adverse developments of the futures position. When the arbitrageur does not have access to sufficient capital if prices diverge, he may be forced to close the position and incurs a loss. Tuckman and Vila (1992) point out that arbitrage trading in futures markets may generate holding costs even in the absence of margin calls. This is because margin deposits may not earn interest.

Draper and Fung (2003) analyze the potential role of governments with respect to mispricing, and find that their role may be twofold. First, institutional constraints

---

[12] With respect to the nature of the mispricing, Neal (1996) stresses the importance of distinguishing between true and spurious arbitrage opportunities.

[13] See e.g., Mitchell et al. (2002).

[14] Sofianos (1993, p. 6) notes that most arbitrage positions are closed before expiration, "(...) following profitable mispricing reversals."

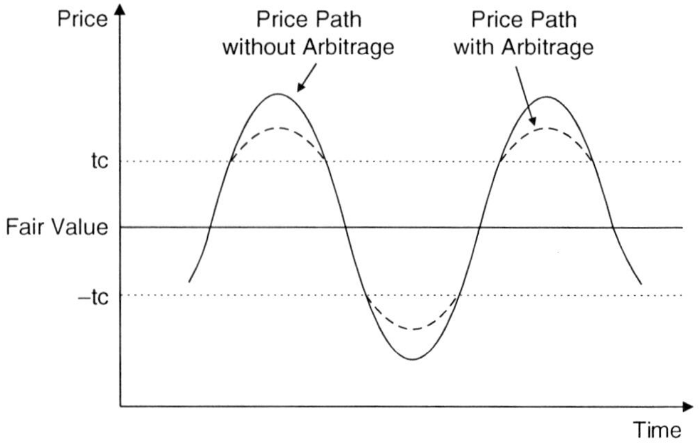

Fig. 5.3 Arbitrage with transaction and holding costs

on, for example, short selling might limit the effectiveness of arbitrage. Second, discretionary government action, in foreign exchange and interest rate markets for example, introduces an additional risk factor, which adds to the idiosyncratic risk faced by arbitrageurs. Another factor that worsens the idiosyncratic risk is the specialization of arbitrageurs. According to Mitchell et al. (2002), imperfect information and market frictions often encourage the specialization of arbitrageurs. This restricts the arbitrageur's ability to diversify away the risk. Risk averse arbitrageurs will, therefore, tend to reduce arbitrage trades.[15]

Figure 5.3 shows the effects of holding costs on the amount of mispricing. As already illustrated in Fig. 5.2, there are no arbitrage trades conducted within the transaction costs bounds. However, outside these bounds, arbitrage pressure is not infinite, but reduced by holding costs. Therefore, the price path does not equal the dotted horizontal lines representing the transaction costs bounds. The price path with arbitrage and transaction, as well as holding costs, is between the wave-like curve without arbitrage and the transaction costs bounds. Hence, mispricing is reduced, but not eliminated. In this regard, Pontiff (2006, p. 40) notes:

> "The mispricing equilibrium with holding costs is a richer description of reality than the transaction cost equilibrium – arbitrage occurs frequently, yet mispricing continues. In equilibrium, arbitrageurs and mispricing co-exist."

5.2.3 Noise, Positive Feedback Trading, and Herding

The second rationale for potential persistent deviations from equilibrium and for nonlinear dynamics is noise trader behavior.[16] Noise traders can be either irrational

[15] For more details on specialization and idiosyncratic risk, see Mashruwala, Rajgopal, and Shevlin (2006), Mendenhall (2004) and Wurgler and Zhuravskaya (2002).

[16] For a recent survey of the literature, see e.g., Dow and Gorton (2006), Hughen and McDonald (2005) and Lo and Lin (2005).

or rational. Irrational noise traders are generally defined as traders who base their trading decisions on irrelevant information[17], on fads and sentiment[18], or on technical analysis and chartism[19], rather than on economic fundamentals.[20]

The importance of fads and sentiments is well recognized in the finance literature. Hirshleifer (1975) argues that it is natural to associate speculation with optimistic, and hedging with pessimistic, opinion. Trading activity based on optimistic opinion or overconfidence can lead to increased deviations of prices from equilibrium, in particular if traders behave like a herd. Herding means that traders do not act randomly, but probably make decisions in similar ways.[21] The rationale for herding was previously emphasized by Kaldor (1939, p. 2) who notes that:

> "If the proportion of speculative transactions in the total is large, it may become, in fact, more profitable for the individual speculator to concentrate on forecasting the psychology of other speculators, rather than the trend of the non-speculative elements."

This trading strategy has also been captured by Keynes' metaphor of the beauty contest, where "(...) each competitor has to pick, not those faces which he himself finds prettiest, but those which he thinks likeliest to catch the fancy of the other competitors."[22] Another rationale for herding concerns market power. If large speculators are able to influence and, therefore, manipulate prices, other traders will follow them.[23] Shiller (2000) points out that individuals might follow the herd even if they know that they rely on false information. According to him, "(...) people are ready to believe the majority view or to believe authorities even when they plainly contradict matter-of-fact judgment."[24]

Non-fundamental trading strategies, such as technical analysis and chartism, can be used to forecast the psychology of other speculators.[25] In fact, chartism is often used to measure a swing in market psychology.[26] Moreover, these trading strategies are widely used in financial markets. Taylor (1992, p. 304) reports that "a very high

---

[17] DeLong, Shleifer, Summers, and Waldmann (1990).

[18] Shiller (1984).

[19] Bauer and Herz (2005).

[20] The idea that noise traders are irrational leads to some important questions about their existence. Rational agents could take advantage of the irrational traders who trade at incorrect prices, based on non-fundamental information. This would drive noise traders out of the competitive asset market. "Noise traders should not survive, and so cannot play the role envisioned for them" (Dow and Gorton, 2006, p. 4). Irrational noise traders can therefore only exist if there are some frictions. For more information on the survival of irrational noise traders, see DeLong, Shleifer, Summers, and Waldmann (1991).

[21] Herding can be defined as investors following a common signal, see Nofsinger and Sias (1999).

[22] Keynes (1986, p. 156). See also the discussion in Sanyal (2005).

[23] For more information on market manipulation, see Hart (1977), Jarrow (1992, 1994), Kumar and Seppi (1992) and Pirrong (1995).

[24] Shiller (2000, p. 151).

[25] Shiller (2000) argues that the psychology of other speculators is often predictable. See also Saadi et al. (2006).

[26] For more information on technical analysis, see e.g., Ludden (1999) and Murphy (1986).

proportion of chief dealers view technical and fundamental analysis as complementary forms of analysis and a substantial proportion suggest that technical advice may be self-fulfilling."[27] This self-fulfilling character of technical analysis is in particular due to trend-following indicators and, hence, may further increase herding.

Reasons for rational noise trading include trading for liquidity, hedging strategies, portfolio insurance, and stop-loss orders.[28] Dow and Gorton (1997) argue that professional traders and fund managers often act like rational noise traders. In their model, agency problems lead managers to trade even though they would be better off doing nothing because their uninformed clients cannot distinguish "actively doing nothing" from "simply doing nothing." DeLong et al. (1990) model the interrelation of rational speculators and positive feedback traders and find that rational speculation can be destabilizing in the presence of positive feedback traders.[29] Price increases induced by rational speculators trading activity will lead to imitation by positive feedback traders. The subsequent price rise therefore consists of a rational part and a part which results from positive feedback traders flowing into the market.

Traders, irrational and rational, "(...) who do not use or misperceive the fundamentals (...)"[30] pose an additional risk to arbitrageurs. Noise trader risk has at least two facets: First, noise traders make the assets they trade more risky (i.e., more volatile).[31] Second, momentum trading (or trend chasing) by noise traders may lead to overreactions of asset prices and therefore to increased deviations from fair values. The length of the path to equilibrium gets less predictable for arbitrageurs who, in turn, are more reluctant to take a position contrary to noise traders. Hence, noise trader risk can significantly add to the holding risk faced by arbitrageurs.

5.3 Vector Autoregression Analysis of Futures Trading Activity

5.3.1 Data

In this section, nonlinearities in the relationship between weekly settlement price changes and weekly data on trader positions in Australian Dollar (AUD), Canadian Dollar (CAD), Swiss Francs (CHF), Euro (EUR), Japanese Yen (JPY), and Mexican

---

[27] Shiller (1987) argues that technical analysis played an important role in market movements during the October 1987 stock market crash.

[28] See e.g., Dow and Gorton (1997) and Vitale (2000). For further approaches, see Romer (1993).

[29] Positive feedback traders are noise traders who follow a positive feedback strategy – that is they buy when prices rise, and sell when prices fall. See e.g., Cutler, Poterba, and Summers (1990) and Nofsinger and Sias (1999).

[30] Taylor (1992, p. 305).

[31] With regard to increased volatility, DeLong, Shleifer, Summers, and Waldmann (1987, p. 1) write that "many prominent market participants see asset markets as little more than casinos." See also Sias, Starks and Tiniç (2001).

Peso (MXP) futures contracts are investigated. The futures contracts are traded at the Chicago Mercantile Exchange (CME). Futures price data are obtained from Datastream. The returns Δp_t are measured as follows:

$$\Delta p_t = 100 * ln\left(\frac{p_t}{p_{t-1}}\right), \tag{5.1}$$

with p_t the futures settlement price of the respective currency future in t. The trader position data are obtained from the Commodity Futures Trading Commission's (CFTC) Commitments of Traders (COT) report.

5.3.2 *Speculation Versus Hedging*

This subsection investigates the effects of price shocks on the proportion of hedgers' and speculators' trading volume in currency futures markets. The "speculation-hedging-ratio" shr_t is defined as:

$$shr_t = \frac{speculation(t)}{hedging(t)}, \tag{5.2}$$

where $speculation(t)$ and $hedging(t)$ contain both long and short positions of speculators (i.e., noncommercial traders) and hedgers (i.e., commercial traders) in t. Continuous returns Δshr_t are computed using the following expression:

$$\Delta shr_t = 100 * ln\left(\frac{shr_t}{shr_{t-1}}\right). \tag{5.3}$$

Table 5.1 presents summary statistics, ARCH-LM and unit root tests for the Δp_t and Δshr_t series. The ARCH-LM test statistics suggest that there is no conditional heteroskedasticity in the return series. The augmented Dickey Fuller (ADF) test and Kwiatkowski, Phillips, Schmidt, and Shin (KPSS) test confirm that the series are stationary.

In order to analyze the effects of price shocks on the "speculation-hedging-ratio," Granger causality tests are conducted, and impulse response functions based on vector autoregressions (VAR) are computed. The number of lags of the VARs are determined from the Akaike, Hannan-Quinn, and Schwartz information criteria. Table 5.2 presents the results of the Granger causality tests. The noncausality null hypothesis can only be rejected for the MXP speculation and the AUD speculation series, using a 10% significance level. On the basis of these tests, no causal relation can be diagnosed for the remaining series.

Figure 5.4 presents the impulse response functions. The impulse responses of all but the JPY series show positive reactions of the "speculation-hedging-ratio" to price changes. These results suggest that there is an increase in speculation compared to hedging resulting from price increases. For the AUD and the MXP series, this increase in the share of speculation in the futures market is statistically significant.

Table 5.1 Summary statistics, ARCH-LM, and unit root tests for the VAR analysis of speculation versus hedging

Series		Sample	Obs.	Mean	Min.	Max.	Std. Dev.	Skewness	Kurtosis	ARCH-LM	ADF	KPSS
AUD	Δp_t	01/02/2001–01/31/2006	249	0.1215	−4.8198	4.6606	1.5437	−0.2274	3.0336	0.4587	−11.4920	0.1273
	Δshr_t	01/02/2001–01/31/2006	249	0.4225	−182.626	121.640	28.5966	−0.2311	11.2443	0.6612	−13.7920	0.0147
CAD	Δp_t	10/06/1992–01/31/2006	693	0.0117	−3.2677	3.2873	0.8597	0.1139	3.8011	0.0863	−18.5669	0.6166
	Δshr_t	10/06/1992–01/31/2006	693	0.0041	−126.202	107.198	25.3487	0.3175	6.1694	0.2042	−20.9293	0.0091
CHF	Δp_t	10/06/1992–01/24/2006	689	0.0001	−5.6229	9.0289	1.5800	0.2933	4.8108	0.6733	−19.2500	0.1561
	Δshr_t	10/06/1992–01/24/2006	689	−0.0453	−100.913	133.020	28.7837	0.9085	6.3194	0.7527	−23.3018	0.0054
EUR	Δp_t	01/12/1999–01/31/2006	366	0.0136	−3.9630	3.9679	1.3766	−0.0116	3.0029	0.7273	−13.3658	0.4246
	Δshr_t	01/12/1999–01/31/2006	366	0.0094	−72.4531	102.556	23.5705	0.9382	6.3925	0.2794	−16.0257	0.0326
JPY	Δp_t	10/06/1992–01/31/2006	694	0.0037	−6.2483	9.3058	1.5940	0.6945	6.6184	0.0828	−17.8842	0.0710
	Δshr_t	10/06/1992–01/31/2006	694	0.0180	−88.4167	109.021	24.3235	0.5866	6.0440	0.2322	−21.7218	0.0061
MXP	Δp_t	03/26/1996–01/31/2006	514	−0.0482	−11.2723	6.3680	1.5694	−1.9096	11.8692	0.1056	−16.7165	0.0537
	Δshr_t	03/26/1996–01/31/2006	514	0.3121	−204.842	138.427	31.8583	−1.6181	11.0497	0.0631	−20.4522	0.0204

Note: The ARCH-LM test is used for testing the null hypothesis of no conditional heteroskedasticity. ARCH-LM results are in p-values. ADF and KPSS are the test statistics of the augmented Dickey Fuller and the Kwiatkowski, Phillips, Schmidt, and Shin test. The ADF test rejects the null hypothesis of nonstationarity if the test statistic is negative and the absolute value of the test statistic exceeds the critical value of the respective significance level: 1%: −2.56; 5%: −1.94; 10%: −1.62. The KPSS test rejects the null hypothesis of stationarity if the test statistic exceeds the critical value of the respective significance level: 1%: 0.739; 5%: 0.463; 10%: 0.347. For more information on the tests applied here, see Lütkepohl and Krätzig (2004)

Table 5.2 Granger causality test for the "speculation-hedging-ratio"

	AUD	CAD	CHF	EUR	JPY	MXP
Test value	3.8277	0.7622	1.9215	0.0179	0.2815	11.7560
p-value	0.0510	0.3828	0.1468	0.8935	0.5958	0.0000

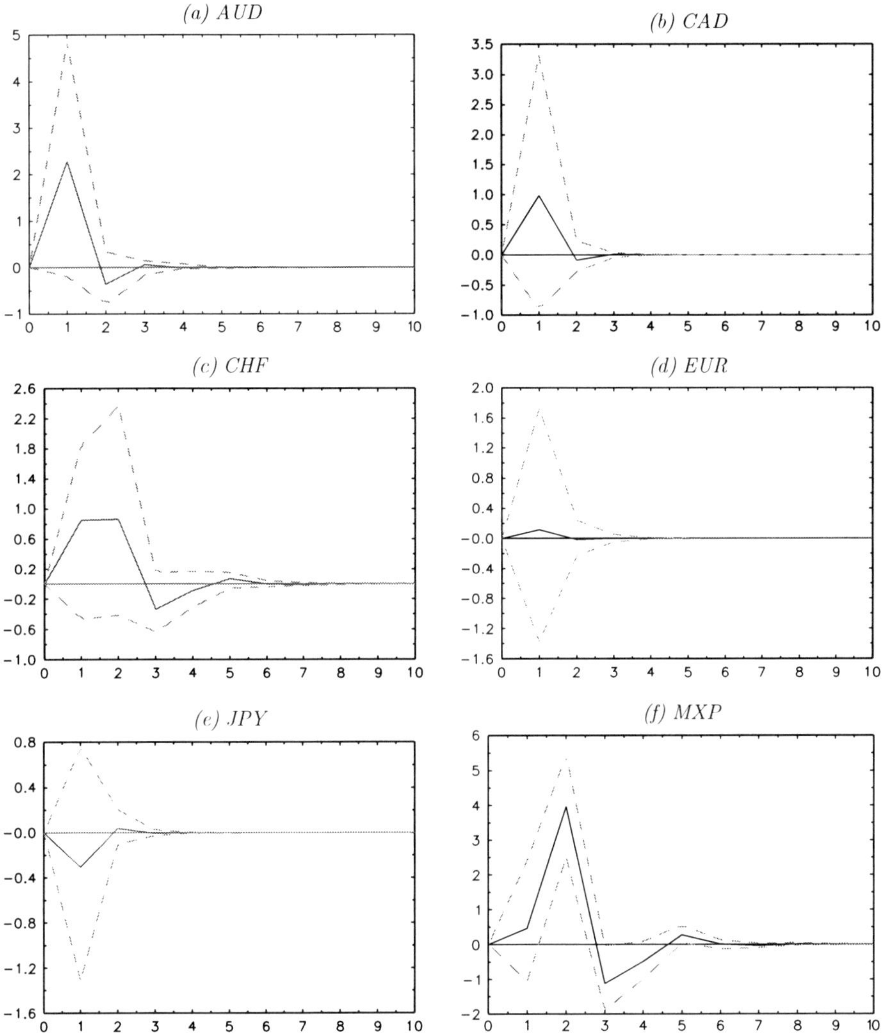

Fig. 5.4 Impulse responses: Effect of price shocks on the "speculation-hedging-ratio"

5.3.3 *Long Versus Short Speculation*

Based on the previous findings with respect to price effects on the "speculation-hedging-ratio," one should not jump to any conclusions concerning the stability of the markets. Up to now, total trading volume of hedgers and speculators was examined. No distinction was made between short and long speculation. For example, suppose that speculators react to an increase in prices by going short in the currency futures. Taking this contrary position may limit the size of disequilibrium and eventually lead prices to return to equilibrium. A closer look at speculators' long and short positions in response to price increases is appropriate. Therefore, the "long-short-speculation-ratio" $slsr_t$ is defined as:

$$slsr_t = \frac{long - speculation(t)}{short - speculation(t)}. \tag{5.4}$$

Continuous returns $\Delta slsr_t$ are then computed:

$$\Delta slsr_t = 100 * ln\left(\frac{slsr_t}{slsr_{t-1}}\right). \tag{5.5}$$

Table 5.3 presents summary statistics, ARCH-LM, and unit root tests for the Δp_t and $\Delta slsr_t$ series.[32] The ARCH-LM test statistics suggest that there is no conditional heteroskedasticity except for the CAD series and the EUR and MXP $\Delta slsr_t$ series. The ADF and KPSS tests confirm that the series are stationary.

The Granger causality tests presented in Table 5.4 and the impulse response functions shown in Fig. 5.5 unambiguously suggest a statistically significant positive effect of price increases on the "long-short-speculation-ratio." Hence, speculators go long in the currency futures in response to the price shocks and, therefore, bet on further price rises.

5.4 Logistic Smooth Transition Regression Analysis of Long Speculation

The results of the previous section suggest a positive effect of price increases on the "long-short-speculation-ratio." That is, the effect on long speculative positions is stronger than on short positions. In this section, the interrelation of long speculation and futures prices will be investigated in more detail. Therefore, a new variable representing the continuous returns of long speculation is defined as:

$$\Delta sl_t = 100 * ln\left(\frac{long - speculation(t)}{long - speculation(t-1)}\right). \tag{5.6}$$

Table 5.5 presents summary statistics, ARCH-LM, and unit root tests for the Δp_t and Δsl_t series. The question is whether the reaction of long speculation Δsl_t to

[32] Note that, compared to the previous section, here, the Mexican Peso series are shorter. The estimation is conducted over the sample period May 9, 2000 to January 31, 2006 because of low liquidity prior to May 2000.

Table 5.3 Summary statistics, ARCH-LM, and unit root tests for the VAR analysis of long versus short speculation

Series		Sample	Obs.	Mean	Min.	Max.	Std. Dev.	Skewness	Kurtosis	ARCH-LM	ADF	KPSS
AUD	Δp_t	01/02/2001–01/31/2006	219	0.1381	−4.8198	4.6606	1.5787	−0.2350	3.0332	0.3944	−10.7692	0.1601
	$\Delta sl sr_t$	01/02/2001–01/31/2006	219	0.1377	−306.772	287.586	79.5862	−0.1982	5.2400	0.5156	−11.7958	0.0185
CAD	Δp_t	10/06/1992–01/31/2006	684	0.0146	−3.2677	3.3457	0.8739	0.1963	3.9601	0.0016	−18.3586	0.6631
	$\Delta sl sr_t$	10/06/1992–01/31/2006	684	0.6097	−421.484	301.069	74.5487	−0.2380	6.8158	0.0000	−20.2528	0.0119
CHF	Δp_t	10/06/1992–01/24/2006	680	0.0001	−5.6229	9.0289	1.5921	0.2841	4.7377	0.7361	−19.2986	0.0119
	$\Delta sl sr_t$	10/06/1992–01/24/2006	680	0.0305	−483.634	402.266	97.5262	−0.5221	7.4348	0.9159	−19.2489	0.0073
EUR	Δp_t	01/12/1999–01/31/2006	366	0.0136	−3.9630	3.9679	1.3766	−0.0116	3.0029	0.7273	−13.3658	0.4246
	$\Delta sl sr_t$	01/12/1999–01/31/2006	366	0.1843	−338.804	306.270	55.3401	−0.4536	10.7931	0.0000	−15.7426	0.0141
JPY	Δp_t	10/06/1992–01/31/2006	694	0.0037	−6.2483	9.3058	1.5940	0.6945	6.6184	0.0828	−17.8842	0.0710
	$\Delta sl sr_t$	10/06/1992–01/31/2006	694	−0.2224	−276.666	426.629	69.3895	0.3177	7.5651	0.2231	−19.2603	0.0111
MXP	Δp_t	05/09/2000–01/31/2006	299	−0.0278	−5.3057	6.3680	1.2166	−0.1824	6.7141	0.7588	−12.9827	0.1134
	$\Delta sl sr_t$	05/09/2000–01/31/2006	299	0.4426	−280.660	353.980	82.9965	0.2162	6.5828	0.0017	−12.4666	0.0283

Note: The ARCH-LM test is used for testing the null hypothesis of no conditional heteroskedasticity. ARCH-LM results are in p-values. ADF and KPSS are the test statistics of the augmented Dickey Fuller and the Kwiatkowski, Phillips, Schmidt, and Shin test. The ADF test rejects the null hypothesis of nonstationarity if the test statistic is negative and the absolute value of the test statistic exceeds the critical value of the respective significance level: 1%: −2.56; 5%: −1.94; 10%: −1.62. The KPSS test rejects the null hypothesis of stationarity if the test statistic exceeds the critical value of the respective significance level: 1%: 0.739; 5%: 0.463; 10%: 0.347. For more information on the tests applied here, see Lütkepohl and Krätzig (2004)

Table 5.4 Granger causality test for the "long-short-speculation-ratio"

	AUD	CAD	CHF	EUR	JPY	MXP
Test value	4.1941	8.1212	15.6060	15.4464	19.4856	5.2639
p-value	0.0412	0.0003	0.0001	0.0001	0.0000	0.0221

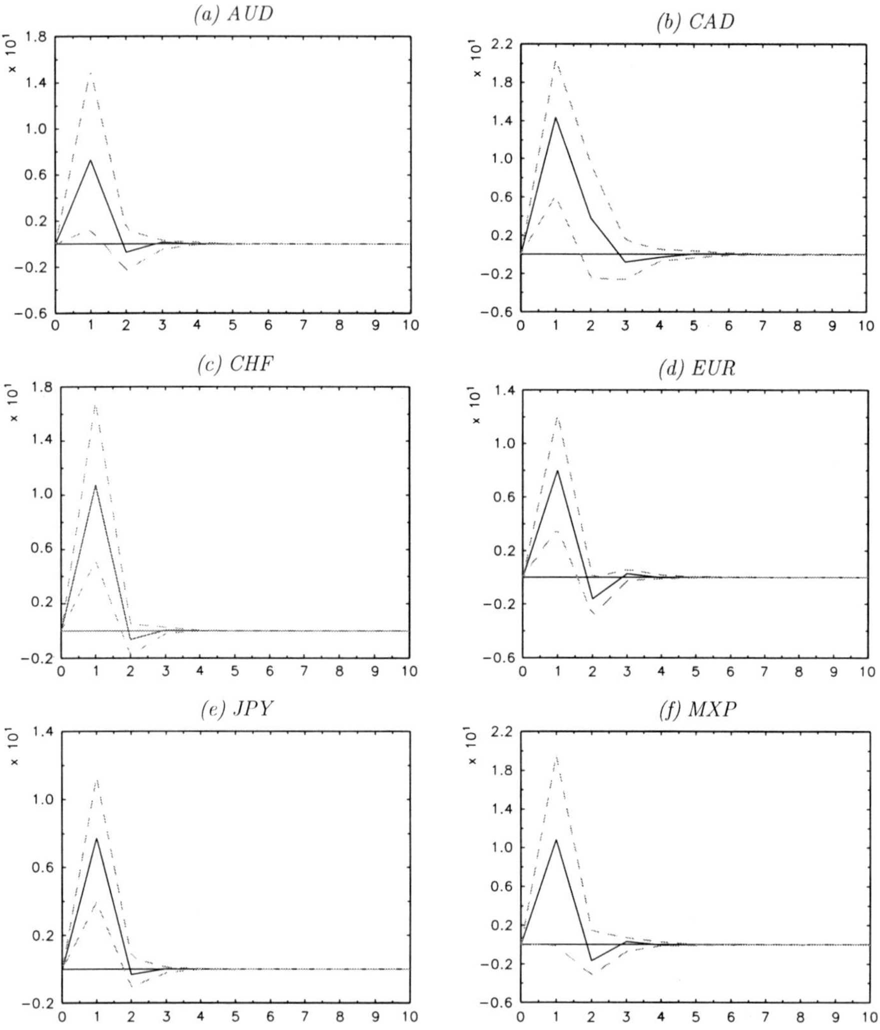

Fig. 5.5 Impulse responses: Effect of price shocks on the "long-short-speculation-ratio"

price shocks Δp_t depends on the underlying price regime. In order to obtain a useful characterization of the dynamics that, however, allows for a simple interpretation of the results, the logistic smooth transition regression model is chosen for the investigation. The empirical analysis in the following sections is based on the modelling

Table 5.5 Summary statistics, ARCH-LM, and unit root tests for the LSTR analysis

Series		Sample	Obs.	Mean	Min.	Max.	Std. Dev.	Skewness	Kurtosis	ARCH-LM	ADF	KPSS
AUD	Δp_t	01/02/2001–01/31/2006	249	0.1215	−4.8198	4.6606	1.5437	−0.2274	3.0336	0.4587	−11.4920	0.1273
	Δsl_t	01/02/2001–01/31/2006	249	0.8610	−125.802	154.426	31.6939	0.6299	7.5138	0.9657	−11.3483	0.0222
CAD	Δp_t	10/06/1992–01/31/2006	693	0.0117	−3.2677	3.2873	0.8597	0.1139	3.8011	0.0863	−18.5669	0.6166
	Δsl_t	10/06/1992–01/31/2006	693	0.6331	−186.183	203.459	37.0903	0.1519	8.2565	0.2810	−20.1534	0.0121
CHF	Δp_t	10/06/1992–01/24/2006	684	0.0001	−5.6229	9.0289	1.5871	0.2863	4.7686	0.7195	−19.2376	0.1546
	Δsl_t	10/06/1992–01/24/2006	684	0.1762	−470.048	413.517	70.7334	−0.5573	10.1125	0.0310	−20.0937	0.0093
EUR	Δp_t	01/12/1999–01/31/2006	366	0.0136	−3.9630	3.9679	1.3766	−0.0116	3.0029	0.7273	−13.3658	0.4246
	Δsl_t	01/12/1999–01/31/2006	366	0.9643	−175.360	202.909	27.6166	0.2223	18.2858	0.0000	−16.4374	0.0385
JPY	Δp_t	10/06/1992–01/31/2006	694	0.0037	−6.2483	9.3058	1.5940	0.6945	6.6184	0.0828	−17.8842	0.0710
	Δsl_t	10/06/1992–01/31/2006	694	0.1253	−270.049	390.385	56.7553	0.5627	10.2736	0.0496	−20.9125	0.0106
MXP	Δp_t	05/09/2000–01/31/2006	299	−0.0278	−5.3057	6.3680	1.2166	−0.1824	6.7141	0.7588	−12.9827	0.1134
	Δsl_t	05/09/2000–01/31/2006	299	1.1863	−248.491	280.940	54.3431	0.5587	10.0802	0.0000	−12.8852	0.0171

Note: The ARCH-LM test is used for testing the null hypothesis of no conditional heteroskedasticity. ARCH-LM results are in p-values. ADF and KPSS are the test statistics of the augmented Dickey Fuller and the Kwiatkowski, Phillips, Schmidt, and Shin test. The ADF test rejects the null hypothesis of nonstationarity if the test statistic is negative and the absolute value of the test statistic exceeds the critical value of the respective significance level: 1%: −2.56; 5%: −1.94; 10%: −1.62. The KPSS test rejects the null hypothesis of stationarity if the test statistic exceeds the critical value of the respective significance level: 1%: 0.739; 5%: 0.463; 10%: 0.347. For more information on the tests applied here, see Lütkepohl and Krätzig (2004) cycle outlined by Teräsvirta (1994, 1997, 1998, 2004), van Dijk, Teräsvirta, and Franses (2002), and Lütkepohl and Krätzig (2004).

5.4.1 The LSTR Model

The LSTR model is a regime-switching model that is well suited to modelling the dynamics of expansion and contraction regimes.[33] The standard LSTR model is defined as

$$y_t = \phi' z_t + \theta' z_t G(\gamma, c, \tau_t) + u_t, \quad u_t \sim iid(0, \sigma^2), \tag{5.7}$$

where $z_t = (w_t', x_t')'$ is a vector of explanatory variables with $w_t' = (1, y_{t-1}, \ldots, y_{t-n})'$, and $x_t' = (x_{1t}, \ldots, x_{kt})'$, which is a vector of exogenous variables. $\phi = (\phi_1, \ldots, \phi_m)$ and $\theta = (\theta_1, \ldots, \theta_m)$ are parameter vectors. The transition between the alternative regimes is controlled by the logistic transition function

$$G(\gamma, c, \tau_t) = \left(1 + exp\left\{-\frac{\gamma}{\hat{\sigma}_{\tau_t}^K} \prod_{k=1}^{K} (\tau_t - c_k)\right\}\right)^{-1}, \quad \gamma > 0, \tag{5.8}$$

which is a bounded function between 0 and 1. Equations (5.7) and (5.8), jointly define the LSTR1 ($K = 1$) or LSTR2 ($K = 2$) model. If $K = 1$, there are two regimes where the parameters $(\phi + \theta G(\gamma, c, \tau_t))$ change monotonically as a function of the transition variable τ_t from ϕ (if $G(\gamma, c, \tau_t) = 0$) to $\phi + \theta$ (if $G(\gamma, c, \tau_t) = 1$). Hence, if $K = 1$, the values of 0 and 1 of the transition function identify two distinct regimes. The transition between these two regimes occurs either smoothly or suddenly. The parameter γ determines how rapid the transition from zero to unity is and, thus, the smoothness of the transition. When $\gamma \rightarrow +\infty$, the transition from one regime to the other occurs almost instantly at $\tau_t = c$. The transition parameter c determines where the transition occurs. The estimated value of c marks the half-way point between the lower regime $G(\gamma, c, \tau_t) = 0$ and the upper regime $G(\gamma, c, \tau_t) = 1$. If $K = 2$, there are three regimes where the two outside regimes are identical, but different to the middle one.[34] The choice of K will be based on linearity tests discussed in the next section.

5.4.2 Testing Linearity Against LSTR

The modelling cycle outlined by Teräsvirta (1994, 1998, 2004) consists of three stages: Specification, estimation, and evaluation. Specification comprises testing linearity against LSTR and, if linearity is rejected, the choice of $K = 1$ or $K = 2$

[33] See e.g., McMillan (2005) and Pérez-Rodríguez, Torra, and Andrada-Félix (2005).

[34] For more information on the LSTR2 model, see e.g., Teräsvirta (2004) and Teräsvirta, van Dijk, and Medeiros (2005).

Table 5.6 Testing linearity against LSTR

	Transition variable	F	F4	F3	F2	Suggested model
AUD	Δp_t	0.0037	0.1280	0.2121	0.0021	LSTR1
CAD	Δp_t	0.2587	0.8891	0.0101	0.7011	Linear
CHF	Δp_t	0.0280	0.4624	0.1178	0.0176	LSTR1
EUR	Δp_{t-9}	0.0005	0.1742	0.4563	0.0000	LSTR1
JPY	Δp_t	0.0167	0.1294	0.4197	0.0085	LSTR1
MXP	Δp_{t-1}	0.0000	0.0000	0.0004	0.0006	LSTR1

referring to (5.8). The choice of $K = 1$ or $K = 2$ (or between LSTR1 and LSTR2, respectively) is based on a series of F-tests.[35]

The linearity tests for the AUD, CAD, CHF, EUR, JPY, and MXP series are conducted for up to ten lags. The variables with the smallest p-values are chosen as transition variables. The p-values of the linearity tests together with the suggested transition variable and the suggested model are presented in Table 5.6. The test results reveal strong evidence of nonlinearities in all except the CAD series (p-value: 0.2587). In regard to the AUD, CHF, and JPY series, using Δp_t as transition variable results in the smallest p-value. However, for the EUR series, Δp_{t-9} is the appropriate transition variable, and for the MXP series Δp_{t-1} is the appropriate transition variable. Moreover, the results suggest to choose an LSTR1 model for all series where linearity is rejected.

5.4.3 *Estimation Results*

In the next step of the modelling cycle, the parameter structure of the model is specified. A number of LSTR models with a variety of different lags are estimated for the AUD, CHF, EUR, JPY, and MXP speculation series and variables with poor explanatory power are excluded from the final specifications.[36]

5.4.3.1 AUD – Speculation Dynamics

The estimation results of the final specification for the AUD series are reported in (5.9) together with a number of statistics.

$$\begin{aligned}\Delta sl_t = &\underset{(0.52)}{35.58} - \underset{(0.55)}{0.06}\,\Delta sl_{t-1} - \underset{(0.79)}{0.02}\,\Delta sl_{t-2} - \underset{(0.09)}{0.14}\,\Delta sl_{t-3}\\ &- \underset{(0.64)}{0.04}\,\Delta sl_{t-4} + \underset{(0.28)}{0.04}\,\Delta sl_{t-5} - \underset{(0.08)}{0.12}\,\Delta sl_{t-6} + \underset{(0.65)}{0.07}\,\Delta sl_{t-7}\end{aligned}$$

[35] For more details on the F-tests, see Teräsvirta (2004, p. 227).

[36] There is no strict formal procedure to determine the lag structure for LSTR models. See e.g., Granger and Teräsvirta (1993) and McMillan (2005).

$$+\underset{(0.53)}{0.05}\,\Delta sl_{t-8}+\underset{(0.04)}{23.86}\Delta p_t+\underset{(0.18)}{2.86}\,\Delta p_{t-1}+\underset{(0.23)}{2.22}\,\Delta p_{t-2}$$
$$-\underset{(0.31)}{1.63}\,\Delta p_{t-4}-\underset{(0.77)}{0.57}\,\Delta p_{t-5}-\underset{(0.00)}{4.45}\,\Delta p_{t-8}$$
$$+[\underset{(0.00)}{-980.01}+\underset{(0.64)}{0.94}\,\Delta sl_{t-1}-\underset{(0.90)}{0.24}\,\Delta sl_{t-2}+\underset{(0.35)}{1.91}\,\Delta sl_{t-3}$$
$$+\underset{(0.36)}{2.30}\,\Delta sl_{t-4}-\underset{(0.35)}{1.82}\,\Delta sl_{t-5}+\underset{(0.53)}{0.95}\,\Delta sl_{t-6}-\underset{(0.00)}{2.82}\,\Delta sl_{t-7}$$
$$-\underset{(0.48)}{1.41}\,\Delta sl_{t-8}+\underset{(0.17)}{159.59}\Delta p_t+\underset{(0.98)}{0.80}\,\Delta p_{t-1}-\underset{(0.87)}{4.92}\,\Delta p_{t-2}$$
$$+\underset{(0.60)}{14.43}\Delta p_{t-4}+\underset{(0.95)}{1.81}\,\Delta p_{t-5}+\underset{(0.22)}{54.57}\Delta p_{t-8}]$$
$$[1+exp\{-(\underset{(NaN)}{1.08}\,/\hat{\sigma}^{1}_{\Delta p})(\Delta p_t-\underset{(NaN)}{4.96})\}]^{-1}. \tag{5.9}$$

$$T=241,\ \ \hat{\sigma}=27.47,\ \ R^2=0.36,\ \ AIC=6.74,\ \ pLM_{ARCH}(1)=0.89,$$
$$pLM_{ARCH}(4)=0.71,\ \ pLJB=0.00,\ \ pLM_{AR}(1)=0.30,\ \ pLM_{AR}(4)=0.66.$$

The p-values of the coefficients appear in parentheses. T is the sample size; $\hat{\sigma}$ is the estimated standard deviation of the residuals; R^2 is the coefficient of determination; AIC is the Akaike information criterion; $pLM_{ARCH}(q)$ is the p-value of the LM test of no ARCH up to order q; $pLJB$ is the p-value of the Lomnicki–Jarque–Bera normality test; and $pLM_{AR}(q)$ is the p-value of the LM test of no error autocorrelation up to order q. The assumption of normality is rejected. However, there is no evidence of ARCH and autocorrelation.

The estimation results presented in (5.9) suggest that the transition occurs when Δp_t is close to five ($c = 4.96$). Since this value of the transition variable is not close to 0, this result does not suggest a contraction and an expansion regime.[37] However, the logistic transition function $G(\gamma, c, \tau_t)$ does not reach the value of 1. This can be seen in Fig. 5.6, which shows the transition function plotted against its argument (Δp_t). Since every point in Fig. 5.6 represents an observation, one can easily retrace the realizations of the transition function. Most observations are in the intermediate range of Δp_t, between -3 and 3. Moreover, there seems to be an equal number of observations for $\Delta p_t < 0$ and $\Delta p_t > 0$. The values of the transition function range from 0 to approximately 0.2, with the speed of transition being rather slow ($\gamma = 1.08$). Therefore, for the range $0 < G(\gamma, c, \tau_t) < 0.2$, a smooth transition from a contraction to an expansion regime can be identified.

---

[37] Note that the transition variable Δp_t is the natural logarithm of the difference between the futures settlement price at time t and the settlement price at t minus one week, since weekly data are analyzed. Positive values of Δp_t, therefore, represent an increase in futures prices, while negative values of Δp_t represent a fall in futures prices. A value of the transition variable close to 0 would, therefore, point to a structural break between contractions and expansions.

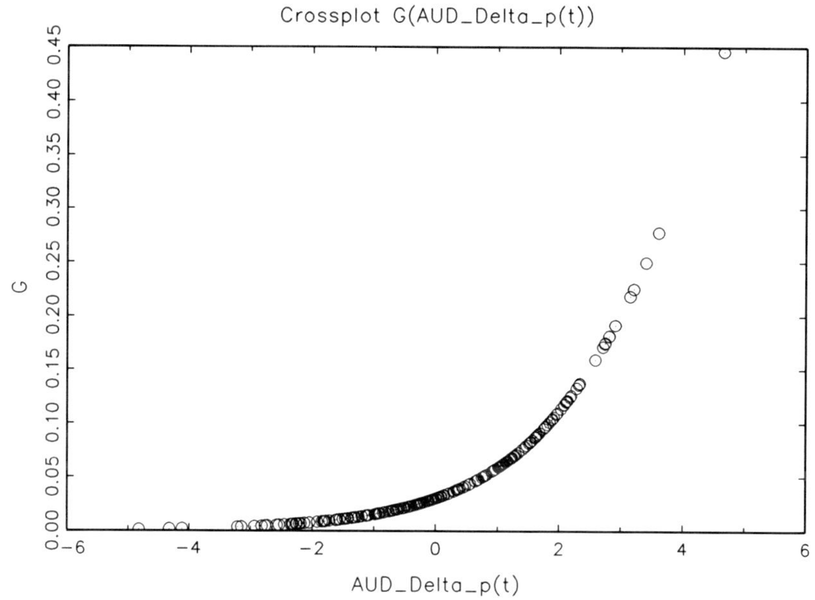

Fig. 5.6 AUD transition function plotted against transition variable Δp_t

The coefficient estimates are presented in (5.9). When the logistic transition function $G(\gamma, c, \tau_t)$ equals 0, only the linear part of the model (i.e., the first four rows of (5.9)) enter the regression model. If $G(\gamma, c, \tau_t) > 0$, then the entire equation is used for the estimation, where the rows five to eight in (5.9) are multiplied with the value of the transition function. The effects of price changes on long speculation in contractions with $G(\gamma, c, \tau_t) = 0$ are therefore:

$$\begin{aligned}\Delta sl_t = & \ldots + 23.86\Delta p_t + 2.86\Delta p_{t-1} + 2.22\Delta p_{t-2} \\ & - 1.63\Delta p_{t-4} - 0.57\Delta p_{t-5} - 4.45\Delta p_{t-8}.\end{aligned}$$

If $G(\gamma, c, \tau_t) > 0$, the regression model reads as follows:

$$\begin{aligned}\Delta sl_t = & \ldots + (23.86 + 159.59 * G(\gamma, c, \tau_t))\Delta p_t + (2.86 + 0.80 * G(\gamma, c, \tau_t))\Delta p_{t-1} \\ & + (2.22 - 4.92 * G(\gamma, c, \tau_t))\Delta p_{t-2} + (-1.63 + 14.43 * G(\gamma, c, \tau_t))\Delta p_{t-4} \\ & + (-0.57 + 1.81 * G(\gamma, c, \tau_t))\Delta p_{t-5} + (-4.45 + 54.57 * G(\gamma, c, \tau_t))\Delta p_{t-8}.\end{aligned}$$

The effect of price increases on long speculation trading volume is positive and much larger in expansions than in the contraction regime. However, most of the estimates are not significant at any level. Nevertheless, these findings might indicate that speculators react to price increases by betting on further price rises. Price increases that act as a signal to speculators might, therefore, lead to positive feedback trading during booms.

5.4.3.2 CHF – Speculation Dynamics

The estimation results for the CHF series are presented in the following equation:

$$
\begin{aligned}
\Delta sl_t =\ & \underset{(0.53)}{7.45} - \underset{(0.00)}{0.21}\,\Delta sl_{t-1} - \underset{(0.00)}{0.44}\,\Delta sl_{t-3} - \underset{(0.00)}{0.24}\,\Delta sl_{t-4} - \underset{(0.00)}{0.25}\,\Delta sl_{t-5} \\
&+ \underset{(0.00)}{22.31}\,\Delta p_t + \underset{(0.00)}{9.29}\,\Delta p_{t-1} + \underset{(0.00)}{10.92}\Delta p_{t-3} + \underset{(0.09)}{5.70}\,\Delta p_{t-4} \\
&+ \underset{(0.06)}{5.68}\,\Delta p_{t-5} - \underset{(0.00)}{8.58}\,\Delta p_{t-6} - \underset{(0.01)}{7.44}\,\Delta p_{t-7} \\
&+ [\underset{(0.61)}{-6.24} + \underset{(0.06)}{0.15}\,\Delta sl_{t-1} + \underset{(0.00)}{0.46}\,\Delta sl_{t-3} + \underset{(0.04)}{0.15}\,\Delta sl_{t-4} + \underset{(0.00)}{0.25}\,\Delta sl_{t-5} \\
&- \underset{(0.29)}{6.82}\,\Delta p_t - \underset{(0.37)}{3.27}\,\Delta p_{t-1} - \underset{(0.00)}{12.05}\,\Delta p_{t-3} - \underset{(0.13)}{5.85}\,\Delta p_{t-4} \\
&- \underset{(0.22)}{4.46}\,\Delta p_{t-5} + \underset{(0.12)}{5.43}\,\Delta p_{t-6} + \underset{(0.12)}{5.21}\,\Delta p_{t-7}] \\
&\quad [1 + exp\{-(\underset{(NaN)}{5797.91} / \hat{\sigma}^1_{\Delta p})(\Delta p_t + \underset{(NaN)}{0.88})\}]^{-1}.
\end{aligned}
\tag{5.10}
$$

$$T = 676,\ \hat{\sigma} = 62.52,\ R^2 = 0.25,\ AIC = 8.30,\ pLM_{ARCH}(1) = 0.53,$$
$$pLM_{ARCH}(4) = 0.00,\ pLJB = 0.00,\ pLM_{AR}(1) = 0.23,\ pLM_{AR}(4) = 0.02.$$

The null hypothesis of normality, as well as the assumption of no ARCH and no autocorrelation, are rejected up to order four. However, there is no ARCH and autocorrelation at one lag.

Figure 5.7 shows a sudden transition from the lower to the upper regime. In fact, there are no observations at intermediate values of the transition function $G(\gamma, c, \tau_t)$. The transition occurs at values of Δp_t close to 0. That means the lower regime is the contraction regime and the upper regime represents expansions.

The estimation results presented in (5.10) support the finding of a rapid transition ($\gamma = 5{,}797.91$) around $\Delta p_t = 0$ ($c = -0.88$). The effects of price changes on trading volume in the contraction regime, where $G(\gamma, c, \tau_t) = 0$, are

$$
\begin{aligned}
\Delta sl_t =\ & \ldots + 22.31\Delta p_t + 9.29\Delta p_{t-1} + 10.92\Delta p_{t-3} + 5.70\Delta p_{t-4} \\
& + 5.68\Delta p_{t-5} - 8.58\Delta p_{t-6} - 7.44\Delta p_{t-7},
\end{aligned}
$$

and in the expansion regime, where $G(\gamma, c, \tau_t) = 1$, are the following:

$$\Delta sl_t = \ldots + (22.31 - 6.82)\Delta p_t + (9.29 - 3.27)\Delta p_{t-1}$$

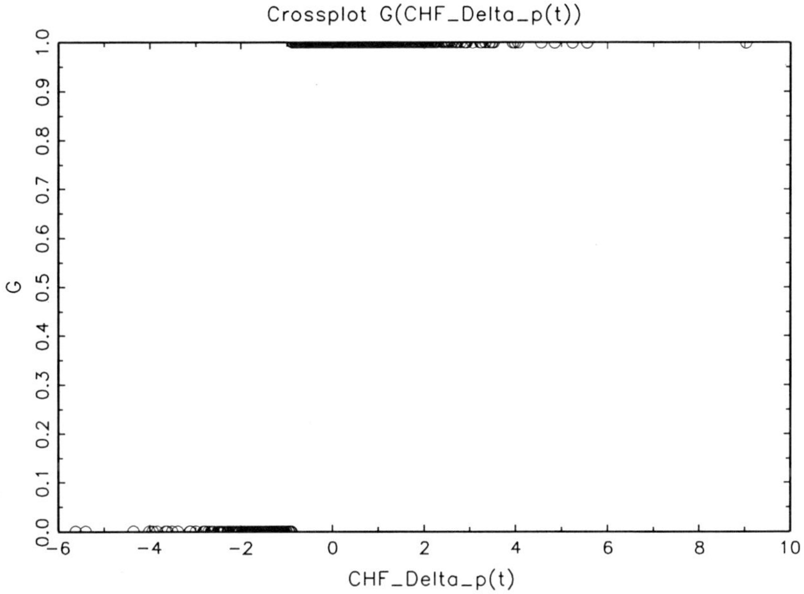

Fig. 5.7 CHF transition function plotted against transition variable Δp_t

$$
\begin{aligned}
&+ (10.92 - 12.05)\Delta p_{t-3} + (5.70 - 5.85)\Delta p_{t-4} \\
&+ (5.68 - 4.46)\Delta p_{t-5} + (-8.58 + 5.43)\Delta p_{t-6} \\
&+ (-7.44 + 5.21)\Delta p_{t-7} \\
= &\ldots + 15.49\Delta p_t + 6.02\Delta p_{t-1} - 1.13\Delta p_{t-3} - 0.15\Delta p_{t-4} \\
&+ 1.22\Delta p_{t-5} - 3.15\Delta p_{t-6} - 2.23\Delta p_{t-7}.
\end{aligned}
$$

These results suggest that the impact of price increases on long speculation is not stronger during expansions. Therefore, the former results with respect to the AUD series cannot be supported. For example, the estimated parameters of Δp_{t-3} and Δp_{t-4} change from positive, during contractions, to negative in the expansion regime. Hence, the overall reaction of trading volume to price changes seems to be more moderate during expansions.

5.4.3.3 EUR – Speculation Dynamics

The empirical results for the EUR series are shown in the following equation:

$$
\begin{aligned}
\Delta sl_t = &\underset{(0.10)}{4.25} - \underset{(0.08)}{0.21}\,\Delta sl_{t-1} + \underset{(0.01)}{0.24}\,\Delta sl_{t-3} + \underset{(0.00)}{0.35}\,\Delta sl_{t-5} + \underset{(0.04)}{0.21}\,\Delta sl_{t-7} \qquad (5.11) \\
&+ \underset{(0.00)}{0.22}\,\Delta sl_{t-8} - \underset{(0.05)}{0.19}\,\Delta sl_{t-9} + \underset{(0.00)}{6.55}\,\Delta p_t - \underset{(0.90)}{0.21}\,\Delta p_{t-1} - \underset{(0.75)}{0.53}\,\Delta p_{t-2}
\end{aligned}
$$

$$
\begin{aligned}
&- \underset{(0.48)}{1.13}\,\Delta p_{t-3} - \underset{(0.38)}{1.63}\,\Delta p_{t-5} - \underset{(0.05)}{3.61}\,\Delta p_{t-6} - \underset{(0.00)}{5.09}\,\Delta p_{t-7} \\
&+ [\underset{(0.09)}{-5.17} + \underset{(0.52)}{0.09}\,\Delta sl_{t-1} - \underset{(0.00)}{0.41}\,\Delta sl_{t-3} - \underset{(0.00)}{0.45}\,\Delta sl_{t-5} - \underset{(0.05)}{0.26}\,\Delta sl_{t-7} \\
&- \underset{(0.00)}{0.40}\,\Delta sl_{t-8} + \underset{(0.22)}{0.15}\,\Delta sl_{t-9} - \underset{(0.77)}{0.58}\,\Delta p_{t} + \underset{(0.24)}{2.56}\,\Delta p_{t-1} + \underset{(0.61)}{1.00}\,\Delta p_{t-2} \\
&+ \underset{(0.66)}{0.88}\,\Delta p_{t-3} + \underset{(0.45)}{1.71}\,\Delta p_{t-5} + \underset{(0.15)}{3.11}\,\Delta p_{t-6} + \underset{(0.00)}{5.34}\,\Delta p_{t-7}] \\
&\quad [1 + exp\{-(\underset{(NaN)}{5.24}\,/\hat{\sigma}^{1}_{\Delta p})(\Delta p_t + \underset{(NaN)}{0.89})\}]^{-1}.
\end{aligned}
$$

$$T = 356,\ \ \hat{\sigma} = 18.52,\ \ R^2 = 0.35,\ \ AIC = 5.91,\ \ pLM_{ARCH}(1) = 0.11,$$
$$pLM_{ARCH}(4) = 0.24,\ \ pLJB = 0.00,\ \ pLM_{AR}(1) = 0.17,\ \ pLM_{AR}(4) = 0.20.$$

The assumption of normality is again rejected, and there is no evidence of ARCH and autocorrelation.

Figure 5.8 shows a smooth transition from the lower to the upper regime ($\gamma = 5.24$). The transition takes place at $c = -0.89$, which is again close to 0. These results, therefore, suggest a smooth transition from a contraction to an expansion regime. In the lower regime (i.e., the contraction regime with $G(\gamma, c, \tau_t) = 0$), the coefficient estimates are:

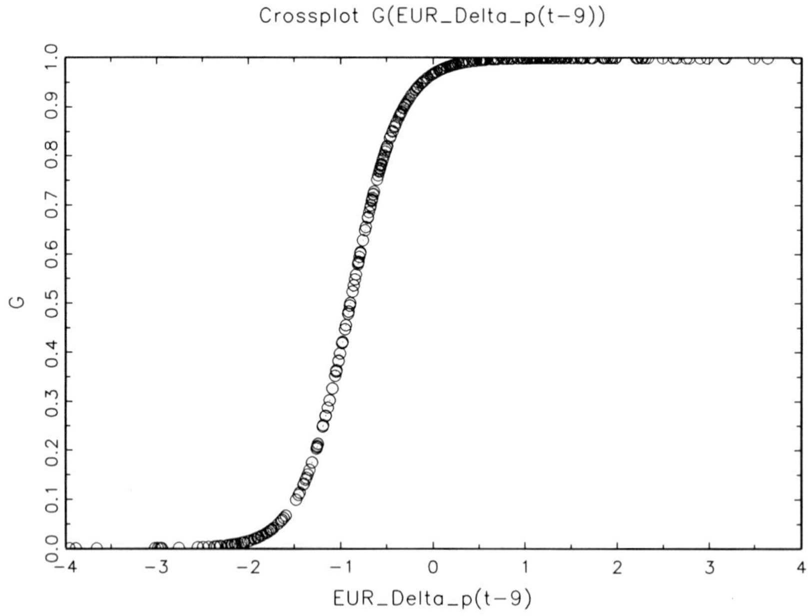

Fig. 5.8 EUR transition function plotted against transition variable Δp_{t-9}

$$\Delta sl_t = \ldots + 6.55\Delta p_t - 0.21\Delta p_{t-1} - 0.53\Delta p_{t-2} - 1.13\Delta p_{t-3} - 1.63\Delta p_{t-5} - 3.61\Delta p_{t-6} - 5.09\Delta p_{t-7}. \tag{5.12}$$

When $G(\gamma, c, \tau_t) = 1$, the coefficient estimates are:

$$\begin{aligned}\Delta sl_t &= \ldots + (6.55 - 0.58)\Delta p_t + (-0.21 + 2.56)\Delta p_{t-1} \\ &\quad + (-0.53 + 1.00)\Delta p_{t-2} + (-1.13 + 0.88)\Delta p_{t-3} \\ &\quad + (-1.63 + 1.71)\Delta p_{t-5} + (-3.61 + 3.11)\Delta p_{t-6} \\ &\quad + (-5.09 + 5.34)\Delta p_{t-7} \\ &= \ldots + 5.97\Delta p_t + 2.35\Delta p_{t-1} + 0.47\Delta p_{t-2} - 0.25\Delta p_{t-3} \\ &\quad + 0.08\Delta p_{t-5} - 0.50\Delta p_{t-6} + 0.25\Delta p_{t-7}. \end{aligned} \tag{5.13}$$

The sum of the coefficients of the price variables in the lower regime is negative (-5.65), indicating a negative relationship between prices and trading volume. In the expansion regime, the sum of the coefficients is 8.37. Thus, the regression results reveal a clear structural break in the effects of prices on trading volume from negative effects in the contraction regime to positive ones during expansions.

5.4.3.4 JPY – Speculation Dynamics

The equation shows the estimation results for the JPY series:

$$\begin{aligned}\Delta sl_t &= \underset{(0.56)}{-1.91} - \underset{(0.02)}{0.10}\,\Delta sl_{t-1} - \underset{(0.14)}{0.06}\,\Delta sl_{t-2} - \underset{(0.00)}{0.18}\,\Delta sl_{t-3} - \underset{(0.00)}{0.13}\,\Delta sl_{t-4} \\ &\quad + \underset{(0.32)}{0.04}\,\Delta sl_{t-5} - \underset{(0.02)}{0.11}\,\Delta sl_{t-6} + \underset{(0.54)}{0.02}\,\Delta sl_{t-7} + \underset{(0.10)}{0.07}\,\Delta sl_{t-9} \\ &\quad - \underset{(0.10)}{0.00}\,\Delta sl_{t-10} + \underset{(0.00)}{7.11}\,\Delta p_t + \underset{(0.06)}{2.97}\,\Delta p_{t-1} - \underset{(0.20)}{2.07}\,\Delta p_{t-2} - \underset{(0.01)}{4.28}\,\Delta p_{t-5} \\ &\quad - \underset{(0.11)}{2.47}\,\Delta p_{t-7} - \underset{(0.04)}{3.20}\,\Delta p_{t-9} - \underset{(0.16)}{2.16}\,\Delta p_{t-10} \\ &\quad + [\underset{(0.17)}{9.04} - \underset{(0.15)}{0.11}\,\Delta sl_{t-1} - \underset{(0.02)}{0.18}\,\Delta sl_{t-2} + \underset{(0.12)}{0.12}\,\Delta sl_{t-3} + \underset{(0.73)}{0.02}\,\Delta sl_{t-4} \\ &\quad - \underset{(0.00)}{0.26}\,\Delta sl_{t-5} - \underset{(0.18)}{0.10}\,\Delta sl_{t-6} - \underset{(0.00)}{0.21}\,\Delta sl_{t-7} - \underset{(0.00)}{0.31}\,\Delta sl_{t-9} \\ &\quad - \underset{(0.00)}{0.28}\,\Delta sl_{t-10} - \underset{(0.82)}{0.82}\,\Delta p_t + \underset{(0.09)}{4.58}\,\Delta p_{t-1} + \underset{(0.00)}{7.35}\,\Delta p_{t-2} + \underset{(0.46)}{1.97}\,\Delta p_{t-5} \\ &\quad + \underset{(0.03)}{6.10}\,\Delta p_{t-7} + \underset{(0.04)}{5.72}\,\Delta p_{t-9} + \underset{(0.15)}{4.22}\,\Delta p_{t-10}] \\ &\quad [1 + exp\{-(\underset{(NaN)}{2919.04}/\hat{\sigma}^1_{\Delta p})(\Delta p_t - \underset{(NaN)}{0.52})\}]^{-1}. \end{aligned} \tag{5.14}$$

$$T = 684,\ \ \hat{\sigma} = 51.43,\ \ R^2 = 0.23,\ \ AIC = 7.93,\ \ pLM_{ARCH}(1) = 0.00,$$
$$pLM_{ARCH}(4) = 0.00,\ \ pLJB = 0.00,\ \ pLM_{AR}(1) = 0.10,\ \ pLM_{AR}(4) = 0.03.$$

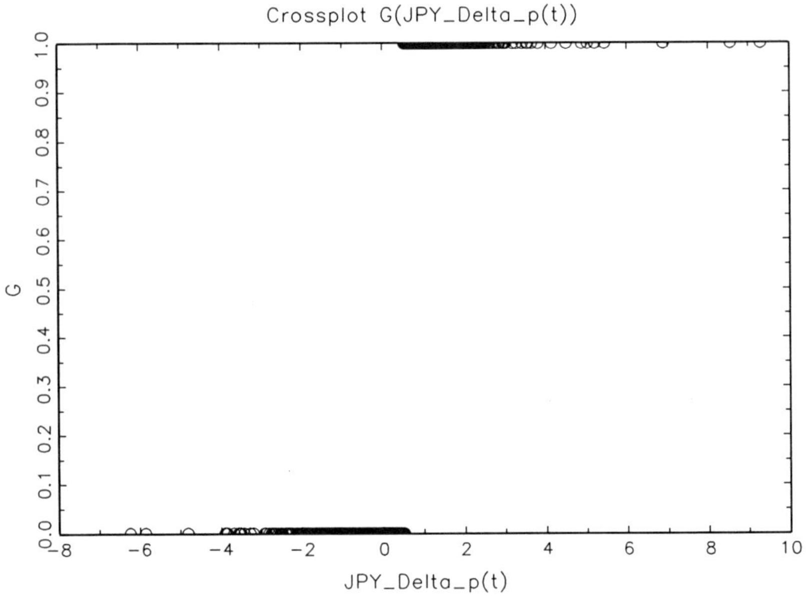

Fig. 5.9 JPY transition function plotted against transition variable Δp_t

The null hypothesis of normality as well as the assumption of no ARCH and the assumption of no autocorrelation up to order four are rejected.

As evident from Fig. 5.9, which shows the transition function plotted against the transition variable Δp_t, the sample is split into approximately equal parts between the two regimes. The transition is rapid ($\gamma = 2{,}919.04$) and takes place close to 0 ($c = 0.52$). The estimation results for the contraction regime are:

$$\begin{aligned} \Delta sl_t &= \ldots + 7.11\Delta p_t + 2.97\Delta p_{t-1} - 2.07\Delta p_{t-2} - 4.28\Delta p_{t-5} \\ &\quad - 2.47\Delta p_{t-7} - 3.20\Delta p_{t-9} - 2.16\Delta p_{t-10}, \end{aligned} \tag{5.15}$$

and for the expansion regime are:

$$\begin{aligned} \Delta sl_t &= \ldots + (7.11 - 0.82)\Delta p_t + (2.97 + 4.58)\Delta p_{t-1} \\ &\quad + (-2.07 + 7.35)\Delta p_{t-2} + (-4.28 + 1.97)\Delta p_{t-5} \\ &\quad + (-2.47 + 6.10)\Delta p_{t-7} + (-3.20 + 5.72)\Delta p_{t-9} \\ &\quad + (-2.16 + 4.22)\Delta p_{t-10} \\ &= \ldots + 6.29\Delta p_t + 7.55\Delta p_{t-1} + 5.28\Delta p_{t-2} - 2.31\Delta p_{t-5} \\ &\quad + 3.63\Delta p_{t-7} + 2.52\Delta p_{t-9} + 2.06\Delta p_{t-10}. \end{aligned} \tag{5.16}$$

This result suggests a structural break between a negative relationship between prices and trading volume in the lower regime, and a positive relationship between prices and trading volume in the upper regime. The coefficients of the price variables sum up to −4.1 in the contraction regime and to 25.02 in the expansion regime. These findings support the results for the EUR series. Here again the effect of price changes on trading volume is positive and much stronger during expansions, pointing to positive feedback trading in booms.

5.4.3.5 MXP – Speculation Dynamics

The last series to be analyzed is the MXP series. The regression results are:

$$\begin{aligned}
\Delta sl_t = {} & \underset{(0.13)}{3.94} - \underset{(0.07)}{0.10}\,\Delta sl_{t-1} - \underset{(0.00)}{0.31}\,\Delta sl_{t-2} - \underset{(0.00)}{0.16}\,\Delta sl_{t-3} - \underset{(0.52)}{0.03}\,\Delta sl_{t-5} \\
& - \underset{(0.00)}{0.15}\,\Delta sl_{t-8} + \underset{(0.00)}{21.64}\,\Delta p_t + \underset{(0.00)}{12.36}\,\Delta p_{t-1} + \underset{(0.00)}{9.51}\,\Delta p_{t-2} \\
& + \underset{(0.01)}{6.04}\,\Delta p_{t-3} - \underset{(0.50)}{1.70}\,\Delta p_{t-5} - \underset{(0.23)}{2.63}\,\Delta p_{t-6} \\
& + [-\underset{(0.48)}{15.74} + \underset{(0.04)}{0.42}\,\Delta sl_{t-1} + \underset{(0.00)}{0.85}\,\Delta sl_{t-2} - \underset{(0.00)}{0.68}\,\Delta sl_{t-3} - \underset{(0.04)}{0.34}\,\Delta sl_{t-5} \\
& + \underset{(0.38)}{0.14}\,\Delta sl_{t-8} + \underset{(0.68)}{4.03}\,\Delta p_t - \underset{(0.96)}{0.43}\,\Delta p_{t-1} - \underset{(0.24)}{10.41}\,\Delta p_{t-2} \\
& - \underset{(0.95)}{0.58}\,\Delta p_{t-3} + \underset{(0.00)}{36.20}\,\Delta p_{t-5} + \underset{(0.00)}{32.67}\,\Delta p_{t-6}] \\
& [1 + exp\{-(\underset{(NaN)}{30.21} / \hat{\sigma}^1_{\Delta p})(\Delta p_{t-1} - \underset{(NaN)}{1.35})\}]^{-1}.
\end{aligned} \tag{5.17}$$

$$T = 291,\ \hat{\sigma} = 40.87,\ R^2 = 0.45,\ AIC = 7.50,\ pLM_{ARCH}(1) = 0.00,$$
$$pLM_{ARCH}(4) = 0.00,\ pLJB = 0.00,\ pLM_{AR}(1) = 0.43,\ pLM_{AR}(4) = 0.61.$$

The assumption of no ARCH and normality are rejected but there is no autocorrelation. Figure 5.10 shows a rather rapid transition ($\gamma = 30.21$) from the lower to the upper regime. The transition occurs at $c = 1.35$. Most observations are in the lower regime.

The estimation results for the lower regime are:

$$\begin{aligned}
\Delta sl_t = {} & \ldots + 21.64\Delta p_t + 12.36\Delta p_{t-1} + 9.51\Delta p_{t-2} \\
& + 6.04\Delta p_{t-3} - 1.70\Delta p_{t-5} - 2.63\Delta p_{t-6},
\end{aligned} \tag{5.18}$$

and for the upper regime are the following:

$$\begin{aligned}
\Delta sl_t = {} & \ldots + (21.64 + 4.03)\Delta p_t + (12.36 - 0.43)\Delta p_{t-1} \\
& + (9.51 - 10.41)\Delta p_{t-2} + (6.04 - 0.58)\Delta p_{t-3} \\
& + (-1.70 + 36.20)\Delta p_{t-5} + (-2.63 + 32.67)\Delta p_{t-6} \\
= {} & \ldots + 25.67\Delta p_t + 11.93\Delta p_{t-1} - 0.90\Delta p_{t-2} \\
& + 5.46\Delta p_{t-3} + 34.50\Delta p_{t-5} + 30.04\Delta p_{t-6}.
\end{aligned} \tag{5.19}$$

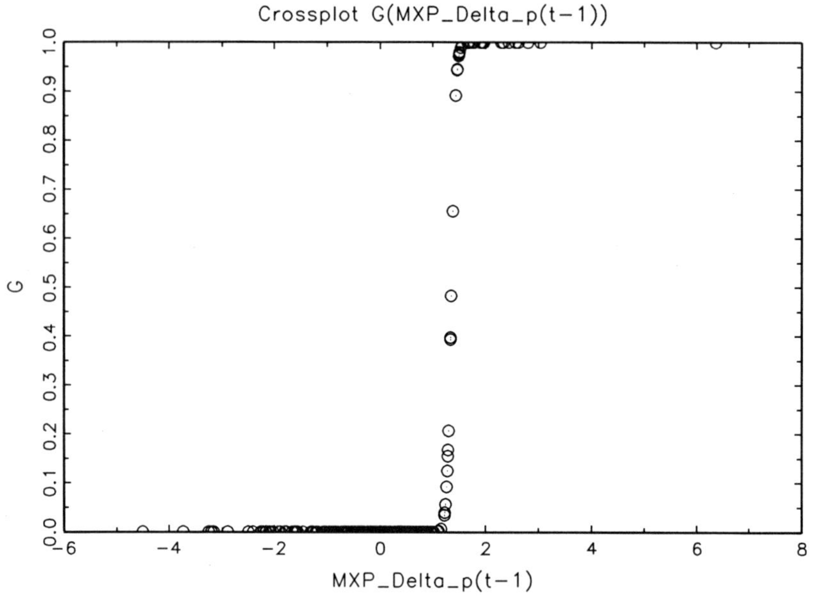

Fig. 5.10 MXP transition function plotted against transition variable Δp_{t-1}

The sum of the price variables in the lower regime is 45.22 and 106.70 in the upper regime. Again, the effect of price changes on trading volume is positive and much stronger during expansions.

5.4.4 Misspecification Tests

Table 5.7 presents test results from diagnostic tests for no remaining nonlinearity and parameter constancy. The test results from the linearity test suggest that there is no remaining nonlinearity in all but the MXP series. However, the results for the MXP series do not point to an LSTR2 model (i.e., the rejection of F3 is not the strongest). Since the linearity test suggests an LSTR1 model, and linearity is most strongly rejected assuming Δp_{t-1} is the transition variable, the structure of the model is not changed. Moreover, parameter constancy is not rejected for the MXP series. Parameter constancy is only rejected for the EUR series if $K = 1$ and $K = 3$. The rejection of parameter constancy is indicative of general misspecification. However, according to Teräsvirta (2004, p. 234), "(...) there is no unique way of responding to a rejection." Therefore, and because the linearity tests do not indicate a misspecification of the model, this is not followed up.

Table 5.7 Test for no remaining nonlinearity and parameter constancy

	Linearity				Parameter constancy		
	F	F4	F3	F2	$K = 1$	$K = 2$	$K = 3$
AUD	0.2729	0.5970	0.3317	0.1355	0.1949	0.5518	0.2611
CHF	0.0736	0.0696	0.0230	0.9553	0.4148	0.3380	0.4924
EUR	0.5485	0.6554	0.0629	0.9028	0.0034	0.1127	0.0325
JPY	0.4013	0.2722	0.1595	0.9088	0.9516	0.9959	0.9893
MXP	0.0250	0.0417	0.5300	0.0394	0.2998	0.4558	0.8909

Note: The table contains p-values of F-variants from LM diagnostic tests for no remaining nonlinearity and parameter constancy. Concerning the test for no remaining nonlinearity, the following decision rules apply: F represents the general test for no remaining nonlinearity. If the null hypothesis of no remaining nonlinearity is rejected, a sequence of null hypotheses (corresponding to F4, F3, and F2) is tested. If the rejection of F3 is the strongest, select an LSTR2 model, otherwise an LSTR1 model is appropriate (see Teräsvirta, 1998). The results of the parameter constancy test are given for three different transition functions with $K = 1,2,3$

5.5 A Catastrophe Theory Approach

The empirical results in the previous section suggest the following stylized facts:

- Price shocks lead to an increased proportion of speculators in futures markets.
- Speculators bet on further price increases and therefore behave like positive feedback traders.
- The behavior of speculators is regime dependent. At least for the AUD, EUR, JPY, and MXP series, the results suggest that the reaction of the quantity of speculation to price rises is much larger in the expansion regime.

In this section, these empirical findings, together with the theoretical consideration concerning the interaction of arbitrage and noise trading, are modelled in a cusp catastrophe approach. Catastrophe theory is chosen because it is able to capture the nonlinearities found through the LSTR analysis as well as the complex interrelation of arbitrageurs and noise traders in a relatively parsimonious model. The usefulness of catastrophe theory for modelling nonlinear and complex relations is, for example, discussed in Granger and Teräsvirta (1993, pp. 32–33), who note:

> "Some nonlinear generators (...) have the property that a small change in parameter values can lead to large changes in the long-run properties, from one fixed point to another quite different one, or from a fixed point to a cycle. This effect is called a bifurcation and reflects the idea that as one searches over parameter values one is actually considering models with quite different long run properties. (...) This is the basis of catastrophe theory (...). In just a few of these cases very substantial changes in the motion of the process can occur with small changes in parameter values, hence the use of the word 'catastrophe'."

The modelling approach in this section is closely related to the work of Zeeman (1974).[38] In his work he models the consequences of the interaction between two types of investors for the stability of a stock exchange.[39] The two types of traders are fundamentalists and chartists (i.e., speculators). The approach in this section differs from the one chosen by Zeeman (1974) by considering three different types of traders. Here, traders are divided into speculators, hedgers, and arbitrageurs. While speculators equal the chartists in Zeeman's model and hedgers might be compared to Zeeman's fundamentalists, the role of arbitrage has not yet been investigated in this type of model. In fact, corrective trades of arbitrageurs are at the center of this investigation. The variables are defined as follows:

- P: Futures settlement price changes is the dependent variable.
- AP: Arbitrage pressure is the "splitting factor." That means, when arbitrage pressure (i.e., the amount of corrective trades) decreases, a critical point is reached where the surface of the graphical representation splits (i.e., bifurcates). For strong values of arbitrage pressure (i.e., if $AP \geq 0$ in this model), changes are smooth. However, for negative values of AP discontinuities may occur. It is assumed that transaction costs and especially holding costs reduce arbitrage pressure.[40]
- TP: Traders net long positions.[41] Traders include speculators, hedgers, and arbitrageurs. TP is the normal factor in the model. This means that for large positive and negative values of TP changes are relatively smooth. For intermediate values of TP catastrophic changes can occur.

---

[38] See also the discussion of Zeeman's model in Aschinger (1995, 2001).

[39] Other applications of catastrophe theory include research concerning business cycles (Varian, 1979), competitive dynamics (Dou & Ghose, 2006; Kauffman & Oliva, 1994; Oliva, Day, & MacMillan, 1988), industrial adoption decisions (Herbig, 1991), anxiety levels in pre-university students (Haslett, Smyrnios, and Osborne, 1998), and ceremonial pig giving cycles in the New Guinea Highlands (Thompson, 1980).

[40] See the discussion in Sect. 5.2. Speculators and hedgers also face transaction costs. However, their trading positions are not effected that much by these costs. This is because of two reasons. First, expected prices play a crucial role with regard to expected gains from trading. In contrast to speculators, arbitrageurs expect prices to equal their equilibrium value. They will therefore, in the absence of holding costs, take positions contrary to the trend as soon as prices cross the transaction costs bounds. Their gain is the difference between the mispricing and the transaction costs. Speculators, on the other hand, expect prices to cross the transaction costs bounds and deviate from equilibrium even further. That is why they go long (short) in the futures contracts if prices rise (fall). Since their expected price is further away from equilibrium than the transaction costs, it does not matter if the actual price is below the transaction costs. Second, compared to hedgers, gains from arbitrage trades are essential to arbitrageurs. Hedgers follow a selective hedging strategy, as discussed in Chap. 3. Hedgers' motivation to trade in futures markets is therefore not solely based on expected gains, but also on risk aversion, especially with respect to the commitment in the spot market. Therefore, transaction costs play a minor role for hedgers. In this context, Dow and Gorton (1997) state that hedgers are often regarded as rational noise traders since they do not base their trading decisions solely on expected gains.

[41] Note that negative values of TP represent net short positions.

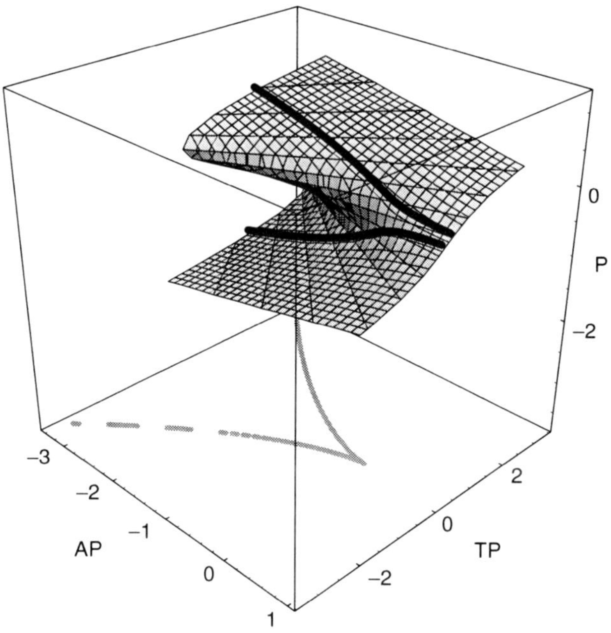

Fig. 5.11 The catastrophe model, bifurcation, and divergence

5.5.1 The Cusp Catastrophe Model and Underlying Hypotheses

It is beyond the scope and purpose of this section to give a detailed description of catastrophe theory. Hence, only a brief overview of the cusp catastrophe model is presented. In mathematical terminology, the cusp function used in this investigation is $F(P, AP, TP) = P^4 + AP * P^2 - TP * P$, where AP and TP are independent and P is the dependent variable. The partial derivative of $F(P, AP, TP)$ with respect to P gives the three-dimensional response surface. This surface is presented in Fig. 5.11 together with two important characteristics of the cusp catastrophe model.[42]

The dashed gray lines in Fig. 5.11 represent the bifurcation set in the $AP - TP - plane$. This bifurcation set shows that reduced arbitrage pressure may lead to increased misalignment of traders positions. Assume that, for any reason, speculators go net long in the currency futures contract ($TP > 0$). If arbitrage intensity was infinite ($AP \geq 0$), arbitrageurs would take positions contrary to speculators. The overall net long positions of traders (i.e., speculators, hedgers, and arbitrageurs) would, therefore, be 0. However, in the presence of transaction and holding costs arbitrageurs might not instantly exploit arbitrage opportunities ($AP < 0$). In this situation, misalignment of net trader positions might occur. The second important

[42] Appendix C presents the program code for the computation of Fig. 5.11.

property of the model is represented by the thick black lines in Fig. 5.11. The black lines show the divergence in the $P - AP - plane$. For the computation of the black lines, the variable TP is set constant at $TP = 0.1$ and $TP = -0.1$. These slightly different values of TP lead to large changes in state (i.e., in P) as AP decreases. Hence, small changes in the path may produce totally different trajectories and, therefore, quite different forms of system behavior.

In order to study the dynamic flows in the model, it is important to define the exact relation between P, AP, and TP. The following Hypotheses are closely related to Zeeman (1974):

> *Hypothesis 1:* The price P responds much faster to changes in arbitrage pressure AP and trader positions TP than AP and TP respond to P. Prices react instantly whereas the reaction of traders is much slower.

> *Hypothesis 2:* If arbitrage pressure is strong ($AP \geq 0$), then the balanced net positions of traders ($TP = 0$) will cause the settlement price to be static ($P = 0$). This is the stable equilibrium.

> *Hypothesis 3:* Reduced arbitrage pressure ($AP < 0$) leads to instability. In mathematical terminology, for large negative values of AP and intermediate values of TP the response dimension (i.e., the dependent variable P) can take on two possible values. This area of bimodality is where sudden, discontinuous catastrophe shifts are possible.

> *Hypothesis 4:* Arbitrageurs do not react instantly to mispricing because of transaction costs. They enter the market when prices cross the transaction costs bounds (i.e., the band of inactivity).

> *Hypothesis 5:* Speculators are positive feedback traders. They go long in the futures contracts when prices increase, and short otherwise. Moreover, they react faster to price changes than hedgers.

> *Hypothesis 6:* Positive feedback trading increases the holding costs faced by arbitrageurs. Holding costs limit arbitrage.

> *Hypothesis 7:* The stronger the mispricing, the more arbitrageurs will enter the market and take positions contrary to speculators. Moreover, hedgers who recognize the growing instability in the market will tend to insure themselves against further mispricing by taking contrary positions.[43]

5.5.2 *The Chain of Events*

Based on the hypotheses presented, the following chain of events can be constructed. It is related to the chain's graphical illustration shown in Fig. 5.12.

---

[43] Like the activity of arbitrageurs, trading activity of hedgers increases with increasing mispricing. This hypothesis is in line with the selective hedging theory. In this context, Working (1953, p. 320) notes that: "Except in firms that have a strict rule against taking hedgable risks, it is common, therefore, for stocks to be carried unhedged at times, when the responsible individual expects a price advance, and for the stocks of the commodity to be hedged at other times. Some individuals and firms hedge stocks only when they are particularly fearful of price decline."

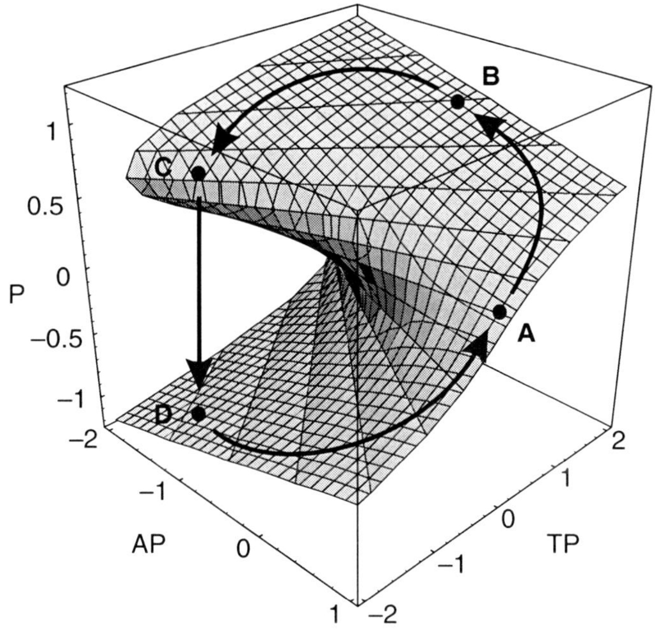

Fig. 5.12 The chain of events in the cusp catastrophe model

1. The economy is initially in equilibrium (see point A in Fig. 5.12). The futures settlement price equals its fair value. Hence, long and short positions are balanced ($TP = 0$). There is no mispricing and, therefore, no arbitrage. In this situation a price shock occurs which pushes the settlement price above its equilibrium value ($P \uparrow$).
2. Arbitrageurs do not react to the initial mispricing because of transaction costs.[44] That means the mispricing does not exceed the critical value, represented by the transaction costs bounds. Speculators react to the price increase by flowing into the market. Hence, the "speculation-hedging-ratio" increases. Moreover, speculators go long (i.e., act like positive feedback traders). The value of net long positions of all traders (speculators, hedgers, and arbitrageurs) increases ($TP \uparrow$). This leads to further price rises and, therefore, deepens the mispricing ($P \uparrow\uparrow$).
3. Now, the price path crosses arbitrageurs' transaction costs bounds. Arbitrageurs engage in trading and take positions contrary to speculators. However, arbitrage is still limited by holding costs. Moreover, holding costs increase with growing positive feedback trading ($AP \downarrow$). This means that, due to increased speculation, noise trader risk, as well as increasing horizon risk resulting from an increase

[44] Note that transaction costs and holding costs faced are arbitrageurs are treated separately. Transaction costs represent a clear barrier prices have to cross before arbitrageurs become actively involved in the market. Holding costs include several factors arbitrageurs have to consider. See Sect. 5.2.

in net long positions (which pushes prices further away from equilibrium), limits arbitrage. Since arbitrage is limited, prices still increase ($P \uparrow$; point B in Fig. 5.12).
4. In this situation, hedgers realize the extent of the mispricing and the overall risk in the market. They react to the increasing prices by going short. Like the arbitrageurs, hedgers take positions contrary to positive feedback traders. The "speculation-hedging-ratio" and the value of net long positions decreases ($TP \downarrow$).
5. The decrease in the "speculation-hedging-ratio" encourages arbitrageurs to exploit the mispricing. Prices begin to fall ($P \downarrow$). Speculators follow hedgers and arbitrageurs by going short, too ($TP \downarrow\downarrow$). This abrupt short selling leads to a crash in prices ($P \downarrow\downarrow$; from point C to point D in Fig. 5.12).
6. Now, prices are below their fair value. Arbitrageurs go long in futures contracts as soon as potential gains exceed the transaction costs. However, arbitrage is again limited by holding costs. Hedgers, who want to protect themselves against further price decreases, go long as well. Prices begin to rise again, and speculators go long ($P \uparrow$, $TP \uparrow$). The more the price path approaches equilibrium, the more holding costs are reduced and arbitrage pressure increases ($AP \uparrow$). Finally, the price path reaches equilibrium. Long and short positions of traders are again in equilibrium and there are no arbitrage opportunities.

5.6 Discussion

This chapter deals with the behavior of futures traders. In particular, the response of the quantity of trading volume to price changes is analyzed. The empirical investigation proceeds in three steps. The results are threefold. First, the fraction of speculators in all but the Japanese Yen currency futures market increases responding to a rise in settlement prices. Second, speculators go long in these futures contracts, i.e., they bet on further price increases and, thus, act like positive feedback traders. Third, the reaction of trading volume to price shocks depends on the price regime. Nonlinearities are found in all markets except the Canadian Dollar futures market. The results of the LSTR analysis suggest that positive feedback trading is even more profound in booms, at least for the Australian Dollar, the Euro, the Japanese Yen, and the Mexican Peso series. These results present strong evidence that price increases lead speculators to behave like a herd of positive feedback traders. This behavior will potentially discourage arbitrageurs from taking positions contrary to the speculators. The resulting deepening of the mispricing may, in turn, lead to a long path back to equilibrium.

A hypothetical chain of events, based on these empirical findings, is then modelled by using cusp catastrophe theory. This parsimonious model is able to capture the nonlinear dynamics and the complexity that is associated with the interrelation of arbitrage and noise trading. The model is particularly useful because delays (in arbitrage) and reversibility (of traders' positions) are characteristic features of the dynamics. It is shown that in the absence of arbitrage positive feedback trading can lead to radical drops (i.e., crashes) in prices. With growing arbitrage pressure, the transition from one state to the other gets smoother. However, the results based on this hypothetical chain of events have to be interpreted with caution. In this regard, Herbig (1991, p. 128) notes that:

> "Catastrophe Theory is the study of discontinuous transitions and is a qualitative, not a quantitative, descriptor. It is analogous to a map without scale; a mountain may be seen to the left but the exact distance to the peak is unknown. The map will tell you what to expect but not how far away or how high it is."

Nevertheless, the hypotheses on which this model is based are plausible with respect to economic theory and at least partly based on empirical findings. The catastrophe model is an appropriate tool for capturing nonlinearities and complexity, and for presenting some interesting accounts and explanations for instability.

Chapter 6
Conclusions

A hedger is a trader who simultaneously holds positions in spot and futures markets in order to reduce spot exposure. However, he does not necessarily minimize the initial spot risk. The minimization of risk is just one single possible outcome from a wide range of potential hedging strategies. Nevertheless, hedging less than the initial spot commitment does not mean that the hedger turns into a speculator. This is because he still holds positions in both markets, with the result that his overall exposure to risk is smaller than if he would only trade in the spot market. Risk is reduced, but not eliminated.

The microeconomic part of this thesis focuses on the determinants of firms' optimal hedging strategies. The impact of price expectations, risk aversion, and hedging costs are particularly important. If hedgers expect spot prices to move in their favor they will be less willing to hedge, since potential returns in the spot market are offset by losses in the futures position. In the presence of hedging costs, the overall profit of the hedged position would be negative if earnings and losses in spot and futures markets were perfectly balanced. Hence, under risk neutrality, companies will not hedge unless there are other incentives to hedge that outweigh the costs. These incentives include taxes, bankruptcy costs and underinvestment problems among others. The models presented in the microeconomic part of this thesis assume a priori that the hedging firm is risk averse.

In Chap. 2, the impact of price expectations and hedging costs on a firm's optimal hedging strategy are investigated in an expected utility framework. The importing firm can trade futures contracts in order to manage the spot currency risk. The model suggests that the size of the importer's hedging position should depend positively on backwardation. In the absence of hedging costs and price biases, the firm hedges its currency exposure fully, while it overhedges (underhedges) if the futures market exhibits backwardation (contango). This result changes, however, if hedging costs are introduced into the model. With hedging costs, the importer hedges fully only if the futures market exhibits backwardation to some degree. Nevertheless, an increase in backwardation should, ceteris paribus, lead the importing firm to increase its trading volume in long futures contracts. The empirical analysis in Chap. 2 investigates the impact of two measures of backwardation on hedgers' trading volume in long and short futures contracts. The results offer little support for the hypotheses

A. Röthig, *Microeconomic Risk Management and Macroeconomic Stability*, Lecture Notes in Economics and Mathematical Systems,
DOI 10.1007/978-3-642-01565-6_6,

suggested by economic theory that short (long) hedging activity depends negatively (positively) on backwardation.

The model presented in Chap. 3 builds on the representative importer's hedging problem introduced in Chap. 2. The mean-variance approach to hedging is applied in order to gain additional insights into the determinants of the importing firm's optimal hedging strategy. First, the optimal hedge is derived and decomposed into a pure hedge component and a speculative component. The speculative component contains firm specific characteristics, such as the degree of risk aversion and price expectations. It approaches zero if the hedger is infinitely risk averse, or if he does not expect prices to move in his favor. The pure hedge component depends on variances and covariances of spot and futures prices. Hence, the pure hedge component is identical for all firms and can be calculated using price data. It is shown in Chap. 3 that this pure hedge equals the so called minimum-variance hedge. Since the pure hedge, or minimum-variance hedge, respectively, is identical for all firms, differences between firms' hedging strategies depend solely on their individual speculative demand. The derived optimal hedge ratio, consisting of the speculative and the pure hedge component, is used to construct a Marshallian-type demand curve. This demand function for futures contracts, plus a stylized futures supply function, are then used to derive the hedgers' surplus. It is shown that risk aversion impacts the hedgers' surplus positively, while hedging costs have a negative effect on the surplus. In general, the investigations in Chaps. 2 and 3 show that, even in the presence of risk aversion, firms do not necessarily fully hedge their spot exposure. Expectations and hedging costs still play an important role in determining the firm's optimal hedging strategy. A wide range of selective hedging strategies from no hedging, over partial hedging, to full hedging and overhedging might be optimal.

From a macroeconomic perspective, firms' hedging activity has an impact on the sensitivity of investment to risk. Suppose that a firm's investment is exposed to currency risk. By choosing the optimal hedging strategy, the firm decides over the vulnerability of its investment to exchange rate changes. The less the firm hedges, the more vulnerable it is in the case of an adverse exchange rate shock. The macroeconomic approach, therefore, supplements the microeconomic discussion on optimal hedging strategies by analyzing the consequences of firms' risk management strategies on investment. This, in turn, allows for a further investigation of how an adverse shock can potentially affect output.

The analysis in Chap. 4 is concerned with the question of how output is affected by an exchange rate shock, depending on several alternative realizations of investment functions which are based on different risk management scenarios. Corporate hedging activity and speculation are investigated in a Mundell–Fleming–Tobin type currency crisis model. Using this model, a direct linkage between microeconomic risk management and macroeconomic stability is established. Three different types of financial derivatives are examined and compared to each other: Futures, forwards, and options. The shape of the investment function depends on which financial derivative is used by the firm, and how it is used. The investment function, in turn, is an important component of the goods market equilibrium curve. It is shown in the model that corporate hedging activity can serve to reduce adverse effects of exchange rate shocks and capital flight on output. Especially nonlinear derivatives such as options are found to be valuable, since they allow for output expansions after favorable exchange rate changes while still protecting against adverse shocks.

The behavior and interaction of different types of traders is of crucial importance for economic stability. Suppose that firms tend to follow a selective hedging strategy. Important aspects, like price expectations and risk aversion, may change over time. Moreover, market sentiment and, therefore, the behavior of other traders might play some role if traders tend to herding and to positive feedback trading. If risk management strategies are at least partly based on optimistic or pessimistic opinion, analyzing the behavior and interaction of traders in disequilibrium might be even more important than in equilibrium. The interaction and behavior of futures market traders is investigated in Chap. 5. The empirical part of this chapter shows that a shock in currency futures prices leads to an increased proportion of speculators in these markets. Moreover, speculators tend to go long in futures contracts in response to a price rise, and, therefore, bet on further price increases. The third empirical finding suggests that the behavior of speculators is regime dependent. The impact of price changes on speculators' trading volume in futures contracts is much stronger during price expansions, pointing to positive feedback trading during booms. A hypothetical chain of interaction between traders, based on these empirical findings, is then incorporated into a cusp catastrophe model. In addition to hedgers and speculators, arbitrageurs play an important role in the model. Transaction and holding costs can discourage arbitrageurs to exploit arbitrage opportunities. If arbitrageurs are inactive, weak arbitrage pressure will not prevent further mispricing, especially in the presence of positive feedback traders. The rather complex interplay between arbitrage, selective hedging, and positive feedback speculation is examined using catastrophe theory. The catastrophe approach is particularly useful, since delays in trading activity and reversibility of traders' positions are characteristic features of the model. The results show that, depending on the behavior of traders in response to a price shock, instability might increase and lead to a long path back to equilibrium.

While the determinants of firms' optimal hedging strategies on the micro level are well understood, there is rarely any literature dealing with macroeconomic consequences of microeconomic risk management. The model presented in Chap. 4 can be regarded as a starting point for a detailed analysis of the interrelation between financing, risk management, investment, and output. The analysis could be extended to the medium run, allowing for dynamic hedging activity in a stochastic environment. Nonlinearities in traders' behavior, as discussed in Chap. 5, are a further important aspect with respect to economic stability. Analyzing market microstructure in conjunction with behavioral economics and finance could lead to a better understanding of instability, panics and crashes. It is important to realize that spot and futures markets are linked by arbitrageurs and hedgers. Arbitrageurs and hedgers, therefore, might perform as a transmission channel between financial and real activity. A more rigorous analysis of macroeconomic consequences of microeconomic risk management is, however, left for future research.

Appendix A
A Geometric Approach to the Hedgers' Surplus

This section presents an alternative derivation of the hedgers' surplus. The demand for futures contracts, as derived in Chap. 3, is

$$h = \frac{\tilde{f}_1 - f_0 - c}{2\lambda V(\tilde{f}_1)} + \frac{Cov(\tilde{e}_1, \tilde{f}_1)}{V(\tilde{f}_1)}, \tag{A.1}$$

where the size of the spot commitment is set to $x = 1$. Solving for c yields the demand function, presented in Fig. 3.5.

$$c = \tilde{f}_1 - f_0 - 2\lambda h V(\tilde{f}_1) + 2\lambda Cov(\tilde{e}_1, \tilde{f}_1). \tag{A.2}$$

The intersection of the demand function with the y-axis is calculated by setting $h = 0$:

$$c = \tilde{f}_1 - f_0 + 2\lambda Cov(\tilde{e}_1, \tilde{f}_1). \tag{A.3}$$

The supply function is the horizontal line with $c = c_s$. Supply and demand equilibrium is

$$c_s = \tilde{f}_1 - f_0 - 2\lambda h V(\tilde{f}_1) + 2\lambda Cov(\tilde{e}_1, \tilde{f}_1). \tag{A.4}$$

Solving for the optimal hedging position h^* yields

$$h^* = \frac{\tilde{f}_1 - f_0 - c_s}{2\lambda V(\tilde{f}_1)} + \frac{Cov(\tilde{e}_1, \tilde{f}_1)}{V(\tilde{f}_1)}. \tag{A.5}$$

The triangle area left of the demand function and above the supply function can then be computed as

$$\begin{aligned} HS &= 0.5(\tilde{f}_1 - f_0 + 2\lambda Cov(\tilde{e}_1, \tilde{f}_1) - c_s)h^* \\ &= 0.5(\tilde{f}_1 - f_0 + 2\lambda Cov(\tilde{e}_1, \tilde{f}_1) - c_s)(\frac{\tilde{f}_1 - f_0 - c_s}{2\lambda V(\tilde{f}_1)} + \frac{Cov(\tilde{e}_1, \tilde{f}_1)}{V(\tilde{f}_1)}) \\ &= \frac{0.25(-\tilde{f}_1 + f_0 + c_s - 2\lambda Cov(\tilde{e}_1, \tilde{f}_1))^2}{\lambda V(\tilde{f}_1)}. \end{aligned} \tag{A.6}$$

A. Röthig, *Microeconomic Risk Management and Macroeconomic Stability*,
Lecture Notes in Economics and Mathematical Systems,
DOI 10.1007/978-3-642-01565-6_A,

Solving (A.5) for $Cov(\tilde{e}_1, \tilde{f}_1)$

$$Cov(\tilde{e}_1, \tilde{f}_1) = \frac{-\tilde{f}_1 + f_0 + c_s + 2\lambda h V(\tilde{f}_1)}{2\lambda}, \tag{A.7}$$

and inserting into (A.6) yields

$$\begin{aligned} HS &= \frac{0.25(-\tilde{f}_1 + f_0 + c_s - 2\lambda(\frac{-\tilde{f}_1 + f_0 + c_s + 2\lambda h V(\tilde{f}_1)}{2\lambda}))^2}{\lambda V(\tilde{f}_1)} \\ &= \frac{0.25(-2\lambda h V(\tilde{f}_1))^2}{\lambda V(\tilde{f}_1)} \\ &= \lambda h^2 V(\tilde{f}_1), \end{aligned} \tag{A.8}$$

which is equivalent to the result in Sect. 3.2.

Appendix B
Stability Analysis

The stability properties of the MFT model in Chap. 4 can be established from the eigenvalues of the Jacobian matrix, along with the trace and the determinant of the Jacobian.

Given a set of n equations in n variables

$$\begin{aligned} y_1 &= f_1(x_1,\ldots,x_n) \\ y_2 &= f_2(x_1,\ldots,x_n) \\ \ldots \\ y_n &= f_n(x_1,\ldots,x_n), \end{aligned} \tag{B.1}$$

the Jacobian matrix (or matrix of partial derivatives, respectively) is given by:

$$J = \begin{bmatrix} \frac{\delta y_1}{\delta x_1} & \cdots & \frac{\delta y_1}{\delta x_n} \\ \vdots & \ddots & \vdots \\ \frac{\delta y_n}{\delta x_1} & \cdots & \frac{\delta y_n}{\delta x_n} \end{bmatrix}. \tag{B.2}$$

Assume the Jacobian of a 2×2 system is

$$J = \begin{bmatrix} a & b \\ c & d \end{bmatrix}. \tag{B.3}$$

The eigenvalues are the roots of the characteristic equation

$$\lambda^2 - \underbrace{(a+d)}_{trJ} * \lambda + \underbrace{(a*d - b*c)}_{detJ} = 0, \tag{B.4}$$

A. Röthig, *Microeconomic Risk Management and Macroeconomic Stability*,
Lecture Notes in Economics and Mathematical Systems,
DOI 10.1007/978-3-642-01565-6_B,

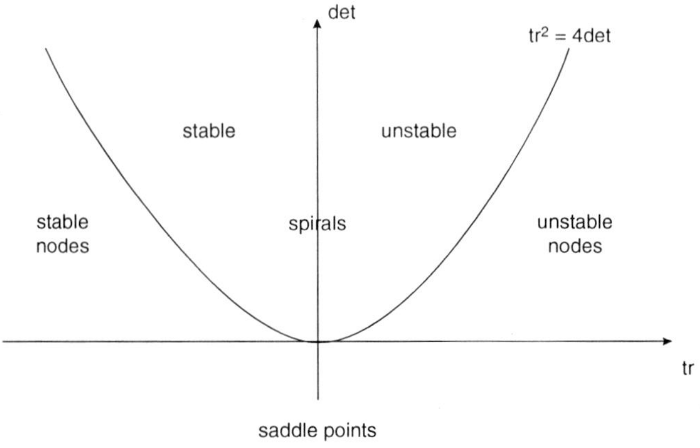

Fig. B.1 The trace-determinant plane

where trJ is the trace of J and $detJ$ is the determinant of J. The eigenvalues are therefore given by[1]

$$\lambda_{\pm} = \frac{1}{2}\left(trJ \pm \sqrt{(trJ)^2 - 4detJ}\right). \tag{B.5}$$

Knowing the trace and the determinant allows to calculate the eigenvalues of the matrix and, hence, investigate the stability of the system. For a graphical representation see the trace-determinant-plane in Fig. B.1.[2]

These stability properties apply only in the neighborhood of the equilibrium under investigation. For systems with multiple equilibria, the neighborhood of each equilibrium must be investigated individually. In order to analyze the stability of the equilibria of the different IS-AA outcomes discussed above, the Jacobian matrix of the basic IS-AA model (4.1) and (4.4) is derived. The starting point of this investigation is the IS-AA diagram without hedging:

$$\begin{aligned} IS: &\quad C(Y - \delta\bar{K} - \bar{T}) + I(e) + \bar{G} + NX(Y, \bar{Y}^*, e) - Y = 0, \\ AA: &\; \underbrace{g(r(Y, M_0) - \bar{r}^* - \beta_\varepsilon \underbrace{(\frac{e_0}{e} - 1)}_{\varepsilon}}_{\xi}, \underbrace{M_0 + B_0 + eF_{p0}}_{W_p}) - eF_p = 0. \end{aligned}$$

The Jacobian is

$$J = \begin{bmatrix} \frac{\delta IS}{\delta Y} & \frac{\delta IS}{\delta e} \\ \frac{\delta AA}{\delta Y} & \frac{\delta AA}{\delta e} \end{bmatrix}, \tag{B.6}$$

[1] See Hirsch, Smale, and Devaney (2004, p. 62).

[2] For similar graphical representations, see e.g., Hirsch et al. (2004, p. 63), Flaschel and Groh (1996, p. 129), Chiarella, Flaschel, Groh, and Semmler (2000, p. 257), and Asada, Chiarella, Flaschel, and Franke (2003, p. 17).

and, therefore,

$$J = \begin{bmatrix} \beta_Y[C_Y + NX_Y - 1] & \beta_Y[I_e + NX_e] \\ \beta_e[g_\xi * r_Y] & \beta_e[-g_\xi * \varepsilon_e + (g_{W_p} - 1) * F_{p0}] \end{bmatrix}. \tag{B.7}$$

Considering $g_\xi < 0$, $r_Y > 0$, $g_{W_p} \in [0,1]$, and $\varepsilon_e \leq 0$, the Jacobian has the following signs:

$$J = \begin{bmatrix} - & ? \\ - & - \end{bmatrix}. \tag{B.8}$$

The stability of the equilibria (E_1, E_2, E_3) depends on the sign of "?" in the Jacobian and, therefore, on the question which effect (NX_e or I_e) dominates the other. In equilibrium E_1 and E_3, the IS curve is upward sloping and $NX_e > I_e$ holds. In this case, the "?" has a positive sign:

$$J_{NX_e > I_e} = \begin{bmatrix} - & + \\ - & - \end{bmatrix}. \tag{B.9}$$

The determinant and the trace of the Jacobian (with $NX_e > I_e$) are

$$\begin{aligned} detJ_{NX_e > I_e} &= ((-) * (-)) - ((+) * (-)) = + > 0, \\ trJ_{NX_e > I_e} &= (-) + (-) = - < 0. \end{aligned} \tag{B.10}$$

Because the determinant is positive ($det(J_{(E_{1,3})}) > 0$), and the trace is negative ($tr(J_{(E_{1,3})}) < 0$), equilibria E_1 and E_3 are stable.

In equilibrium E_2, the IS curve is backward bending, since $I_e > NX_e$. Here, the sign of "?" is negative:

$$J_{I_e > NX_e} = \begin{bmatrix} - & - \\ - & - \end{bmatrix}. \tag{B.11}$$

The determinant and the trace of the Jacobian (with $I_e > NX_e$) are[3]

$$detJ_{I_e > NX_e} = \underbrace{((-) * (-))}_{a*d} - \underbrace{((-) * (-))}_{b*c} = - < 0, \tag{B.12}$$

$$trJ_{I_e > NX_e} = (-) + (-) = - < 0. \tag{B.13}$$

The determinant in (B.12) is negative, because it is assumed that $b * c$ is larger than $a * d$. This means that,

$$\frac{\delta IS}{\delta e} * \frac{\delta AA}{\delta Y} > \frac{\delta IS}{\delta Y} * \frac{\delta AA}{\delta e}. \tag{B.14}$$

It can be shown that (B.14) holds true by using the graphical representation of the "neighborhood" of equilibrium E_2, presented in Fig. B.2. Figure B.2 illustrates the effect of changes of Y and e on the IS and AA curve. Therefore, Fig. B.2 allows to

[3] Note that the terms $a * d$ and $b * c$ correspond to the stylized Jacobian in (B.3).

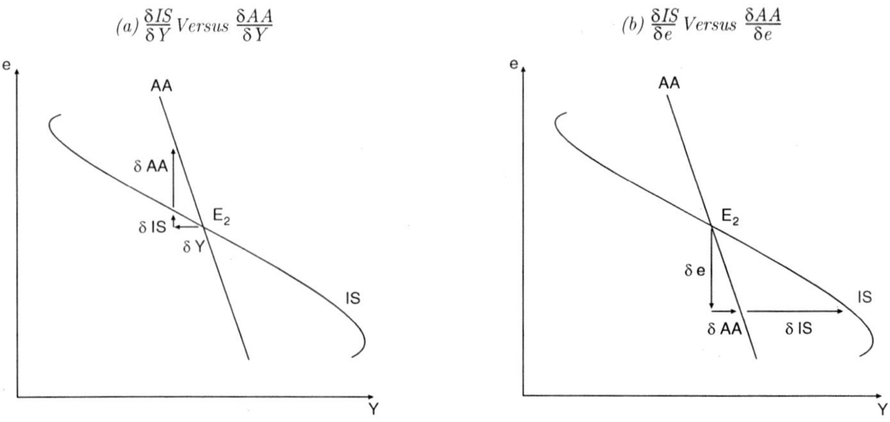

Fig. B.2 The "neighborhood" of E_2

qualitatively compare $\frac{\delta IS}{\delta Y}$ to $\frac{\delta AA}{\delta Y}$ and $\frac{\delta IS}{\delta e}$ to $\frac{\delta AA}{\delta e}$. The effect of changes in Y is larger on the AA curve than on the IS curve

$$\frac{\delta AA}{\delta Y} > \frac{\delta IS}{\delta Y}, \tag{B.15}$$

and variations in e affect the IS curve stronger than the AA curve

$$\frac{\delta IS}{\delta e} > \frac{\delta AA}{\delta e}. \tag{B.16}$$

Therefore, (B.14) holds true. The determinant in (B.12) is negative and equilibrium E_2 is a saddle point.[4] Since slight deviations from this steady state level can result in an economic boom or a crisis, this equilibrium is unstable.

Up to now, all cases $NX_e \neq I_e$ have been investigated. Here, for the sake of completeness, the case $NX_e = I_e$ is discussed. If $NX_e = I_e$, the Jacobian is:

$$J_{NX_e=I_e} = \begin{bmatrix} - & 0 \\ - & - \end{bmatrix}, \tag{B.17}$$

with

$$\begin{aligned} detJ_{NX_e=I_e} &= ((-)*(-)) - ((0)*(-)) = + > 0, \\ trJ_{NX_e=I_e} &= (-)+(-) = - < 0. \end{aligned} \tag{B.18}$$

This equilibrium is stable, since $detJ_{NX_e=I_e} > 0$ and $trJ_{NX_e=I_e} < 0$.

[4] See the trace-determinant plane in Fig. B.1.

Appendix C
The Computation of the Catastrophe Surface

This section presents the "Mathematica" program code for the computation of Fig. 5.11 in Chap. 5. For a detailed description on how to implement catastrophe models in "Mathematica," see Sanns (2000).

First, the cusp function is defined, and its partial derivative with respect to P is computed.

```
F[P_, AP_, TP_] := P^4 + AP*P^2 - TP*P

D1F[P_, AP_, TP_] := Evaluate[D[F[P, AP, TP], P]]
```

Then, the surface of the cusp catastrophe model can be drawn using the following commands.

```
<< "Graphics`Master`"

CriticalPoints =
  ContourPlot3D[D1F[P, AP, TP], {AP, -2, 1}, {TP, -2, 2},
  {P, -2, 2}, PlotPoints -> 6, ViewPoint -> {2, -2, 1.5},
  Axes -> True, AxesLabel -> {"AP", "TP", "P"},
  DefaultFont -> 14, BoxRatios -> {2, 2, 2},
  ColorOutput -> CMYKColor]
```

Next, the bifurcation set can be computed as follows.

```
D2F[P_, AP_, TP_] := Evaluate[D[D1F[P, AP, TP], P]] D2F[P, AP, TP]

scnd = ContourPlot3D[D2F[P, AP, TP], {AP, -2, 1},
  {TP, -2, 2}, {P,-2, 2}, Axes -> True,
  AxesLabel -> {"AP", "TP", "P"}, PlotPoints -> 6,
  ViewPoint -> {2, -2, 1.5}]

compose1 = Show[CriticalPoints, scnd]

solu = Solve[{D1F[P, AP, TP] == 0, D2F[P, AP, TP] == 0}, {AP, TP}]

solu1 = Flatten[solu]

{s, t} = {AP, TP} /. solu1
```

A. Röthig, *Microeconomic Risk Management and Macroeconomic Stability*,
Lecture Notes in Economics and Mathematical Systems,
DOI 10.1007/978-3-642-01565-6_C, © Springer-Verlag Berlin Heidelberg 2009

```
foldline =
  ParametricPlot3D[
  {s, t, P, {Thickness[0.005], RGBColor[1, 0, 0]}},
  {P, -0.75, 0.75}, DefaultFont -> 14]

compose2 = Show[compose1, foldline]

cusp = ParametricPlot[{s, t}, {P, -1, 1}, AxesLabel -> {"AP", "TP"},
    AspectRatio -> 1]

cusp3D = ParametricPlot3D[
  {s, t, -3.7, {Thickness[0.01],
  Dashing[{0.01, 0.05, 0.05, 0.05}],
  GrayLevel[0.5]}}, {P, -0.751, 0.75},
  DefaultFont -> 14]
```

Finally, the following program lines can be used to compute the divergence.

```
Clear[P, AP]

eps = 0.1

vconst = -0.1

L = Solve[D1F[P, AP, vconst] == 0, {AP}]

compon = AP /. %

AP1 = compon[[1]]

diverg1 =
  ParametricPlot3D[
  {AP1, vconst, P + eps, {Thickness[0.015]}},
  {P, -1, -0.05}, PlotRange -> {{-1, 1}, {-1, 1}, {-1, 1}}]

Clear[vconst]

vconst = 0.1

L = Solve[D1F[P, AP, vconst] == 0, {AP}]

compon = AP /. %

AP1 = compon[[1]]

diverg2 =
  ParametricPlot3D[
  {AP1, vconst, P + eps, {Thickness[0.015]}},
  {P, 0.05, 1}, PlotRange -> {{-1, 1}, {-1, 1}, {0, 1}}]

All = Show[CriticalPoints, diverg1, diverg2, cusp3D,
  ColorOutput -> CMYKColor]
```

Bibliography

Abhyankar, A., Copeland, L. S., & Wong, W. (1997). Uncovering nonlinear structure in real-time stock-market indexes: The S&P 500, the DAX, the Nikkei 225, and the FTSE-100. *Journal of Business and Economic Statistics, 15*, 1–14.
Adam-Müller, A. F. A. (1997). Export and hedging decisions under revenue and exchange rate risk: A note. *European Economic Review, 41*, 1421–1426.
Adam-Müller, A. F. A. (2000). Hedging price risk when real wealth matters. *Journal of International Money and Finance, 19*, 549–560.
Adam, T. R., & Fernando, C. S. (2006). Hedging, speculation, and shareholder value. *Journal of Financial Economics, 81*, 283–309.
Aghion, P., Bacchetta, P., & Banerjee, A. (2000a). *Currency crises and monetary policy in an economy with credit constraints*. Centre for Economic Policy Research, Discussion Paper Series, 2529.
Aghion, P., Bacchetta, P., & Banerjee, A. (2000b). A simple model of monetary policy and currency crises. *European Economic Review, 44*, 728–738.
Aghion, P., Bacchetta, P., & Banerjee, A. (2004). A corporate balance sheet approach to currency crises. *Journal of Economic Theory, 119*, 6–30.
Albuquerque, R. (2003). *Optimal currency hedging*. Simon School of Business, University of Rochester.
Allan, F., & Gale, D. (1994). *Financial innovation and risk sharing*. Cambridge: The MIT Press.
Allayannis, G., & Weston, J. P. (2001). The use of foreign currency derivatives and firm market value. *Review of Financial Studies, 14*, 243–276.
Allayannis, G., Ihrig, J. & Weston, J. P. (2001). Exchange-rate hedging: Financial versus operational strategies. *American Economic Review, 91*, 391–395.
Anderson, R. W., & Danthine, J. P. (1981). Cross hedging. *Journal of Political Economy, 89*, 1182–1196.
Anderson, R. W., & Danthine, J. P. (1983). Hedger diversity in futures markets. *Economic Journal, 93*, 370–389.
Arango, L. E., & Melo, L. F. (2006). Expansions and contractions in Brazil, Colombia, and Mexico: A view through nonlinear models. *Journal of Development Economics, 80*, 501–517.
Asada, T., Chiarella, C., Flaschel, P., & Franke, R. (2003). *Open economy macrodynamics*. Berlin: Springer.
Aschinger, G. (1995). *Börsenkrach und Spekulation: eine ökonomische Analyse*. München: Verlag Franz Vahlen.
Aschinger, G. (2001). *Währungs- und Finanzkrisen: Entstehung, Analyse und Beurteilung aktueller Krisen*. München: Verlag Franz Vahlen.
Aslanidis, N., Osborn, D. R., & Sensier, M. (2002). *Smooth transition regression models in UK stock returns*. Royal Economic Society Annual Conference, 11, http://econpapers.repec.org/paper/ecjac2002/11.htm
Aslanidis, N., Osborn, D. R., & Sensier, M. (2003). *Explaining movements in UK stock prices: How important is the US market?* The University of Manchester, Discussion Paper Series, 27.

Baron, D. P. (1970). Price uncertainty, utility, and industry equilibrium in pure competition. *International Economic Review, 11*, 463–480.

Battermann, H. L., Broll, U., & Wahl, J. E. (2002). Insurance demand and the elasticity of risk aversion. *OR Spectrum, 24*, 145–150.

Bauer, C., & Herz, B. (2005). Technical trading, monetary policy, and exchange rate regimes. *Global Finance Journal, 15*, 281–302.

Bauer, W., & Ryser, M. (2004). Risk management strategies for banks. *Journal of Banking and Finance, 28*, 331–352.

Beatty, A. (1999). Assessing the use of derivatives as part of a risk-management strategy. *Journal of Accounting and Economics, 26*, 353–357.

Benavente, J. M., Johnson, C. A., & Morandé, F. G. (2003). Debt composition and balance sheet effects of exchange rate depreciations: A firm-level analysis for Chile. *Emerging Markets Review, 4*, 397–416.

Benninga, S., Eldor, R., & Zilcha, I. (1984). The optimal hedge ratio in unbiased futures markets. *Journal of Futures Markets, 4*, 155–159.

Benninga, S., Eldor, R., & Zilcha, I. (1985). Optimal international hedging in commodity and currency forward markets. *Journal of International Money and Finance, 4*, 537–552.

Benson, K., & Oliver, B. (2004). Management motivation for using financial derivatives in Australia. *Australian Journal of Management, 29*, 225–242.

Bernanke, B. S., & Gertler, M. (1990). Financial fragility and economic performance. *Quarterly Journal of Economics, 105*, 87–114.

Bernanke, B. S., & Gertler, M. (1995). Inside the black box: The credit channel of monetary policy transmission. *Journal of Economic Perspectives, 9*, 27–48.

Bernanke, B. S., & Lown, C. S. (1991). The credit crunch. *Brookings Papers on Economic Activity, 91*, 205–279.

Bernanke, B. S., Gertler, M., & Gilchrist, S. (1996). The financial accelerator and the flight to quality. *Review of Economics and Statistics, 78*, 1–15.

Bernanke, B. S., Gertler, M., & Gilchrist, S. (1999). The financial accelerator in a quantitative business cycle framework. In J. B. Taylor, & M. Woodford (Eds.), *Handbook of Macroeconomics*. Amsterdam: Elsevier.

Biais, B., Glosten, L., & Spatt, C. (2005). Market microstructure: A survey of microfoundations, empirical results, and policy implications. *Journal of Financial Markets, 8*, 217–264.

Blanchard, O. J., & Fischer, S. (1989). *Lectures on macroeconomics*. Cambridge: MIT.

Bodnar, G. M., Hayt, G. S., Marston, R. C., & Smithson, C. W. (1995). Wharton survey of derivatives usage by U.S. non-financial firms. *Financial Management, 24*, 104–114.

Bond, S., Elston, J. A., Mairesse, J., & Mulkay, B. (2003). Financial factors and investment in Belgium, France, Germany, and the United Kingdom: A comparison using company panel data. *Review of Economics and Statistics, 85*, 153–165.

Bonomo, M., Martins, B., & Pinto, R. (2003). Debt composition and exchange rate balance sheet effect in Brazil: A firm level analysis. *Emerging Markets Review, 4*, 368–396.

Briys, E., & de Varenne, F. (1998). Optimal hedging and the partial loss offset provision. *European Financial Management, 4*, 321–333.

Briys, E., & Schlesinger, H. (1993). Optimal hedging when preferences are state dependent. *Journal of Futures Markets, 13*, 441–451.

Briys, E., Crouhy, M., & Schlesinger, H. (1990). Optimal hedging under intertemporally dependent preferences. *Journal of Finance, 45*, 1315–1324.

Briys, E., Crouhy, M., & Schlesinger, H. (1993). Optimal hedging in a futures market with backround noise and basis risk. *European Economic Review, 37*, 949–960.

Broll, U. (1997). Cross hedging in currency forward markets: A note. *Journal of Futures Markets, 17*, 475–482.

Broll, U., & Eckwert, B. (1996). Cross hedging of exchange rate risk. *Review of International Economics, 4*, 282–286.

Broll, U., & Eckwert, B. (1998). Export and hedging decision with state-dependend utility. *International Review of Economics and Finance, 7*, 247–253.

Broll, U., & Eckwert, B. (2000). Market structure and multiperiod hedging. *International Review of Economics and Finance, 9*, 291–298.
Broll, U., & Wahl, J. E. (1992). Hedging with synthetics, foreign-exchange forwards, and the export decision. *Journal of Futures Markets, 12*, 511–517.
Broll, U., & Wong, K. P. (2002). Optimal full-hedging under state-dependend preferences. *Quarterly Review of Economics and Finance, 42*, 937–943.
Broll, U., Chow, K. W., & Wong, K. P. (2001). Hedging and nonlinear risk exposure. *Oxford Economic Papers, 53*, 281–296.
Broll, U., Wahl, J. E., & Wong, W. K. (2006). Elasticity of risk aversion and international trade. *Economics Letters, 92*, 126–130.
Broll, U., Wahl, J. E., & Zilcha, I. (1995). Indirect hedging of exchange rate risk. *Journal of International Money and Finance, 14*, 667–678.
Brooks, C. (2002). *Introductory econometrics for finance*. Cambridge: Cambridge University Press.
Brown, G. W., & Toft, K. B. (2002). How firms should hedge. *Review of Financial Studies, 15*, 1283–1324.
Brüggemann, R. (2006). Sources of German unemployment: A structural vector error correction analysis. *Empirical Economics, 31*, 409–431.
Brüggemann, R., Lütkepohl, H., & Saikkonen, P. (2006). Residual autocorrelation testing for vector error correction models. *Journal of Econometrics, 134*, 579–604.
Burnside, C., Eichenbaum, M., & Rebelo, S. (2001). Hedging and financial fragility in fixed exchange rate regimes. *European Economic Review, 45*, 1151–1193.
Calomiris, C. W., & Hubbard, R. G. (1990). Firm heterogeneity, internal finance, and credit rationing. *Economic Journal, 100*, 90–104.
Camacho, M. (2004). Vector smooth transition regression models for US GDP and the composite index of leading indicators. *Journal of Forecasting, 23*, 173–196.
Carranza, L. J., Cayo, J. M., & Galdón-Sánchez, J. E. (2003). Exchange rate volatility and economic performance in Peru: A firm level analysis. *Emerging Markets Review, 4*, 472–496.
Céspedes, L. F., Chang, R., & Velasco, A. (2000). *Balance sheets and exchange rate policy*. National Bureau of Economic Research, NBER Working Paper Series, 7840.
Chatrath, A., Song, F., & Adrangi, B. (2003). Futures trading activity and stock price volatility: Some extensions. *Applied Financial Economics, 13*, 655–664.
Chew, L. (1996). *Managing derivative risks: The use and abuse of leverage*. Baffins Lane: Wiley.
Chiarella, C., Flaschel, P., Groh, G., & Semmler, W. (2000). *Disequilibrium, growth and labor market dynamics: Macro perspectives*. Berlin: Springer.
Clifton, E. V. (1985). The currency futures market and interbank foreign exchange trading. *Journal of Futures Markets, 5*, 375–384.
Cochrane, J. H. (2001). *Asset pricing*. Princeton: Princeton University Press.
Collins, R. A. (1997). Toward a positive economic theory of hedging. *American Journal of Agricultural Economics, 79*, 488–499.
Copeland, T. E., Weston, J. F., & Shastri, K. (2005). *Financial theory and corporate policy*. Boston: Pearson.
Corsetti, G., Pesenti, P., & Roubini, N. (1998a). *Paper tigers? A model of the Asian crisis*. National Bureau of Economic Research, NBER Working Paper Series, 6783.
Corsetti, G., Pesenti, P., & Roubini, N. (1998b). *What caused the Asian currency and financial crisis? Part I: A macroeconomic overview*. National Bureau of Economic Research, NBER Working Paper Series, 6833.
Corsetti, G., Pesenti, P., & Roubini, N. (1998c). *What caused the Asian currency and financial crisis? Part II: The policy debate*. National Bureau of Economic Research, NBER Working Paper Series, 6834.
Cummins, J. D., Phillips, R. D., & Smith, S. D. (1998). *Derivatives and corporate risk management: Participation and volume decision in the insurance industry*. The Wharton Financial Institutions Center, Working Paper Series, 98–19.

Cutler, D. M., Poterba, J. M., & Summers, L. H. (1990). Speculative dynamics and the role of feedback traders. *American Economic Review, 80*, 63–68.

Danthine, J. P. (1978). Information, futures prices, and stabilizing speculation. *Journal of Economic Theory, 17*, 79–98.

DeLong, J. B., Shleifer, A., Summers, L. H., & Waldmann, R. J. (1987). *The economic consequences of noise traders*. National Bureau of Economic Research, NBER Working Paper Series, 2395.

DeLong, J. B., Shleifer, A., Summers, L. H., & Waldmann, R. J. (1990). Positive feedback investment strategies and destabilizing rational speculation. *Journal of Finance, 45*, 379–395.

DeLong, J. B., Shleifer, A., Summers, L. H., & Waldmann, R. J. (1991). The survival of noise traders in financial markets. *Journal of Business, 64*, 1–19.

DeMarzo, P. M., & Duffie, D. (1995). Corporate incentives for hedging and hedge accounting. *Review of Financial Studies, 8*, 743–771.

Diamond, P. A., & Stiglitz, J. E. (1974). Increases in risk and in risk aversion. *Journal of Economic Theory, 8*, 337–360.

Dodd, R. (2000). *The role of derivatives in the East Asian financial crisis*. Center for Economic Policy Analysis, CEPA Working Paper Series III, 20.

Dodd, R. (2002). *Derivatives, the shape of international capital flows and the virtues of prudential regulation*. World Institute for Development Economic Research, United Nations University, Discussion Paper, 93.

Dolde, W. (1993). The trajectory of corporate financial risk management. *Journal of Applied Corporate Finance, 6*, 33–41.

Dou, W., & Ghose, S. (2006). A dynamic nonlinear model of online retail competition using cusp catastrophe theory. *Journal of Business Research, 59*, 838–848.

Dow, J., & Gorton, G. (1997). Noise trading, delegated portfolio management, and economic welfare. *Journal of Political Economy, 105*, 1024–1050.

Dow, J., & Gorton, G. (2006). *Noise traders*. National Bureau of Economic Research, NBER Working Paper Series, 12256.

Draper, P., & Fung, J. K. W. (2003). Discretionary government intervention and the mispricing of index futures. *Journal of Futures Markets, 23*, 1159–1189.

Duffie, D. (1989). *Futures markets*. Englewood Cliffs: Prentice Hall.

Duffie, D., & Singleton, K. J. (2003). *Credit risk: Pricing, measurement, and management*. Princeton: Princeton University Press.

Eaker, M. R., & Grant, D. M. (1987). Cross-hedging foreign currency risk. *Journal of International Money and Finance, 6*, 85–105.

Echeverry, J. C., Fergusson, L., Steiner, R., & Aguilar, C. (2003). 'Dollar' debt in Colombian firms: Are sinners punished during devaluations? *Emerging Markets Review, 4*, 417–449.

Ederington, L. H. (1979). The hedging performance of the new futures market. *Journal of Finance, 34*, 157–170.

Ederington, L., H., & Lee, J. H. (2002). Who trades futures and how: Evidence from the heating oil futures market. *Journal of Business, 75*, 353–373.

Ehrhardt, M. C., Jordan, J. V., & Walkling, R. A. (1987). An application of arbitrage pricing theory to futures markets: Tests of normal backwardation. *Journal of Futures Markets, 7*, 21–34.

Eiteman, D. K., Stonehill, A. I., & Moffett, M. H. (2004). *Multinational business finance* (10th ed.). Boston: Pearson.

Ericsson, N. R. (1999). Empirical modeling of money demand. In H. Lütkepohl, & J. Wolters (Eds.), *Money demand in Europe* (pp. 29–49). Heidelberg: Physika.

Fatemi, A., & Luft, C. (2002). Corporate risk management costs and benefits. *Global Finance Journal, 13*, 29–38.

Fazzari, S. M., Hubbard, R. G., & Petersen, B. C. (1988). Financing constraints and corporate investment. *Brookings Papers on Economic Activity, 88*, 141–195.

Feder, G., Just, R. E., & Schmitz, A. (1980). Futures markets and the theory of the firm under price uncertainty. *Quarterly Journal of Economics, 94*, 317–328.

Fender, I. (2000a). *Corporate hedging: The impact of financial derivatives on the broad credit channel of monetary policy*. BIS Working Papers, 94.

Fender, I. (2000b). *The impact of corporate risk management on monetary policy transmission: Some empirical evidence*. BIS Working Papers, 95.

Flaschel, P., & Groh, G. (1996). *Keynesianische Makroökonomik: Unterbeschäftigung, Inflation und Wachstum*. Berlin: Springer.

Flaschel, P., & Semmler, W. (2006). Currency crisis, financial crisis, and large output loss. In C. Chiarella, P. Flaschel, R. Franke, & W. Semmler (Eds.), *Quantitative and empirical analysis of nonlinear dynamic macromodels*. Amsterdam: Elsevier.

Fort, R., & Quirk, J. (1988). Normal backwardation and the inventory effect. *Journal of Political Economy, 96*, 81–99.

Franckle, C. T. (1980). The hedging performance of the new futures market: Comment. *Journal of Finance, 35*, 1273–1279.

Frechette, D. L. (2000). The demand for hedging and the value of hedging opportunities. *American Journal of Agricultural Economics, 82*, 897–907.

Frechette, D. L., & Fackler, P. L. (1999). What causes commodity price backwardation? *American Journal of Agricultural Economics, 81*, 761–771.

Friberg, R. (1998). In which currency should exporters set their prices? *Journal of International Economics, 45*, 59–76.

Friberg, R. (1999). *Exchange rates and the firm: Strategies to manage exposure and the impact of EMU*. London: MacMillan.

Froot, K. A., Scharfstein, D. S., & Stein, J. C. (1993). Risk management: Coordinating corporate investment and financing policies. *Journal of Finance, 48*, 1629–1658.

Froot, K. A., Scharfstein, D. S., & Stein, J. C. (1994). A framework for risk management. *Harvard Business Review, 72*, 91–102.

Fung, H. G., & Leung, W. K. (1991). The use of forward contracts for hedging currency risk. *Journal of International Financial Management and Accounting, 3*, 78–92.

Galiani, S., Yeyati, E. L., & Schargrodsky, E. (2003). Financial dollarization and debt deflation under a currency board. *Emerging Markets Review, 4*, 340–367.

Galindo, A., Panizza, U., & Schiantarelli, F. (2003). Debt composition and balance sheet effects of currency depreciations: A summary of the micro evidence. *Emerging Markets Review, 4*, 330–339.

Garber, P. M. (1998). *Derivatives in international capital flows*. National Bureau of Economic Research, NBER Working Paper Series, 6623.

Gay, G. D., & Nam, J. (1998). The underinvestment problem and corporate derivatives use. *Financial Management, 27*, 53–69.

Géczy, C., Minton, B. A., & Schrand, C. (1997). Why firms use currency derivatives. *Journal of Finance, 52*, 1323–1354.

Gemmill, G., & Thomas, D. C. (2002). Noise trading, costly arbitrage, and asset prices: Evidence from closed-end funds. *Journal of Finance, 57*, 2571–2594.

Gertler, M., & Gilchrist, S. (1994). Monetary policy, business cycles, and the behavior of small manufacturing firms. *Quarterly Journal of Economics, 109*, 309–340.

Goodhart, C. (2000). *Commentary: Crises: The price of globalization?* Global economic integration: Opportunities and challanges. Federal Reserve Bank of Kansas City, 107–110.

Graham, J. R., & Rogers, D. A. (2002). Do firms hedge in response to tax incentives? *Journal of Finance, 57*, 815–839.

Granger, C. W. J., & Teräsvirta, T. (1993). *Modelling nonlinear economic relationships*. Oxford: Oxford University Press.

Gruben, W. C., & Welch, J. H. (2001). *Banking and currency crisis recovery: Brazil's turnaround of 1999*. Federal Reserve Bank of Dallas, Economic and Financial Review, Fourth Quarter, 12–23.

Guay, W. R. (1999). The impact of derivatives on firm risk: An empirical examination of new derivative users. *Journal of Accounting and Economics, 26*, 319–351.

Guay, W. R., & Kothari, S. P. (2003). How much do firms hedge with derivatives? *Journal of Financial Economics, 70*, 423–461.

Haigh, M. S., & Holt, M. T. (2000). Hedging multiple price uncertainty in international grain trade. *American Journal of Agricultural Economics, 82*, 881–896.

Hall, A. D., Skalin, J., & Teräsvirta, T. (2001). A nonlinear time series model of El Niño. *Environmental Modelling and Software, 16*, 139–146.

Hardy, C. O., & Lyon, L. S. (1923). The theory of hedging. *Journal of Political Economy, 31*, 276–287.

Hart, O. D. (1977). On the profitability of speculation. *Quarterly Journal of Economics, 91*, 579–597.

Harvey, C., & Roper, A. (1999). *The Asian bet*. In A. Harwood, R. Litan, & M. Pomerleano (Eds.), Financial markets and development: The crisis in emerging markets. Washington: Brookings Institution Press.

Haslett, T., Smyrnios, K. X., & Osborne, C. (1998). A cusp catastrophe analysis of anxiety levels in pre-university students. *Journal of Psychology, 132*, 5–24.

Hauser, R. J., & Neff, D. (1993). Export/import risks at alternative stages of U.S. grain export trade. *Journal of Futures Markets, 13*, 579–595.

Haushalter, D., Klasa, S., & Maxwell, W. F. (2007). The influence of product market dynamics on a firm's cash holdings and hedging behavior. *Journal of Financial Economics, 84*, 797–825.

Hawtrey, R. G. (1940). A symposium on the theory of the forward market: Mr. Kaldor on the forward market. *Review of Economic Studies, 7*, 196–201.

Heifner, R. G. (1972). Optimal hedging levels and hedging effectiveness in cattle feeding. *Agricultural Economic Research, 24*, 25–35.

Heifner, R. G. (1973). *Hedging potential in grain storage and livestock feeding*. U.S. Department of Agriculture, Agricultural Economic Report No. 238.

Herbig, P. A. (1991). A cusp catastrophe model of the adoption of an industrial innovation. *Journal of Product Innovation Management, 8*, 127–137.

Hicks, J. R. (1939). *Value and capital*. London: Oxford University Press.

Hirsch, M. W., Smale, S., & Devaney, R. L. (2004). *Differential equations, dynamical systems & an introduction to chaos* (2nd ed.). Amsterdam: Elsevier.

Hirshleifer, J. (1975). Speculation and equilibrium: Information, risk, and markets. *Quarterly Journal of Economics, 89*, 519–542.

Hirshleifer, J. (1977). The theory of speculation under alternative regimes of markets. *Journal of Finance, 32*, 975–999.

Holmes, M. J. (2002). Are there non-linearities in US-Latin American real exchange behavior? *Estudios de Economía, 29*, 177–190.

Holthausen, D. M. (1979). Hedging and the competitive firm under price uncertainty. *American Economic Review, 69*, 989–995.

Hu, X., & Schiantarelli, F. (1998). Investment and capital market imperfections: A switching regression approach using U.S. firm panel data. *Review of Economics and Statistics, 80*, 466–479.

Hughen, J. C., & McDonald, C. G. (2005). Who are the noise traders? *Journal of Financial Research, 28*, 281–298.

Hull, J. C. (2000). *Options, futures, and other derivatives* (4th ed.). Upper Saddle River: Prentice Hall.

Inci, A. C., & Lu, B. (2007). Currency futures-spot basis and risk premium. *Journal of International Financial Markets, Institutions and Money, 17*, 180–197.

Ishii, Y. (1977). On the theory of the competitive firm under price uncertainty: Note. *American Economic Review, 67*, 768–769.

Jarrow, R. A. (1992). Market manipulation, bubbles, corners, and short squeezes. *Journal of Financial and Quantitative Analysis, 27*, 311–336.

Jarrow, R. A. (1994). Derivative security markets, market manipulation, and option pricing theory. *Journal of Financial and Quantitative Analysis, 29*, 241–261.

Jeanne, O., & Zettelmeyer, J. (2005). Original sin, balance-sheet crises, and the roles of international lending. In B. Eichengreen, & R. Hausmann (Eds.), *Other people's money: Debt denomination and financial instability in emerging market economies*. Chicago: The University of Chicago Press.

Jensen, M. C., & Meckling, W. H. (1976). Theory of the firm: Managerial behavior, agency costs and ownership structure. *Journal of Financial Economics, 3*, 305–360.

Jin, H. J., & Koo, W. W. (2006). Offshore hedging strategy of Japan-based wheat traders under multiple sources of risk and hedging costs. *Journal of International Money and Finance, 25*, 220–236.

Johnson, L. L. (1957). Price instability, hedging, and trade volume in the coffee futures market. *Journal of Political Economy, 65*, 306–321.

Johnson, L. L. (1960). The theory of hedging and speculation in commodity futures. *Review of Economic Studies, 27*, 139–151.

Kahl, K. H. (1983). Determination of the recommended hedging ratio. *American Journal of Agricultural Economics, 65*, 603–605.

Kaldor, N. (1939). Speculation and economic stability. *Review of Economic Studies, 6*, 1–27.

Kaldor, N. (1940). A symposium on the theory of the forward market: A note on the theory of the forward market. *Review of Economic Studies, 7*, 196–201.

Kauffman, R., & Oliva, T. (1994). Multivariate catastrophe model estimation: Method and application. *Academy of Management Journal, 37*, 206–221.

Kawai, M., & Zilcha, I. (1986). International trade with forward-futures markets under exchange rate and price uncertainty. *Journal of International Economics, 20*, 83–98.

Kawaller, I. G. (1991). Determining the relevant fair value(s) of S&P 500 Futures: A case study approach. *Journal of Futures Markets, 11*, 453–460.

Keynes, J. M. (1930). *A treatise on money, II: The applied theory of money*. London: MacMillan.

Keynes, J. M. (1986). *The general theory of employment, interest and money* (vol. 7). The Collected Writings of John Maynard Keynes. Cambridge: Cambridge University Press.

Kimball, M. S. (1990). Precautionary saving in the small and in the large. *Econometrica, 58*, 53–73.

Kimball, M. S. (1993). Standard risk aversion. *Econometrica, 61*, 589–611.

Knill, A., Minnick, K., & Nejadmalayeri, A. (2006). Selective hedging, information asymmetry, and futures prices. *Journal of Business, 79*, 1475–1501.

Kobold, K. (1986). *Interest rate futures markets and capital market theory*. Berlin: de Gruyter.

Kolb, R. W. (1991). *Options: An introduction*. Miami: Kolb.

Kolb, R. W. (1992). Is normal backwardation normal? *Journal of Futures Markets, 12*, 75–91.

Kolb, R. W. (1996). *Financial derivatives* (2nd ed.). Cambridge: Blackwell Business.

Krugman, P. (1999). *Analytical afterthoughts on the asian crisis*. Mimeo.

Krugman, P. (2000). Crises: The price of globalization? In *Global economic integration: Opportunities and challanges* (pp. 75–106). Federal Reserve Bank of Kansas City.

Kumar, P., & Seppi, D. J. (1992). Futures manipulation with cash settlement. *Journal of Finance, 47*, 1485–1501.

Lapan, H., & Moschini, G. (1994). Futures hedging under price, basis, and production risk. *American Journal of Agricultural Economics, 76*, 465–477.

Larson, D. F. (2007). On inverse carrying charges and spatial arbitrage. *Journal of Futures Markets, 27*, 305–336.

Lence, S. H. (1995a). The economic value of minimum-variance hedges. *American Journal of Agricultural Economics, 77*, 353–364.

Lence, S. H. (1995b). On the optimal hedge under unbiased futures prices. *Economics Letters, 47*, 385–388.

Lence, S. H. (1996). Relaxing the assumptions of minimum-variance hedging. *Journal of Agricultural and Resource Economics, 21*, 39–55.

Lence, S. H., & Hayes, D. J. (1994). The empirical minimum-variance hedge. *American Journal of Agricultural Economics, 76*, 94–104.

Levich, R. M., Hayt, G. S., & Ripston, B. A. (1999). *1998 survey of derivatives and risk management practices by U.S. institutional investors.* New York University, Leonard N. Stern School, Finance Department, Working Paper No. 99–074.

Levy, H., & Markowitz, H. M. (1979). Approximating expected utility by a function of mean and variance. *American Economic Review, 69*, 308–317.

Lien, D., & Wang, Y. (2002). Risk aversion, disappointment aversion, and futures hedging. *Journal of Futures Markets, 22*, 123–141.

Lin, C. M., & Smith, S. D. (2005). *Hedging, financing, and investment decisions: A simultaneous equations framework.* Working Paper 2005-5, Federal Reserve Bank of Atlanta.

Litzenberger, R. H., & Rabinowitz, N. (1995). Backwardation in oil futures markets: Theory and empirical evidence. *Journal of Finance, 50*, 1517–1545.

Lo, W. C., & Lin, K. J. (2005). A review of the effects of investor sentiment on financial markets: Implications for investors. *International Journal of Management, 22*, 708–715.

Longstaff, F. A. (2000). The term structure of very short-term rates: New evidence for the expectations hypothesis. *Journal of Financial Economics, 58*, 397–415.

Ludden, U. (1999). *Technical analysis on foreign exchange markets.* Münster: LIT.

Lundbergh, S., & Teräsvirta, T. (1998). *Modelling economic high-frequency time series with STAR-STGARCH models.* Stockholm School of Economics, SSE/EFI Working Paper Series in Economics and Finance, 291.

Lundbergh, S., & Teräsvirta, T. (2006). A time series model for an exchange rate in a target zone with applications. *Journal of Econometrics, 131*, 579–609.

Lütkepohl, H. (1990). Asymptotic distributions of impulse response functions and forecast error variance decompositions of vector autoregressive models. *Review of Economics and Statistics, 72*, 116–125.

Lütkepohl, H. (2004). Vector autoregressive and vector error correction models. In H. Lütkepohl, & M. Krätzig (Eds.), *Applied time series econometrics* (pp. 86–158). Cambridge: Cambridge University Press.

Lütkepohl, H., & Krätzig, M. (2004). *Applied time series econometrics.* Cambridge: Cambridge University Press.

Lütkepohl, H., Teräsvirta, T., & Wolters, J. (1999). Investigating stability and linearity of a German M1 money demand function. *Journal of Applied Econometrics, 14*, 511–525.

MacMinn, R. D. (1987). Forward markets, stock markets, and the theory of the firm. *Journal of Finance, 42*, 1167–1185.

Martens, M., Kofman, P., & Vorst, T. C. F. (1998). A threshold error-correction model for intraday futures and index returns. *Journal of Applied Econometrics, 13*, 245–263.

Martinez, L., & Werner, A. (2002). The exchange rate regime and the currency composition of corporate debt: The Mexican experience. *Journal of Development Economics, 69*, 315–334.

Mashruwala, C., Rajgopal, S., & Shevlin, T. (2006). Why is the accrual anomaly not arbitraged away? The role of idiosyncratic risk and transaction costs. *Journal of Accounting and Economics, 42*, 3–33.

McKinnon, R. I. (1967). Futures markets, buffer stocks, and income stability for primary producers. *Journal of Political Economy, 75*, 844–861.

McMillan, D. G. (2001). Nonlinear predictability of stock market returns: Evidence from nonparametric and threshold models. *International Review of Economics and Finance, 10*, 353–368.

McMillan, D. G. (2003). Non-linear predictability of UK stock market returns. *Oxford Bulletin of Economics and Statistics, 65*, 557–573.

McMillan, D. G. (2005). Smooth-transition error-correction in exchange rates. *North American Journal of Economics and Finance, 16*, 217–232.

McMillan, D. G., & Speight, A. E. H. (2002). Nonlinear dynamics in high-frequency intraday financial data: Evidence for the UK long gilt futures market. *Journal of Futures Markets, 22*, 1037–1057.

McMillan, D. G., & Speight, A. E. H. (2006). Nonlinear dynamics and competing behavioral interpretations: Evidence from intra-day FTSE-100 index and futures data. *Journal of Futures Markets, 26*, 343–368.

Mejia-Reyes, P., Osborn, D. R., & Sensier, M. (2004). *Modelling real exchange rate effects on output performance in Latin America*. The University of Manchester, Discussion Paper Series, 35.
Mello, A. S., & Parsons, J. E. (2000). Hedging and liquidity. *Review of Financial Studies, 13*, 127–153.
Mendenhall, R. R. (2004). Arbitrage risk and post-earnings-announcement drift. *Journal of Business, 77*, 875–894.
Mian, S. L. (1996). Evidence on corporate hedging policy. *Journal of Financial and Quantitative Analysis, 31*, 419–439.
Miffre, J. (2000). Normal backwardation is normal. *Journal of Futures Markets, 20*, 803–821.
Mishkin, F. S. (1998). *International capital movements, financial volatility, and financial instability*. National Bureau of Economic Research, NBER Working Paper Series, 6390.
Mishkin, F. S. (2000). Comment: The onset of the East Asian financial crisis. In P. Krugman (Eds.), *Currency crises*. Chicago: The University of Chicago Press.
Mitchell, M., Pulvino, T., & Stafford, E. (2002). Limited arbitrage in equity marktes. *Journal of Finance, 57*, 551–584.
Mizen, P., & Vermeulen, P. (2005). *Corporate investment and cash flow sensitivity: What drives the relationship?* European Central Bank, Working Paper Series, 485.
Modigliani, F., & Miller, M. H. (1958). The cost of capital, corporation finance and the theory of investment. *American Economic Review, 48*, 261–297.
Monoyios, M., & Sarno, L. (2002). Mean reversion in stock index futures markets: A nonlinear analysis. *Journal of Futures Markets, 22*, 285–314.
Murphy, J. A. (1986). Futures fund performance: A test of the effectiveness of technical analysis. *Journal of Futures Markets, 6*, 175–185.
Myers, S. C., & Majluf, N. S. (1984). Corporate financing and investment decisions when firms have information that investors do not have. *Journal of Financial Economics, 13*, 187–221.
Nance, D. R., Smith, C. W., & Smithson, C. W. (1993). On the determinants of corporate hedging. *Journal of Finance, 48*, 267–285.
Neal, R. (1996). Direct tests of index arbitrage models. *Journal of Financial and Quantitative Analysis, 31*, 541–562.
Neftci, S. N. (2000). *An Introduction to the mathematics of financial derivatives* (2nd ed.). San Diego: Academic.
Nofsinger, J. R., & Sias, R. W. (1999). Herding and feedback trading by institutional and individual investors. *Journal of Finance, 54*, 2263–2295.
Oliva, T. A., Day, D. L., & MacMillan, I. C. (1988). A generic model of competitive dynamics. *Academy of Management Review, 13*, 374–389.
Onliner, S. D., & Rudebusch, G. D. (1996). Is there a broad credit channel for monetary policy? *FRBSF Economic Review, 1*, 3–13.
Osborn, D. R., & Sensier, M. (2004). *Modelling UK inflation: Persistence, seasonality and monetary policy*. The University of Manchester, Discussion Paper Series, 46.
Peck, A. E. (1975). Hedging and income stability: Concepts, implications, and an example. *American Journal of Agricultural Economics, 57*, 410–419.
Pennings, J. M. E., & Garcia, P. (2004). Hedging behavior in small and medium-sized enterprises: The role of unobserved heterogeneity. *Journal of Banking and Finance, 28*, 951–978.
Pérez-Rodríguez, J. V., Torra, S., & Andrada-Félix, J. (2005). Are Spanish Ibex35 stock future index returns forecasted with non-linear models? *Applied Financial Economics, 15*, 963–975.
Pindyck, R. S. (2001). The dynamics of commodity spot and futures markets: A primer. *Energy Journal, 22*, 1–29.
Pindyck, R. S., & Rubinfeld, D. L. (1998). *Econometric models and economic forecasts*. Singapore: McGraw-Hill.
Pirrong, S. C. (1995). Mixed manipulation strategies in commodity futures markets. *Journal of Futures Markets, 15*, 13–38.
Pontiff, J. (1996). Costly arbitrage: Evidence from closed-end funds. *Quarterly Journal of Economics, November*, 1135–1151.

Pontiff, J. (2006). Costly arbitrage and the myth of idiosyncratic risk. *Journal of Accounting and Economics, 42*, 35–52.

Pratap, S., Lobato, I., & Somuano, A. (2003). Debt composition and balance sheet effects of exchange rate volatility in Mexico: A firm level analysis. *Emerging Markets Review, 4*, 450–471.

Pratt, J. W. (1964). Risk aversion in the small and in the large. *Econometrica, 32*, 122–136.

Proaño, C. R., Flaschel, P., & Semmler, W. (2005). Currency and financial crises in emerging market economies in the medium run. *Journal of Economic Asymmetries, 2*, 105–130.

Radelet, S., & Sachs, J. (2000). The onset of the East Asian financial crisis. In P. Krugman (Eds.), *Currency crises*. Chicago: The University of Chicago Press.

Rødseth, A. (2000). *Open economy macroeconomics*. Cambridge: Cambridge University Press.

Romer, D. (1993). Rational asset-price movements without news. *American Economic Review, 83*, 1112–1130.

Röthig, A. (2004). *Currency futures and currency crises*. Darmstadt Discussion Papers in Economics, 136.

Röthig, A. (2008). *The impact of backwardation on hedgers' demand for currency futures contracts: Theory versus empirical evidence*. Darmstadt Discussion Papers in Economics, 190.

Röthig, A., & Chiarella, C. (2007). Investigating nonlinear speculation in cattle, corn, and hog futures markets using logistic smooth transition regression models. *Journal of Futures Markets, 27*, 719–737.

Röthig, A., Semmler, W., & Flaschel, P. (2007). Hedging, speculation, and investment in balance-sheet triggered currency crises. *Australian Economic Papers, 46*, 224–233.

Röthig, A., Semmler, W., & Flaschel, P. (2009). Corporate currency hedging and currency crises. A. Pyka, U. Cantner, A. Greiner, & T. Kuhn (Eds.), *Recent advances in Neo-Schumpeterian economics: Essays in honour of Horst Hanusch*. Cheltenham: Edward Elgar (Forthcoming).

Rothschild, M., & Stiglitz, J. E. (1970). Increasing risk: A definition. *Journal of Economic Theory, 2*, 225–243.

Rutledge, D. J. S. (1972). Hedgers' demand for futures contracts: A theoretical framework with applications to the United States soybean complex. *Food Research Institute Studies, 11*, 237–256.

Saadi, S., Gandhi, D., & Elmawazini, K. (2006). On the validity of conventional statistical tests given evidence of non-synchronous trading and non-linear dynamics in returns generating process. *Applied Economic Letters, 13*, 301–305.

Samuelson, P. A. (1957). Intertemporal price equilibrium: A prologue to the theory of speculation. *Weltwirtschaftliches Archiv, 79*, 181–221.

Sanders, D. R., Boris, K., & Manfredo, M. (2004). Hedgers, funds, and small speculators in the energy futures market: An analysis of the CFTC's Commitments of Traders reports. *Energy Economics, 26*, 425–445.

Sandmo, A. (1971). On the theory of the competitive firm under price uncertainty. *American Economic Review, 61*, 65–73.

Sanns, W. (2000). *Catastrophe theory with Mathematica: A geometric approach*. Osnabrück: Der Andere Verlag.

Sanyal, A. (2005). *Keynes' metaphor of the newspaper competition: A model*. Macroeconomics 0501015, EconWPA.

Sarno, L. (1999). Adjustment costs and nonlinear dynamics in the demand for money: Italy, 1861–1991. *International Journal of Finance and Economics, 4*, 155–177.

Sarno, L., & Thornton, D. L. (2003). The dynamic relationship between the federal funds rate and the treasury bill rate: An empirical investigation. *Journal of Banking and Finance, 27*, 1079–1110.

Sarno, L., Taylor, M. P., & Peel, D. A. (2003). Nonlinear equilibrium correction in U.S. real money balances, 1869–1997. *Journal of Money, Credit, and Banking, 35*, 787–799.

Schrand, C., & Unal, H. (1998). Hedging and coordinated risk management: Evidence from thrift conversions. *Journal of Finance, 53*, 979–1013.

Sensier, M., Osborn, D. R., & cal, N. (2002). *Asymmetric interest rate effects for the UK real economy*. The University of Manchester, Discussion Paper Series, 10.

Shiller, R. J. (1984). Stock prices and social dynamics. *Brookings Papers on Economic Activity, 2*, 457–510.
Shiller, R. J. (1987). *Investor behavior in the October 1987 stock market crash: Survey evidence.* National Bureau of Economic Research, NBER Working Paper Series, 2446.
Shiller, R. J. (2000). *Irrational exuberance.* Princeton: Princeton University Press.
Shleifer, A. (2000). *Inefficient markets. An introduction to behavioural finance.* Oxford: Oxford University Press.
Shleifer, A., & Vishny, R. W. (1997). The limits of arbitrage. *Journal of Finance, 52*, 35–55.
Sias, R. W., Starks, L. T., & Tiniç, S. M. (2001). Is noise trader risk priced? *Journal of Financial Research, 24*, 311–329.
Skalin, J., & Teräsvirta, T. (1999). Another look at swedish business cycles. *Journal of Applied Econometrics, 14*, 359–378.
Smith, C. W., & Stulz, R. M. (1985). The determinants of firms' hedging policies. *Journal of Financial and Quantitative Analysis, 20*, 391–406.
Sofianos, G. (1993). Index arbitrage profitability. *Journal of Derivatives, Fall*, 6–20.
Stulz, R. M. (1990). Managerial discretion and optimal financing policies. *Journal of Financial Economics, 26*, 3–27.
Taylor, M. P. (1992). The use of technical analysis in the foreign exchange market. *Journal of International Money and Finance, 11*, 304–314.
Telser, L. G. (1986). Futures and actual markets: How they are related. *Journal of Business, 59*, 5–20.
Teräsvirta, T. (1994). Specification, estimation, and evaluation of smooth transition autoregressive models. *Journal of the American Statistical Association, 89*, 208–218.
Teräsvirta, T. (1997). Smooth transition models. In C. Heij, H. Schumacher, B. Hanzon, & K. Praagman (Eds.), *System dynamics in economic and financial models.* Chichester: Wiley.
Teräsvirta, T. (1998). Modeling economic relationships with smooth transition regression. In A. Ullah, & D. E. A. Giles (Eds.), *Handbook of applied economic statistics.* New York: Marcel Dekker.
Teräsvirta, T. (2004). Smooth transition regression modeling. In H. Lütkepohl, & M. Krätzig (Eds.), *Applied time series econometrics.* Cambridge: Cambridge University Press.
Teräsvirta, T., van Dijk, D., & Medeiros, M. C. (2005). Linear models, smooth transition autoregressions, and neural networks for forecasting macroeconomic time series: A re-examination. *International Journal of Forecasting, 21*, 755–774.
Thompson, M. (1980). The geometry of confidence: An analysis of the Enga te and Hagen moka, a complex system of ceremonial pig giving in the New Guinea Highlands. In J. C. Mitchell (Eds.), *Numerical techniques in social anthropology.* Philadelphia: Institute for the Study of Human Issues.
Tse, Y. (2001). Index arbitrage with heterogeneous investors: A smooth transition error correction analysis. *Journal of Banking and Finance, 25*, 1829–1855.
Tuckman, B., & Vila, J. L. (1992). Arbitrage with holding costs: A utility-based approach. *Journal of Finance, 47*, 1283–1302.
Tufano, P. (1998). Agency costs of corporate risk management. *Financial Management, 27*, 67–77.
van Dijk, D., & Franses, P. H. (1999). Modeling multiple regimes in the business cycle. *Macroeconomic Dynamics, 3*, 311–340.
van Dijk, D., Teräsvirta, T., & Franses, P. H. (2002). Smooth transition autoregressive models – a survey of recent developments. *Econometric Reviews, 21*, 1–47.
Varian, H. R. (1979). Catastrophe theory and the business cycle. *Economic Inquiry, 17*, 14–28.
Vitale, P. (2000). Speculative noise trading and manipulation in the foreign exchange market. *Journal of International Money and Finance, 19*, 689–712.
Vrolijk, C. (1997). *Derivatives effect on monetary policy transmission.* International Monetary Fund, IMF Working Paper, WP/97/121.
Vukina, T., Li., D. F., & Holthausen, D. M. (1996). Hedging with crop yield futures: A mean-variance analysis. *American Journal of Agricultural Economics, 78*, 1015–1025.
Working, H. (1953). Futures trading and hedging. *American Economic Review, 43*, 314–343.

Wurgler, J., & Zhuravskaya, E. (2002). Does arbitrage flatten demand curves for stocks? *Journal of Business, 75*, 583–608.

Zeeman, E. C. (1974). On the unstable behaviour of stock exchanges. *Journal of Mathematical Economics, 1*, 39–49.

Zilcha, I., & Broll, U. (1992). Optimal hedging by firms with multiple sources of risky revenues. *Economics Letters, 39*, 473–477.

Breinigsville, PA USA
27 October 2009

226544BV00002B/4/P

9 783642 015649